With a Little Bit of Luck
A Country Boy Growing up in the Years after World War II

Douglas H. Lester

Rock's Mills Press
Rock's Mills, Ontario • Oakville, Ontario
2024

Published by
Rock's Mills Press
www.rocksmillspress.com

Copyright © 2024 by Douglas H. Lester.
All rights reserved. No part of this publication may be reproduced, distributed, or transmitted in any form or by any means, including photocopying, recording, or other electronic or mechanical methods, without the prior written permission of the publisher, except in the case of brief quotations embodied in critical reviews and certain other noncommercial uses permitted by copyright law. For permission requests, contact the publisher at: customer.service@rocksmillspress.com.

For information about trade, library, and bulk orders, please contact the publisher through our website or at: customer.service@rocksmillspress.com.

Contents

Part One

Luck	9
Ignition	10
The Back Stories	12
Looking for a Hero	15
Grampa Lester	16
Grampa Chipps	16
Farm Life	18
When Curiosity Summons	19
Dangerous Pursuits	20
Born Curious	21
Dougie Went A Courtin'	21
Church Routines	22
The Chicken Farm	23
Early School Days	25
Learning the Hard Way	28
Social Dynamics	29
Victoria Day	31
Living Easy	32
The Buchner Farm	34
Barnyard Biology	35
Different Worlds	37
Grade One	37
Shortcuts	39
The Power of Story	39
Adventures on the Chicken Farm	40
The Rhythm of Life	42
Sunday Adventures	44
Our Town	45
Father and Son	46
Christmas Concert	48
Tonsillitis	48
Christmas Magic	49
Ice Skating	50

Birthday Traditions	51
Blossoming Mind	51
Settling In	52
Between a Flock and a Hard Face	53
New Challenges	54
General Conduct	56
The Wider World	57
Mother to the Rescue	58
Summertime	59
One of the Guys	61
My Hero Hugh	61
The Toe Rubbers Escapade	62
The Chick Disaster	63
The Bicycle	64
The Day the Music Died	65
Doc Lester	66
Empty Days	67
Baseball	67
A House of Our Own	68
Doggie Tales	69
Growing Pains	70
The Good Life	71
Comfortable in the Kitchen	73
Ice Hockey	74
Spring Fever	74
Summertime	75
Last Schoolyard Fight	76
Crazyland	77
Redemption	78
Choosing My Path	79
Born Again	80
Leadership Development	81
Working Man	82
The Larger World	83
My Parents as People	84
Role Model	85
The Summer of '59	86
Grade Eight	87
Lazy Hazy Days of Summer	88
Mowing Away Hay	89
Paint Contractor	90
The Brotherhood	91

The Outsider 92
The Test 93
Settling In 93
Cadets 95
Al's Bus 96
University Bound 96
Heart Attack 97
Tobacco Work 98
Measuring Tobacco 99
Unloading Boats 101
The Tobacco Worker's Honeymoon 102
Women at War 104
Music to the Rescue 105
Leadership Lessons 105
Academic Path 107
My Back-Row Buddy 108
Church Routines 109
Sweet Sixteen 110
Missionary Calling 111
A Summer of Possibilities 112
Sucker Busters 114
Coming of Age 115
The Tying Machine 116
Quiet Courage 118
Romance 119
The Bigger World 121
As Good as It Gets 122
A Strange Adventure 123
Finishing with a Bang 127
The Test 129
Manning Up 130
Taking the Lead 135
My Senior Year 137
My Football Career 138
A Hard Rain's A-Gonna Fall 138
Solitary Joy 140
Finishing Well 141
A Summer in the Sun 142
Grampa Chipps Comes to Stay 145
Ending with a Whimper 147
Another Beginning—Another Ending 148
And Now I Become a Man 149

The Dodgers 149
Finding My Path 151
   Numismania 152
My Dark Night 153
The Summer of '65 155
University 156
Summer of '66 160
A Selection of Photographs 163

Part Two

Married Life 175
More Than a Bit of Luck 175
Building a Life 176
Life Moves On 177
Creating Community 179
A Home of our Own 181
Things Fall Apart 182
Stumbling to the Finish Line 184
Butch and Sundance 185
Running For My Life 187
Wishing Doesn't Make It So 187
Now What? 189
The Sunshine That Changed My Life to Spring 190
Cupid Shoots His Arrow 192
Swept Off My Feet 193
Wedding Bells 194
Becoming a Family 195
The Lester-Kempston Bunch 196
Year Two 198
Grampa Norm 200
Settling In 202
Transition Time 202
Mary Lake 205
Cheryl and Doug's Excellent Adventure 206
More Transitions 211
The Year of Moves 213
Summertime and the Livin' is Busy 214
The Waterloo Years 217
Life Goes On 223

Dedicated to
Cheryl, my love, my wife, my kindred spirit.
And our four children who have enriched both our lives.

~ Part One ~

LUCK

I almost didn't get born.

I guess that's true for all of us in one way or another. It seems we all need *a little bit of luck* to get started.

In my case I'm thankful for synchronicity, fate, and a certain yellow bathing suit.

Let me explain.

The woman who ended up being my mother had studied two things—how to be a preacher's wife, and how to teach in a one-room eight-grade school. The preacher's wife thing just didn't happen, so at age twenty-eight, my future mother was the teacher in a one-room school and had mostly given up on the marriage thing.

You see, up until the 1950s, the men who ran rural schools in Ontario required all women teachers to be unmarried. The schoolmarms' agreement that Lillian Chipps had signed stated that her contract would be immediately voided if she married. So, Miss Chipps had accepted her fate and had settling into life as a popular, hard-working, church-involved spinster teacher.

Meanwhile, the man who ended up being my father also had not been lucky at romance. At age twenty-nine, he was aging out of the market. He'd had some romances but, with the uncertainty of a protracted war and his financial status as the second son of a struggling farmer, it looked like he would end up a bachelor. Two of my father's three brothers fought in Europe while my dad had been excused from military service so that he could contribute to the war effort by keeping the family farm producing during the war years. The odds against Howard Lester ever becoming anyone's father had been seriously jeopardized by an unfortunate farm accident the spring he turned twenty-six.

The Lester farm water well, like most rural wells at the time, had been dug by hand, one shovelful at a time with the opening shaped and secured with a circular brick wall to hold back the earth. As a boy, I saw one dug and it was a fascinating process. It was like building an upside-down tower into the ground. As earth was removed one bucket at a time, a brick wall was cemented in place one row at a time to hold back the earth. They just kept digging deeper and deeper into the ground and building the wall until the bottom began to fill with water. In the centre, a pipe reached down to the water and a pump sat on boards at the bottom, pumping water up to the surface to supply the barn and the house. The well on my grandfather's farm was about sixty feet deep.

In the spring of 1942, the pump on my grandfather's farm quit pumping and it was decided that my father, who was the lightest candidate, would be lowered into the well by his father and brother to examine the pump and either repair or replace it. A hundred-foot hay rope was fetched from the barn and rigged to a board so that my future father could be lowered safely down to the bottom.

Shortly after he began his descent something went horribly wrong. The rope snapped and Howard Lester was sent plunging to a likely death. His life was saved when he managed to grab hold of the pipe in the centre to slow his plunge but, when he hit the boards at the bottom, his boots exploded, and his hands and body were left bloodied and bruised. I never heard the details of dad's rescue, but I certainly heard of the damage the fall did. Amazingly no bones were broken, but Howard's testicles took a beating. The examining physician looked him in the eyes and sadly pronounced that it was unlikely his damaged parts would ever produce a child.

It didn't look good. My potential parents were on separate childless paths.

That's when *a little bit of luck* changed everything.

IGNITION

They say that when the conditions are right it only takes one spark to get a fire going. Luckily for me, serendipity provided the conditions for ignition in the summer of 1944.

On a hot August Sunday, twenty-eight-year-old schoolmarm Lillian Chipps, considered by the local school trustees to be married to her career, and by her age and experience a confirmed single, joined some friends for an afternoon swim on the East Beach in Port Burwell, Ontario, a vibrant fishing village on the north shore of Lake Erie. At the time the beach had food stands, a dance hall-pavilion, and a long cement pier reaching out into the harbour. It was a regular summer destination for fishing, teen adventures, family outings, and church picnics. No visit to Port Burwell would be complete without a leisurely stroll to the end of the pier.

As fate would have it, bachelor farmer Howard Lester had taken a day off haying and decided to spend the day at Port Burwell fishing from the pier, swimming, and lounging on the beach. Near the end of the afternoon, as Howard walked the long cement pier, he watched daring swimmers risk a race across the wide harbour and back. A yellow two-piece bathing suit, worn by one of the few women strong enough to join the challenging swim, caught his eye. As Miss Chipps pulled herself onto the warm cement, removed her bathing cap, shook out her hair and took a deep breath, my father was immediately twitterpated.

A flirtatious conversation led to an official date and, after a summer and fall of courting and a winter romance with snow-stuck cars and horse-drawn sleigh rides, my mother and father were married in a simple wedding on Saturday, April 7, 1945, at the farm home of Frank and Minnie Chipps, just east of Courtland, Ontario.

There was no crowd, just Lillian's parents and the required two witnesses. There was no reception or party, although some of my mother's brothers and friends tied tin cans to the '37 Ford and covered the engine in Limburger cheese to add a smoky aroma to their honeymoon drive. Later, some of Dad's Bayham friends arranged a shivaree where the newlyweds were surprised late one evening, escorted from their bed in their pajamas, placed on a horse-drawn wagon, and paraded with hoots and hollers through backroads and the local community.

As marriage was forbidden for women teachers by local trustees, my mother was immediately unemployed. It would be nearly ten years before she was offered another teaching position.

Realizing that starting married life in my widowed grandfather's fiefdom would be neither joyful nor prosperous, my father considered his options and took a job as hired man with a nearby dairy farmer named Frank Lowry. Dad's pay included a rent-free stay in a small white clapboard house on the farm. This safe refuge was where my mother and father spent the first year of their marriage and where I began my life.

Although my parents almost missed the love boat, when the opportunity for marriage and family came their way they wasted no time, and my father's water well incident proved to be no impediment. That was particularly fortunate for me since their union allowed me to experience this thing we call life.

Their desire to start a family produced quick results. Just a little over nine months after their wedding day, I was born on a cold and stormy winter's night—January 18, 1946. Weighing in at ten pounds, six ounces, I was a huge challenge right from the start for my little mother who was five feet, two inches tall and weighed about 120 pounds. However, as I was to learn in the years to come, my mother was strong enough to face any test. I also discovered later that, although she seldom let it be obvious, my mother was fiercely competitive, and producing a large healthy baby would have brought her much joy.

Born just as World War II was winding down, I was one of the first wave of Baby Boomers that filled hospitals and schools from 1946 to 1965. As a Canadian farm boy, I was born in relative safety and privilege compared with my contemporaries in war-ravaged Europe, even though by Canadian standards my parents were living in poverty.

My life had begun. I had been born into a farm family with food and shelter in rural Ontario far from the bustling cities and isolated from the devastation of the war that had shattered lives and much of Europe.

THE BACK STORIES

Over the years, through curiosity and interactions, I managed to pick up bits and pieces of Mom's and Dad's backstories. There were moments while fishing or hunting with my dad, or in the kitchen learning to sew or cook with my mom, when they would share a bit of their early lives.

Dad was a gifted storyteller and when he and his brothers were together, I would always get some interesting snippets from his past. In Dad's later years, we went every year to the world's trap shooting championship in Vandalia, Ohio, where he participated in the open singles competition from the sixteen-yard line. I learned a lot during those long drives, and during lazy evenings as we relaxed at our motel.

Discovering details about my mother's past was much more challenging. My mom's early years were a well-kept secret. Mom never shared anything about her romances, or her successes and failures as a young teacher. She never shared how she was shamed to the point of never singing a note, even though she appeared to enjoy music. I don't think even Dad knew some of these hidden stories.

Although my mother never shared much about the adventures of growing up on a farm with six brothers, or about the motorcycle races, the barnyard rodeos, and the swimming in the creek, over the years through uncles and aunts I did manage to piece together some of her backstory. Born to Frank and Minnie (Voigt) Chipps on September 3, 1915, my mother, Lillian Lena Chipps, was the fourth child in a family of nine. A country girl with six brothers and two sisters, she was quite capable of standing her ground, and there wasn't much she hadn't seen in her nearly thirty years of single life. A gifted student, my mother was the only one of her siblings to complete five years of high school. Mother had dreamed of marrying a preacher and, to follow her dream, she took the extraordinary step of leaving her safe and comfortable farm life to spend a year at Toronto Bible College in order to prepare for her role as a pastor's wife. As a backup plan, she also went to Normal School in London, Ontario, and became an elementary school teacher. By the time she met my father, she had given up on finding a preacher and resigned herself to a life dedicated to teaching in a small rural school and helping with church activities and chores around the farm.

Mother had spent most of her life on the 275-acre family farm near Courtland. A large herd of Holsteins and a variety of pigs, chickens, and geese, along with cats, dogs, and horses, provided food, transportation, and entertainment. The Chipps family farm was the scene of Sunday afternoons that rivalled the wild west. Family and friends gathered after church for an afternoon of good food, conversation, and excitement. Horses were being broken in the coral, motorcycles repaired and raced, guns tested with tin cans for targets, sometimes an excursion to the nearby fishing hole, and after the war, an airplane taxying on a hayfield and heading up into the sky.

My father loved to tell how my mother's brother, John, had taken him for a Sunday afternoon flight that overshot the hayfield runway and bounced them across a ploughed field. The landing jarred every bone in my father's body and gave him a strong aversion to leaving solid ground. To the best of my knowledge, Dad was never on another plane in his entire life.

My father, Howard Eugene Lester, born May 22, 1915, to Sandford and Lenora (Leach) Lester, had a very different early life than my mother. Instead of a consistent homelife in a well-known community, my father's family moved frequently and, for most of his formative years, Dad's father was often away from home travelling as a salesman. Fortunately for Dad and his brothers, his mother was a calm, consistent parent with enough love and caring to give all the boys a good start in life. Dad was the second son in a family of four boys—Alex, then Dad, followed by Fred and Blake. There was another boy, Jack, who died shortly after birth. Dad and his brothers all began life near Eden, Ontario, on a small dairy farm. At the time, Grampa Sandford had a small herd of purebred Jersey cows which he considered to be the aristocrats of the bovine world.

However, by the time my father began school, the farm had been sold and the family had moved south to the small village of Vienna, located a few miles north of Port Burwell. Here, my grandfather ran a pool hall in the front of the house and kept a couple of cows and a few chickens in the small barn outback. My dad loved the mix of farm and village life, but that didn't last long.

When my grandfather was offered an opportunity to become a salesman for Delco Products (a subsidiary of General Motors that manufactured car starters, batteries, and other electrical and electronics hardware), Sandford sold his home and moved the family north to Ingersoll in Oxford County. By this time, all four brothers were in school and, with their English bulldog, Joker, the thriving small town provided a few years of idyllic life. There were stories of swimming holes and toboggan runs, and Joker, with his teeth gripping a lineman's leather pouch being carried up a hydro pole.

Soon, the Lester family was on the move again, off to the edge of Hamilton, where Dad completed his elementary education and had his first job working for a market gardener. In the family's backyard, Dad kept banty chickens, rabbits, and pigeons. With the beginning of the Great Depression, Delco-Light sales declined. (This small generator-battery combination, designed to provide electricity to rural residents not yet connected to the electrical grid had been Grampa's best-selling item). The family moved to Burford, where Dad attended high school for two years. Here my father gained carpentry and farming skills, which became necessary since the next move took the family back to ownership of a dairy farm near Eden.

All I know of Grampa Sandford is from my parents' recollections. Apparently, Grampa was a good talker and an effective salesman. As a Delco representative he made a good income but spent most of it on clothes and automobiles. Grampa was well known and had friends in high places. One of Grampa's buddies, Mitch Hepburn, became Ontario's youngest premier in 1934. About this time, as fate would have it, Grampa Lester inherited a farm from his uncle.

The transition to the farm was not smooth. Sandford's angry aunt had possession of the house and farm buildings and she challenged the will. Dad's family needed to harvest crops and establish ownership which meant setting up a tent and living like squatters for many months. The move also meant the end of Dad's schooling as he and his brother were responsible for most of the farming duties.

The family feud meant that, although they owned the farm, the house took time to become legally theirs. This meant that two of Lester boys and their father and mother started farming while living through the winter in a tent on the corner of the farm without any animals or equipment. Dad never saw this as a hardship. He spoke fondly of weeks of cutting wood with Uncle Alex on the other end of a cross-cut saw. Dad loved to hunt and rabbit stew became an important supplement to a meagre budget.

As soon as the legal issues were settled, Dad raised a large flock of chickens, and they slowly began to fill the stanchions in the barn. As Dad walked the sandy fields plowing and discing, he gathered an impressive collection of Indigenous tools. By the time Dad married, he and Grampa had managed to assemble a herd of dairy cows. A few years after Dad married and moved on, Grampa sold the farm and bought a house in Tillsonburg where he and his second wife, Lucy, lived until his death. He died when I was eighteen.

LOOKING FOR A HERO

As a boy, I looked to the men in my life to inspire and act as role models for me. During the first five years my male influences were limited to my father, grandfathers, a few uncles, and my older cousin George.

The first role model was my father. Since he was farming right out our back door, I had access nearly all the time. As a toddler, my mother had to restrain me as I tried to follow his car to town. In later years, after we had moved to Hawkins Poultry Farm, my dad welcomed me in his workplace, and I learned valuable skills from him and the men he worked with.

GRAMPA LESTER

My Grampa Lester was not one of my heroes. I had almost no relationship with him. Part of that may have to do with his age since he was sixty years old when I was born, but I suspect it was much more than that. His wife of thirty-five years, Lenora, had died suddenly of a stroke in July 1942, four years before I was born. People who knew her told me that she was an amazing cook, a pianist, a loving mother, and a gracious host to the crews that came to their farm during harvest.

Sandford seemed cold and aloof the few times we interacted. Until I was teenager I have only one memory of a visit to his home. I was about four years old. He must have remarried by then, and his second wife, Lucy, must have been there, but I don't remember meeting her. What I do remember was my first Spanish onion sandwich. I cautiously tried it and found it surprisingly good. During that visit, Grampa Sandford gave me an old rocking chair with a corded bottom which I treasured and kept for the next fifty years. Other than a silver dollar for Christmas one year, and a travel bag from his estate in 1964, those were the only gifts I ever received from Grampa.

I suspect that he and Dad had had some difficult times during the years they farmed together, with Sandford wearing white coveralls and Dad doing the lion's share of the work. Grampa seldom came to our home and when he did, he came alone, and his visits were brief. Although my father had given up smoking by the time I was six years old, when Grampa Lester came to our house, Dad would get out a large glass ashtray and Grampa would sit in the corner chair smoking one cigarette after another during his short visit. He never indicated the slightest curiosity about me or my life. He never celebrated a birthday, graduation, or any other event with me, or had any words of support or encouragement.

GRAMPA CHIPPS

My mother's father, Frank Chipps, was one of my early heroes. He was always pleased to see me and he was genuinely interested in my life.

My earliest memory of a trip to Grampa and Gramma Chipps' place was when I was five and my brother Larry was three. We had opened our gifts during our first Christmas at the Hawkins farm and it seemed like we had just started playing with our new toys when we were told playtime was over. It was time to go to Grampa and Gramma Chipps' house.

With pouty faces we left our toys, donned our visiting clothes, and headed through the snow to their little house in Courtland. I can still see and smell that large kitchen when we opened the door. Aunts and older cousins were carrying in food and stuffing pans into the oven and onto the stove. Children and uncles were crowded into two rooms at the front of the house. Laughter and conversation filled every nook.

Somehow, they managed to get over thirty-five of us seated and fed. The food and desserts were plentiful. My sadness over leaving my toys was erased. This Christmas event was repeated for a few more times, with new babies and cousins' beaus and husbands added each year. There were no gifts except for one year when Grampa presented each of his adult children with a large King James Bible. Finally, when there were over sixty of us trying to squeeze into that little house, it was decided they would gather for summer picnics instead, and we were liberated to spend Christmas at home.

Grampa Chipps was sixty-nine years old when I was born. Grampa had married my Gramma, Minnie (Voigt) Chipps, when he was thirty-three and she was twenty-eight. Then he and Gramma began a legacy that involved nine children. By the time I was ten years old they had twenty-six grandchildren. Starting with nothing, my grandfather had managed to purchase a farm near Courtland by the time my mother was a young girl. With long hours and the help of his boys, Grampa became a successful dairy farmer with a large herd of Holstein cattle.

Although I have a photo of my grandmother standing in front of the farmhouse with me in her arms, my earliest memories are of Gramma in a wheelchair, crippled by spinal arthritis, and her and Grampa living in a small insulbrick and stucco home in Courtland.

Though I now realize Grampa was only in his mid-seventies, he and Gramma seemed ancient to my seven-year-old self. I am sure Grampa was still very involved in the nearby farm since his son Lloyd, who took over the farm, was only in his early thirties. I also know that Grampa worked hard in his large garden, which my brother and I enjoyed exploring every time we visited in the summer. He had the largest and most delicious blackberries I have ever enjoyed. He also had a large rhubarb patch, and Larry and I would challenge each other to eat the raw stem and then giggle as our faces puckered.

Although he never dropped into our house for a visit, Grampa Chipps was an important role model. I admired his determination and the way he cooked, cleaned, and cared for my grandmother. He was often singing a hymn as we arrived for a visit, and singing for Grampa and Gramma was part of most visits.

He often told us that he had only borrowed money once in his life and after that, he learned to "cut the cloth the way it lay." After Gramma died in 1963, Grampa gave up his home and lived with each of his daughters for a few years. While living with my Aunt Ruth, Grampa became addicted to TV—especially *Hockey Night in Canada*. Grampa Chipps spent his last years in a nursing home in Tillsonburg, dying just before his ninety-third birthday.

FARM LIFE

Working for Frank Lowry gave Dad and Mom the start they needed, and by the second year of my life, my parents had embarked on a big adventure. A young local farmer, Max Rutherford, had inherited two farms but lacked experience and equipment. It was agreed that he and Dad would farm together on "shares."

Although money was in short supply, my parents were truly happy. They were blessed with a simple faith in God and each other that allowed them to face life's challenges, and to enjoy a long life together. Mother sewed and cooked creatively. They grew a large garden and canned vegetables and fruit. Dad supplied eggs and meat. I never recall missing a meal.

The move to the Culloden area farm meant a large house with an orchard, barn, laneways, and open fields—just what a curious toddler needed in order to begin exploring the bigger world. I have very few memories from the time before my brother arrived when I was two and a half, but early photos show me throwing a ball with my Uncle Alex, playing in the orchard, and enjoying the family dog.

My two earliest memories both involve the arrival of my brother Larry, and both involve me getting into trouble. Shortly after my brother arrived home from the hospital, his basinet was placed on a table. I wanted to examine this lump that had occupied my mother for most of the past year, so I reached up and tipped the basinet to improve my view. Suddenly there was a flurry of activity. Mother swooped in to grab her precious bundle and I was angrily exiled from the area. Two things were obvious at this moment—I was no longer the apple of my mother's eye, and this new member of the family was not ready to be a playmate.

The second memory involves a failed attempt to engage my little brother in outdoor adventures when I was about three. I recall standing on the back porch tapping on the bedroom window hoping to wake him when I was shooed from the area and sternly informed that an afternoon nap was a precious thing.

Without a useful playmate, I was on my own. I followed my father to the barn and the fields, but whether he was plowing or milking I was usually informed of the dangers and forced to watch from a distance. I had more than one teary-eyed rage over not being allowed to go to town with my father. I tried to follow him down the road and my mother was forced to be the arresting officer and jailer—a role I forced her into more often than was fair.

I also tested my mother's patience with my barnyard adventures. She later told me that I returned to the house covered in mud or manure so often she sometimes hosed me down before extracting me from my soiled garments.

WHEN CURIOSITY SUMMONS

Dad loved to tell how one of my adventures as a two-year-old almost proved too much for my young mother, very pregnant with child number two. She had dressed me for show—not for exploration—with stylish shorts and white baby shoes. Somehow, she was delayed in heading to town, and during the lull in the action, I wandered toward the barnyard. Seeing new piglets, I headed into the pigsty to get a better look. When mother called, and I obediently returned to the house, she could not believe her eyes. Her well-dressed young man was now soiled with pig manure nearly to the knees, and the white shoes and socks had disappeared. After some carefully chosen Christian words of rebuke, she used a garden hose to remove most of the filth. Mother often told this story as an example of one of her toughest rescue missions. It was certainly not the last.

When I was three, I faced what I considered my first truly impossible situation. For reasons long lost in the cobwebs of memory, I decided to insert my head into my dresser drawer to get a good look for some lost item. After satisfying my curiosity, I attempted to remove myself from the scene. My head had mysteriously done some sort of *Alice in Wonderland* thing and would not exit through the space it had entered. I tried quietly for some time to extricate myself since, even at three, the male aversion to asking for help was developing well. Then I started to panic.

After a few violent and painful last throes of independence, I began to wail. The siren summoned help in the form of my mother who later quoted me as saying, "Mom, you are never going to get me out of this one." Being a mother, she stifled her desire to laugh (or at least that is the story that I tell myself) and extricated me. In the rescue, I took careful note of her technique, and I am proud to report that I have never been stuck in a dresser drawer again. However, there is a lesson that extends beyond the situation.

You see, the experts have a theory that we are supposed to be able to transfer learning from one situation to another. This may work in theory, but in the real world, most of us have weak long-term memory. For me, that has led to many moments when I realize I just stuck a part of my body in a space that will make it very difficult for me to retrieve it. Each situation has just enough variation on a theme that my brain is too slow in detecting the similarity to a past calamity.

DANGEROUS PURSUITS

Twice, during these early years, my farm explorations were nearly fatal. On one of my attempts to follow Dad to town, I avoided detection by following a lane and the edge of a field. By the time I realized pursuit was in vain, I was lost. To make matters worse, I had wandered into a large cornfield. After hours of frantic searching that involved most of the neighbours, I was found sitting teary-eyed and frightened on a large rock in the middle of the field.

My other exploration was even more dangerous with immediate consequences.

One sunny morning in my fourth summer, I was exploring the barn on my own when I discovered a curry comb hanging on a nail beside our plow horse's stall. With some effort, I managed to reach the comb and decided to groom our horse. I remember starting on his rear flank and moving toward his back right leg. Suddenly, everything went dark, and the next thing I knew, I found myself in the house in bed as if awakening from a gentle sleep. There seemed to be no panic and very little was made of my misadventure. My best guess is that I was close enough to old Toby that I was flung more than kicked and ended up in a crumpled state against the wall. I never did learn how I made it from the barn to the house.

BORN CURIOUS

This penchant for exploration was not limited to the outdoors. My father enjoyed telling the story of my first visit to the farmhouse. My parents were exploring our new home when suddenly I disappeared. Apparently, I had opened the basement door and walked forward into the unknown and fallen into the dark basement. When they heard the wailing, Dad was quoted as saying nonchalantly, "Well, he must be okay if he can make that much noise."

DOUGIE WENT A-COURTIN'

As my time at our first farmhouse was coming to an end, I had one more adventure—this time it was in a whole new territory. During my three years on the Rutherford farms, I had been introduced to the other family's daughter several times. At the ripe old age of four, I decided to go courting. At first, my romantic adventure was proceeding marvelously. I don't recall my entrance or opening lines, but by the time disaster struck I had won the smiles of both mother and sweet Mary and was sitting happily at the kitchen table with cookies and milk.

Just then, who should appear at the door but my mother, whom I had unfortunately neglected to apprise of my agenda. One look at her face revealed that this would not end well for me. With a firm grasp of my arm, and with none of the politeness or grace I had hoped for, I was unceremoniously removed from my bliss and marched toward home. On the way, my mother found a switch and emphasized her anger and disappointment with a series of physical punctuation marks. I guess the cornfield and workhorse incidents had reduced my mother's tolerance for my adventures.

In retrospect, I now realize that our parents were in the final stages of ending their farming partnership and that may have had its own impact on my ill-fated romance. Within weeks, we had left the Rutherford farm and were once again safely ensconced in the hired man's house on the Lowry farm.

I think, after a few years, Dad and Mom realized that the "farming on shares" experiment was a failure—they had shared the risks without much opportunity to own anything. We left the farm penniless with Dad and Mom still owing for some fence posts. By now, my brother Larry was a useful playmate, and we spent a cozy winter in the little white house on the Lowry farm as my father sought a long-term employment opportunity.

CHURCH ROUTINES

From the start, church activities were an important part of our family life. By the time I was born, my parents had already chosen First Baptist Church in Tillsonburg as their place of worship and community, and no matter what else changed in their lives, this was a constant. Our church involvement meant Sunday School and church on Sunday morning, a 7:00 p.m. service on Sunday evening, and Prayer Meeting on Wednesday night.

My father may have strayed a bit before mother saved him from dancehalls and cigarettes, but Dad's mother, Gramma Lenora, had laid a solid foundation during his Ingersoll days and Dad enjoyed being with people of faith and being dressed in a suit one day a week. As we grew older, both our parents were involved in church leadership roles. My father was a Deacon and the Sunday School treasurer. My mother taught the Young Adult Sunday School class and was a dedicated member of the Hilda Lindsay Mission Circle.

Christmas at church was a magical time. The First Baptist Church was still sparkling new during my toddler years, having burned to the ground and been rebuilt shortly after I was born. The basement stage was an amazing performance space with huge curtains. Every Christmas at the annual concert each Sunday School class from toddlers to teens did recitations and put on skits. Through these presentations I gained confidence and a love for drama.

I remember sitting in awe as older teens did skits on stage—especially when they did a shadow show of an operation, with moans and groans that accompanied the shadowy extraction from the body on the operating table of a collection of items, including a saw and hammer, that left me wide-eyed with wonder and delight.

Easter was another special time on the church calendar with a Good Friday service and an Easter Sunday breakfast. Easter Sunday service was a special occasion when many people came to church in new outfits or accessories. Colourful dresses. New hats. New ties.

During my growing up, it was standard for people to dress up for church. Women dressed in their finest dresses. Men in their suits. My brother and I had Sunday slacks, white shirts, clip-on bow ties, and polished shoes. Our hair was parted and slicked with Brylcreem. The preparation and opportunity to wear our finest was a welcome weekly pivot point in the routines of school and work. Church life taught me many important life lessons. I enjoyed polishing the shoes on Saturday. I loved the organ and choir in the morning and the old-fashioned hymn sing with the piano each Sunday night.

THE CHICKEN FARM

On a spring day in 1951, my mother chased me down and scrubbed me so thoroughly behind the ears that seventy years later I still have bodily memories of that morning as we prepared to set out on our next adventure. I didn't know what was happening, but I knew it was important.

Our 1937 Ford sputtered to a halt in the yard of a white stucco house at the front of Roger Hawkins' chicken farm just east of the Tillsonburg town limits. I soon learned that this was to be our new home—or at least part of it was. We were to occupy the back half of the house for the next six years. Our half of the house had two bedrooms, a kitchen large enough for a table for four, a living area with a coal stove, and beyond that a doorway leading to a bathroom and basement which we would share with the husband and wife and their two young daughters who lived in the front of the house. Both parts of the house were accessed through a common entrance door.

As my parents met with my father's new employer I began playing with his son, Hugh. Soon we were laughing and romping like we had known each other for years. The details of my father's employment faded into the background as I basked in the first friendship of my young life. By the time my father and his new boss, Roger, shook hands to finalize their agreement, Hugh and I had forged a bond that would last the rest of Hugh's short life, and impact me for the rest of mine.

Within days we had moved in, with Larry and I sharing a double bed tucked into the corner of the northeast bedroom. Larry occupied the half next to the wall and I had the benefit of easy access and a window to the east, just next to the bed. The window was a source of never-changing enchantment. At night I would fall asleep watching the moon and stars. On cloudy nights the clouds would drift across the sky transporting me to dreamland on puffy ships. On stormy nights lightning would light up the sky and rain would lash our window on the world. In the winter the window would ice over with long fingers of frost beginning at the bottom and moving up the window. As the sun rose in the morning the window would sparkle with delicate crystal designs.

The farm was an amazing rural wonderland for Larry and me. The 100-acre farm included buildings, a huge pasture, and woods. The gravel driveway in front of our house led to the farm gate next to the main barn and extended through the open range to another gate at the edge of the woods. Inside the farm gate was the main barn, a storage barn, and a huge maintenance building where a full-time mechanic kept everything, including tractors, farm trucks, delivery vehicles, and Roger's station wagon, running well.

The farm was only one part of a very successful feed store and poultry operation that had a hatchery and retail egg and feed sales in Tillsonburg and Ingersoll. Each spring, thousands of chicks would arrive to be nurtured and sold once they began laying in September. In the fields behind the barns there was a large open range with small, sheltered roosts scattered throughout where thousands of young hens would spend their first summer as they grew to maturity. In the fall they were either moved into our barns or sold as layers to hobbyists and farmers. The barnyard was always filled with a crew of several men with a variety of responsibilities. Everything on the farm except the laying hens was overseen by a mountain of a man, Mert McClintock.

At Hawkins farm my father had taken on the role of Flock Manager for a flock of 2,000 laying hens housed on three floors of a converted dairy barn. Each floor housed over 600 leghorn chickens bred to lay almost 365 days a year. The south wall of each floor was lined with nesting boxes. Each hen claimed a nesting space and like clockwork returned each day to deposit an egg. Aside from feeding and caring for the chickens, Dad gathered every egg by hand, putting them in large wire baskets that were transported into town where the eggs were sorted, packaged, and sold. Along the north wall of each floor, there was a huge roosting area covered with fencing wire where the chickens gathered each night to sleep. This roosting area, which sat a couple of feet off the floor, also collected the droppings from the chickens. By the time the annual cleaning and whitewashing took place, the ammonia generated by the feces was enough to give my father serious sinus issues and to have a lifelong impact on my ability to detect subtle odors.

My father worked six days a week from seven in the morning till six at night, with basic egg gathering and chores left to his discretion on Sunday. In return, Dad's pay was fifty dollars per week, a rent-free home, all the chickens and eggs needed to feed his family, and a week of summer holidays at a trailer owned by the boss located on the shore of Little Lake in Midland, Ontario.

As Dad's boss's son, Hugh, prepared to begin school we received an unexpected bonus. Since Hugh had turned five in February and lived within the town limits, he was entitled to begin half-day kindergarten in September. However, even though I was five, since I lived outside the town, I would be expected to attend a one-room rural school a few miles down the road. As a rural student, there was no kindergarten. I would begin school with grade one a year later. Hugh's father offered to pay my tuition to attend the town school so that Hugh and I could attend classes together.

So, with a little bit of luck, the country boy got to attend the town school in Tillsonburg—a blessing with implications that would help shape my future.

EARLY SCHOOL DAYS

On the day after my mother's thirty-sixth birthday on September 4, 1951, I began school at Tillson Avenue Public School in Tillsonburg. One of the farm delivery trucks dropped me off at the front of the school and Hugh and I played on the large pavement at the rear until the bell rang and a gray-haired woman, Miss Collins, called the kindergarten children to line up single file to walk into her classroom. Regular attendance at Sunday School had prepared me well as the day began with God Save Our King and the Lord's Prayer. Soon we settled into classroom routines. I enjoyed the classroom learning but it was the dynamics of a huge playground that really captured my attention. Although kindergarten was only half-day, the time before school began and the morning recess provided plenty of time to discover this amazing new world of the town school.

The schoolyard was huge with a Girls' side and a Boys' side, separate baseball diamonds, and a large soccer field at the back next to "Lover's Lane." The school was shaped in a large "L" and the entire inside of the "L" was paved. I watched in amazement as students skipped, bounced balls, rolled marbles, played hopscotch, jacks, and tag. The large playground was filled with activity as over 250 children, ages five to sixteen, played, lounged, and wrestled. Various forms of baseball and soccer were a constant. Older boys raced from the classroom to touch home plate and call out their position in scrub. Others played versions of games where a batter hit balls and all comers collected points for grounders and single bounces. In most versions, if you caught a fly, you were instantly up. But I am getting ahead of myself. The first few days were a blur as some of the older boys Hugh knew from his neighbourhood or children we both knew from Sunday School helped us get oriented.

In industrial post-war Canada our school looked and operated very much like the factories down the street. Kindergarten students entered the classroom at the north end of the school and the finished products emerged from the room next to the main entrance nine years later as work or high school prospects.

One morning, toward the end of the first week, as recess began, one of the older boys gestured for me to come into the hall and he quietly led me further down the production line. There, two rooms south, we peeked into the grade two classroom. To my friend's amusement and my horror, at the back of the class, in the largest desk they could find, sat a tall skinny young man looking lost and forlorn. In the following discussion with my older tutor I was told that unless you could read, write, and do arithmetic you failed in our school. And, if you failed, you stayed behind as your classmates moved on. The unhappy young man, Jimmy, struggled to read and write and so he was condemned to daily humiliation until his sixteenth birthday when he would be legally set free to work full time setting up pins at the local bowling alley, instead of the part-time position he now held when he wasn't confined to his desk at school. I was pretty sure you couldn't fail kindergarten, but I started to fear the *Dick and Jane* world that awaited just across the hall.

The second week, I started to realize that my jeans and high-top leather shoes set me apart from most of my classmates. Instead of Levi's, I wore denims my mother had sewed, and instead of Converse sneakers, I wore lace-up high-top leather boots prescribed by Popham's shoe store to help with my flat feet and weak ankles. My boots became a real issue that Friday during morning recess. A group of kindergarten and grade one boys were enjoying a rollicking game of keep-away with a football that one of the boys had brought from home when my foot hit a chunky grade one boy in the face. He spit out a tooth and went to find the teacher in charge of the yard. I was soon identified as the boy with the boots, and trembling I looked up into the eyes of a giant male teacher who said I was to go to the principal's office on Monday morning. With that, he turned and walked away. The other boys, including the one I had wounded, went back to playing as I stumbled off contemplating my fate and preparing for a long walk home and the longest weekend of my young life.

As soon as I got home, I confessed my crime to my mother, hoping for some comforting words. There were none. She seemed eerily stoic as she said we'd have to talk about it when Dad finished his day's work. In the evening, I retold my sad tale and that I had to go to meet the principal on Monday morning. This was precedent-setting for our family, and it became obvious that my parents were neither going to rescue nor defend me. Other than a "sounds serious" from my father, and "you should be more careful" from my mother, I was clearly on my own. Within a few minutes, it was a typical September evening with Larry and me playing outside until dusk and then coming in for bedtime routines and storytime.

Monday morning, I awoke with a heavy heart. My parents sent me off to school with Ed Sheering in the Hawkins delivery truck with instructions that if I was sent home from school, I should start walking home and stop at Paul George's store so that he could call and let my mother know I was on my way. That was it. Here I was a mile and a half from home with a trip to the office to start my third week at school.

When the school doors were unlocked at 8:30 a.m., I entered the north doors and walked past the safety of my classroom and down the long hall to discover my fate. As I neared my destination, I saw a large man in a blue suit standing in the centre of the hall. I felt like Jacob Two-Two meeting the Hooded Fang. He bent down and looked at me and all I could see was his bushy black eyebrows and penetrating eyes. I expected the worst. As I stood there trembling, he smiled and asked if I was Douglas Lester. I nodded and waited for my punishment. He smiled and told me he had talked to Billy's parents, and they said Billy's tooth was loose anyway. With a reminder to be more careful, I was finished with my first trip to the Principal's Office. It would not be my last.

LEARNING THE HARD WAY

Soon I relaxed and settled into the school routines. I loved the diversity and excitement of the schoolyard and, with Hugh Hawkins as my co-conspirator and constant companion, I grew in confidence each day. However, Hugh arrived mysteriously at school, and unless I had one of my rare sleepovers at his house, he headed home to Lisgar Avenue on his own, and I was on my own, as I walked to the town limits and beyond. The walk was filled with enticing distractions and dangerous interactions with dogs and bullies.

As I look back, I marvel that, as a five-year-old, I was on my own most days on my journey to and from school. Some days, I received a ride with one of the delivery men from the farm to the school, and sometimes, as I walked home, one of the men would stop and offer me a ride as he headed to the farm. Most of the time, however, I walked. The route was simple enough—a half-mile west from our home to the edge of town and then a mile south on Tillson Avenue to the school. The highway and street were tree-lined with sidewalks once I reached town. There were three businesses on my route that could be used as a refuge, or as a temptation if I had enough change to purchase a treat. Buster Scott's garage and store welcomed me as I reached the edge of Tillsonburg. His two temptations were Hires Genuine Root Beer and scooped ice cream cones—each for ten cents. A quarter mile further, Lamos Grocery was a welcome haven, with Helen Lamos always behind the counter with a smile and kindness. Nearer the school, Paul George's Deli was another well-known stop. Walking home was an adventure. There was always a group of us walking, talking, and playing games along the way. I followed others into the stores and even though I seldom had money to spend I was soon known by Paul George, Helen Lamos, and Buster Scott.

Early in October, I learned a painful lesson. As we left the playground and began walking down the sidewalk, another boy, Gary Demeyere, and I bragged about our throwing skills. In a dangerous version of mine-is-bigger-than-yours, we each picked up a small rock and proceeded to prove our prowess by throwing them across the busy street. We watched in horror as one of the stones flew high in the air and landed in the middle of the windshield of a big Buick headed north on Tillson Avenue. The windshield shattered. The man driving stopped in the middle of the street, opened his door, and looked for his attacker. By then Gary and I were running for cover and hid behind the first large tree along the sidewalk. As we peeked out to see what was happening, a large man grabbed each of us by the wrist and demanded our names. Gary's father was a well-known local farmer, so once he was identified he was released to run home. My captor took me to Paul George's store to contact my mother and then he drove me to the farm. I cowered in the distance as George Gyulveszi, one of the richest men in the area, discussed the incident with my father and negotiated a satisfactory settlement for the damage. I watched my father shake hands to seal the agreement. My father held his head high and looked George in the eyes. Dad was only five foot, six inches tall, but at that moment he was a giant in my eyes.

My parents demonstrated grace and love that day that I have tried to emulate ever since. They expressed their disappointment with my pride and lack of judgment and challenged me to be more thoughtful in the future. The reality of the situation was punishment enough. My father had agreed to pay seventy-five dollars to replace the windshield. Since my father was only paid fifty dollars a week, this was a very expensive lesson. I never knew if the other father ever paid a cent, and I never knew whose stone failed to clear the roadway. Once again, I had learned the hard way.

SOCIAL DYNAMICS

A classroom is an amazing little community. Alliances form, friendships blossom and fade. I seemed to get along with almost everybody except for one large girl. I thought Connie was a bully and I avoided her as much as possible. Unfortunately, Connie lived on Tillson Avenue and walked with the same group as I did each day on the way home. To make matters worse she lived almost next door to my kindergarten love interest, Sandy, and to make it even worse, they were friends.

I loved to talk and giggle with my classmates. Most of the time this was met with a stern look or a reminder to stop talking. My chattiness would be an ongoing issue for me in the classroom, although I became more aware and surreptitious as the years went by. Miss Collins ran her classroom well, and most of the time my talkative nature had minor consequences—that was until the day the class weaved a paper mat to take home for Thanksgiving. Once again, I was talking when I was expected to be listening. My punishment was to sit in a corner of the room watching my classmates take strips of coloured paper and create these amazing woven placemats. There was no reprieve. I missed the entire weaving experience and had no gift to take home. That stung, and even though I continued my talkative ways, I realized that art, music, and reading were activities too valuable to squander.

As Christmas approached, I began to lobby my mother for a birthday party at our house for my sixth birthday in January. To my surprise she was more agreeable than I had expected, but when she asked who I would invite there was a problem. The children I knew best were the Tillson Avenue crew—I would invite David, and Hugh, Sharon, and Sandy, and of course my brother Larry and our neighbour, Jennifer. My mother had been listening too well. She had heard me complain about my walking companion, Connie, who lived next to Sandy. She insisted that if I invited Sandy, Connie had to be invited too. I was trapped and I knew it. Connie would have to be included in what proved to be my first and only school friends–based birthday party.

On Saturday, January 19, 1952, the day after my birthday, my guests arrived at noon for lunch and cake. All went well, right up to the presentation of a large chocolate cake and my opportunity to blow out six candles. My mother cut the cake into generous-sized pieces and even before the last piece was served chaos had begun. My mother had mixed several coins from a penny to a quarter into the cake mix. As the word spread around the table, eating the cake became secondary as I watched in horror. I was dumbfounded for several reasons, and these thoughts created a storm in my young brain—*Why would my mother waste so much money when it was so scarce? What if one of my greedy prospectors choked? Why was this intruding mob free to act so differently from what was expected table manners in our home?*

By the time the cake and my visitors were cleaned up, I would have been quite content to usher all my guests out the door, but the worst was yet to come. Like the biblical locusts, my classmates descended upon my room and toys. Our tin-can telephones with their butcher-cord line were stretched across the room and mocked and admired simultaneously. I don't know what became of the girls, but the boys terrified me as they checked out every toy like inspectors looking for defects. I held my breath as they tried out our little train with its fragile tracks. Before the time for the assault expired, there was one more indignity. One of the visitors discovered my Raggedy Andy doll. Handmade by my mother, it had been one of my treasures until my guests asked if I still played with him. Like the disciple Peter in the garden, I treated Andy with disdain, and he soon disappeared from my life. The children left the party giggling and smiling. I put on a brave front, but I was less than thrilled. By the time the last child had left our home, I was an older and wiser six-year-old.

VICTORIA DAY

In our home, summer really began on the May 24th weekend. My father used to say that you put your long underwear on at Thanksgiving and took it off on Victoria Day. All through my childhood years, Victoria Day meant a large bonfire, a wiener roast, firecrackers, fireworks, and a very late night. For the first ten years, the celebration always took place at my Aunt Mabel and Uncle Ken's farm. The home of my mother's older sister, this farm was the place Larry and I went for a holiday or when Mom and Dad had a time away. Aunt Mabel had four children—George, Aletha, Marie, and Val. George was much older, but he was always kind and witty, and we loved being around him. Aletha and Marie spoiled us and encouraged us in music and dealing with Val. Our cousin Val was three years older than me. For Val everything in life was an adventure, and sometimes I was wounded or misled by his enthusiasm. Nevertheless, Val, Larry, and I spent many delightful hours playing in hay mows and along the creek.

On the Monday of the Victoria Day weekend, Dad would hurry through his chores, feeding the chickens and gathering the eggs, and then we would head to Uncle Ken's farm near Springfield. Usually, we would arrive by late afternoon and help gather a few more branches for the huge pile on the driveway. Firecrackers were readily available and inexpensive. The ones I remember best were about the size of a little finger and came ten in a package. Each of these miniature explosives came with its own wick. Our parents were unconcerned as we lit matches and learned how to light and throw a firecracker before it went off in our hands. Each year, on the next day at school, we would see some burned fingers and share tales.

As soon as Uncle Ken and his older son George finished milking the cows, the bonfire was started and several aunts, uncles, and cousins would begin roasting wieners on one of a dozen or more willow branches cut and sharpened for this purpose. Soon firecrackers would be exploding by our feet or under the chair of one of our aunts. It was delightful chaos. We ate hotdogs, chips, and marshmallows until we were stuffed, and by then it was time for sparklers and fireworks. My older cousin, George, who was sixteen years older than me, was in charge of the pyrotechnics. We didn't have a lot, but they were impressive to us. The evening always ended with two fireworks that seemed an anticlimax after watching exploding fireballs high in the sky. One was a spinner nailed to a fence post, that on a good year spun madly as it spit sparks and made a loud hissing sound. Often it just went "fzzzt" while we booed. Then it was time for the Burning Schoolhouse—what a disappointment—just a boxy contraption that sat on a fence post and burned quietly. As it sputtered to a dull ending, I knew the night was over and we bid our farewells and headed home.

LIVING EASY

Both of my parents loved the outdoors, and their enjoyment of the good earth was passed on in every aspect of our lives. Roger Hawkins had allotted our family a small garden plot on the poultry farm just behind the farmyard buildings. On the Saturday of each Victoria Day weekend, it was time to plant our vegetable garden. Before planting day the garden had been plowed and disked, but the heavy clay still had to be pounded into workable soil with rakes and hoes and smoothed before it would be ready for planting. The garden was a family affair, and even at our young age we were enlisted to hoe and dig holes for planting potatoes and beans. With pride, we helped unwind the string and pound in the stakes that marked the rows of carrots and radishes, beans, Swiss chard, corn, and cucumbers. Once planted, the guide string was removed, and a stake was pounded in to mark the row. We placed the seed package on the stake to remind us of what was there until it had sprouted. Most of the vegetables were planted by hand and, as small boys, my brother and I were instructed in the art of carefully distributing the precious seeds. For corn and beans, Dad had an amazing ancient hand planter that poked a hole and then dropped the correct number of kernels or beans into the hole. Although planting day took many hours, I don't ever remember being bored or disinterested. When our help wasn't required, Larry and I had small trucks and cars that we played with on roads and hills we fashioned at the end of the garden. My mother and father were good teachers and clever managers. They gave us enough work to teach responsibility while adding enough Freshie, cookies, and freedom to make it seem like fun. Finally, a wall of red snow fence was placed around our garden to keep rabbits and chickens out.

Summer Sundays were magical. Dad managed to fit his chores around church and still had time for a picnic lunch by a river where he fished, or for a trip to the lake where the family swam and basked in the sun. Once each summer, we would visit the Sand Hills east of Port Burwell where a hundred-foot-high hill of sand provided endless entertainment as we climbed, jumped, and frolicked, ending up on the Lake Erie beach. Both my parents were confident swimmers and we soon learned to dog paddle and body surf in the waves. When brother Larry had had enough, he would start to turn blue, and I would be reluctantly summoned to shore where we would both be wrapped in towels and laid out to dry. Back at the car, we used the car door and a towel as a change room as we removed our bathing suits and changed into our shorts and shirts.

Then good got even better. As a hired man, Dad was given a week's stay at Roger Hawkins' trailer on the shore of Little Lake in Midland, Ontario. As preparation for our holiday, Larry and I could pick out boxes of any type of popular cereal—a welcome break from 358 days of porridge. While in Midland, my father woke before dawn every day so he could row our rented boat to a reed bed and fish for perch and bass as the sun came up. Dad would return by 8:00 a.m. with a few fish and a smile as we gathered for a morning breakfast. Then the day would begin in earnest. My mother was often the organizer of the outings. During our three summers at Midland, there were day trips to Penetanguishene, the Martyrs Shrine, and the Indigenous village of Sainte-Marie among the Hurons. But most of all, there were long lazy days of sunshine and lakeside living. We swam at the beach. We fished and jumped off the wooden dock. Dad and Mom took us in the rowboat where we caught perch, which were pan-fried for supper. Often the day ended with our own little family fire on the beach, roasting marshmallows, and lying on our backs staring at the Big Dipper and a star-studded sky.

I was a skilled fisherman by age six. I had learned how to collect dew worms with a flashlight on the dew-covered grass after dark. I had learned how to select a sapling along a riverbank and with Dad's help to cut it just the right length for my pole. Then I had learned how to tie the fishing line to the end of the pole and wind about thirty feet of line around the pole so I could turn my pole to release or wind in the bait. Next, I learned how to attach a lead sinker and a hook. I learned to tie a hook almost as early as I learned to tie my shoes. Next, I had to learn how to bait the hook, impaling the wriggly worm along the length of the hook so that it was alluring but not easily removed. Then, when I caught a fish, I had to learn how to extricate the hook. The first task was slimy; the second could be dangerous—until I learned how to avoid the spiky pectoral fin and the hook. At Little Lake, aside from bigger perch, we caught beautiful but tiny sunfish that we learned to release unharmed back into the water.

The long sunny days of summer made each day an adventure. Summer was my favourite season as a young boy, and it still is.

THE BUCHNER FARM

My Aunt Mabel and Uncle Ken's farm was a frequent stop for us as young boys. Mom and Dad visited often and would sit and talk for hours. Many times, Mom would bring a Toni perm she had purchased, and Aunt Mabel would trim and perm my mother's hair so it curled tight for several weeks. Then, while the men talked about cows and cars, my mother would return the favour and perm my aunt's hair. Often late in the visit Aunt Mabel would pass on some hand-me-downs from cousin, Val, and since she had a soft heart and a sense of fairness, there was usually a new shirt or toy for brother, Larry. Just as it seemed we were about to leave, Aunt Mabel and her girls would spring into action preparing salmon sandwiches served with tea, fresh milk, cheese, and pie. I remember my wonder at how far my aunt and cousins could spread a small can of salmon mixed with mayonnaise. I also marvelled as a block of cheese covered in mould was cleaned up and served without a second thought.

My aunt and uncle's old two-story house seemed huge compared to our two-bedroom apartment. When Larry and I stayed for a few days, we slept upstairs. There was running water in the Buchner house, but no indoor bathroom. The "toilet" was in the outhouse—a small, crude shack behind the house with a wooden bench with two holes where you sat. I never understood why there were two seats since this was not an experience I wanted to share with anyone. A pole light in the yard was the only light we had as we made our way to and from the outhouse before going to bed. At night, the bedrooms had a chamber pot, which was kept under the bed and allowed a chance to relieve yourself without trekking outdoors. Larry and I slept three in a bed with our cousin Val, and on more than one occasion, I woke up with a thump as I fell out of bed.

The meals at the huge kitchen table were generous, and we enjoyed the hard work and laughter that was part of life on a dairy farm.

BARNYARD BIOLOGY

The farm was the place where I learned about life in its rawest forms. Here, as a young child, I saw birth and death without discussions about fairness or feelings. Life was a cycle. Birth and death were a necessary part of that cycle. On the Hawkins farm, during our six years there, we ate eggs and chickens—lots of eggs and chickens! In the side yard, we had a block of wood with two spikes nailed to the top. Dad would bring a plump chicken that had ceased laying to the house. The doomed chicken's head was placed on the block between the spikes, the neck stretched, and then with a swing of an axe the chicken was quickly dispatched. I was horrified the first time I saw my father or mother chop the head off and hold the chicken in the air as the lifeblood drained onto the grass, but soon it was just part of life as I helped remove the feathers and prepare our Sunday meal.

On the Buchner farm, I saw the life and death drama on even a larger scale. The herd of Holsteins was on constant display as they stood in rows in their stanchions to be fed and milked. I saw the huge bull in its pen with its prominent genitalia and I understood what was involved as I saw calves being born. I saw the manure and urine and milk. We dodged cow patties in the fields and, when they were dry, used them as primitive frisbees. We watched mature calves and older cows loaded onto a butcher's truck and later that week we had roast beef for supper. Life was raw and it was cyclical.

One day, as I was exploring at my uncles' farm, I discovered a nest of duck's eggs just beginning to hatch. Fascinated and curious as a beak and a foot began to break through, I thought I could help. I gently began to break away some of the shell. Soon I was horrified to see blood and then my cousin realized what I was doing and intervened. "You can't help them!" he said, "They have to do it themselves." I was learning the complexity of life and, a few days later as I watched a veterinarian insert his arm deep into a cow to liberate a breached calf, I realized how *complex* the web of life is. Without that intervention, both the calf and its mother might have died. I was learning that, in life, wisdom is knowing when to step back and when to intervene.

Every aspect of life and development was under constant study by Val, Larry, and me, and our laboratory provided endless opportunity. One sunny day, as we watched the young goslings waddle to the creek for a swimming lesson, we got into a discussion about animals and their ability to swim. There was a large cement watering trough at the back of the barn, and soon we were chasing down participants for our experiment. One of us would drop the subject into the water at one end of the water trough and we would evaluate the swimming technique, offering help at the other end, if required. We discovered that although cats are not strong swimmers they did quite well and were amazingly capable of exiting the water on their own. Chickens were a surprise. After comparing their feet with a duck's, we questioned their water worthiness but, surprisingly, with a lot of clucking and a great deal of wing flapping when set free, they proved that, if necessary, even they could survive in the water.

Life on the farm was an endless learning opportunity. One of the last lessons that summer came when Larry and I had our first horseback ride. Our cousin, Marie, was an athlete, and she rode the Buchners' plow horse with ease and elegance. One day, Larry and I convinced her to let us have a ride. With the help of a fence and some assistance from Marie and her older sister Aletha, we sat proudly on the bare back of our steed. Clutching the horse's mane and holding the reins I was in charge as Larry clung behind me. At first, all went well as we ambled to the end of the driveway and, using the reins like my hero Roy Rogers, I turned our mount, and we headed back up the long driveway. We picked up speed and I basked in the joy of the moment. Suddenly, our horse saw a clump of appealing grass, and in one smooth move stopped and lowered its head to nibble. I was still clutching the reins as both me and my brother were hurled into the air. I landed with a thud and as Larry crashed to the ground on top of me our heads banged together. We struggled to our feet and stumbled toward the house. Without discussing it we both knew that if we ever hoped to ride again, we would say we were fine and hope to begin to be able to focus by supper time.

DIFFERENT WORLDS

By the age of six, I had started to realize that just as my parents had different expectations and tolerance levels so did every other adult. Church and Sunday School had taught me a lot already. On Sunday morning the preacher was loud and demanding. He quoted scripture and pounded the pulpit to wake sleepy children and fill everyone with the fear of hellfire. In the formal morning service, the educated and proper Reverend led the singing of the hymns from the official hymnal of the Baptist Convention of Ontario accompanied by a pipe organ. In the evening, the music was led by a taxi driver named Ernie and accompanied by a piano—a wonderful experience as we sang lively songs with upbeat choruses from the brown, less formal, songbook.

GRADE ONE

As I prepared to cross the hall from kindergarten to grade one, I knew this new world would have a new person with her own set of quirks and expectations.

If I had learned that life on the farm was a process of struggle and survival, I was about to discover school in 1950's Ontario was just as demanding. As students, we were constantly graded and compared. Lectures, punishment, and embarrassment were the norm, and students who didn't make the grade were slowly moved through the classes with placement determined more by size than academic progress.

At school, everything from Sunday School attendance to the cleanliness of your fingernails was assessed. Early in grade one, our music skills were evaluated for the first time. Up until then I loved singing and my church experience had indicated that enthusiasm was all that mattered. In our grade one classroom, one day a man named Mr. Fatheringham showed up with a round shiny thing and, when he blew it, we were to hum the same sound. If we failed, we were consigned to the blackbirds or crows, while the robins and bluebirds smiled at their success. I had a good voice and with a little practice I was able to rise through the bird ranks, but even at this young age my socialist sensibilities disliked the process and I ached for those who were publicly humiliated.

I enjoyed learning and social interactions. I discovered that I was good at academics, but I was easily distracted and more interested in my classmates than the wisdom of the teacher. My social justice sentiments began early, and I was quick to feel sorry for students who were disciplined. This sense of concern was particularly keen when I was considered one of the culprits.

I loved the energy and bustle of the playground. There were boys and girls of every size and shape and a constant hum of activity. I had learned to curb my enthusiasm and play with my agemates in ways that were safe and acceptable. I was just getting comfortable with Mrs. Brennan when, after Christmas a new teacher, Mrs. Bissett, arrived and took over the classroom.

Mrs. Bissett was a stern woman who ruled the classroom with fierce expectations. When she or any other adult entered the classroom, we were trained to stand immediately to show our respect. Two of my favourite pastimes, daydreaming and chatting, were forbidden. Each morning began with the "Lord's Prayer" and "God Save the King." Standing at attention meant exactly that—any leaning or fidgeting was met with a personal visit and a quiet reprimand. Suddenly, I did not feel as safe and secure as I had just a few weeks earlier.

My safety concerns were increased one day early in January. One of the girls who sat at the table next to mine came each day in a frilly dress. One day, when the teacher stepped out of the classroom, to the surprise and delight of everyone, our young fashionista quickly climbed onto her group's table and, like a Spanish dancer, did a little dance, punctuated with a flip of her skirt. At the worst possible moment, Mrs. Bissett walked back into the classroom. My goofy smile froze. The situation was doubly dire because our dancer was the daughter of our new teacher. Determined to make an example, the teacher took our performer firmly by the wrist and escorted her to the front of the classroom. Here, teacher and parent, Mrs. Bissett, calmly proceeded to force the young offender to hold her hands out one at a time as she hit her three times on each hand with a heavy black piece of leather. We all watched in stunned silence. This was the first time I heard of "getting the strap." Unfortunately, it would not be the last.

SHORTCUTS

As my life demonstrates, I am curious and gullible and the only thing I can say in my defence is that I usually try not to make the same mistake twice. This was the case as I learned about this thing one of the older boys described as a "shortcut." Eager to try it out, I decided to abandon my usual route home and check out the back streets, convinced that my shortcut would have me home in record time. Unfortunately, the reality fell far short of my eager anticipation, and, after touring some new subdivisions and encountering at least one dead end, I arrived home nearly an hour late and had to listen to a long and detailed instruction from my worried mother on what a real shortcut was.

THE POWER OF STORY

The summer before grade one, Mom and Dad had taken us to the drive-in theatre while on vacation. One short black and white movie touched me in a way that I had never been moved by the few movies I had seen up to that point. It was the story of a boy and a horse and, as a sad but inevitable end began to unfold, I felt a lump in my throat. Tears filled my eyes and my throat ached. It was the first time I had been so moved by a story. I was discovering the power of language and my inner world was being enlivened by rich imagery. This was the beginning of a lifelong love of books and stories.

At our church's Sunday School, I learned the great stories from the Bible, the story of Joseph and his many-coloured robe, Jonah and the whale, David and Goliath, the Plagues of Egypt, Moses parting the sea, Mary and Joseph and the birth in a stable, Jesus turning water into wine, Jesus enduring pain and dying on a cross. Heroic adventures and courageous lives. My imagination grew much faster than my ability to read, but the power of story had lit an inner flame.

Fortunately for me, my mother knew the power of poetry and prose and introduced us to both early on in our lives. So, while at school I was painfully learning to read with the mind-numbing adventures of Dick and Jane, Spot, and Puff, at home my mother was awakening my imagination by reading the wonderful stories of Thornton Burgess. I loved the woodland characters that lived on the edge of Farmer Brown's farm. This was made all the more wonderful since we lived right next door to a real-life Farmer Brown. My mother read with expression, and bedtime stories from the *Family Herald* or one of Burgess's books kept us begging for more. Stories about Johnny Chuck, Peter Cottontail, Unc' Billy Possum, Buster Bear, Paddy the Beaver, Jerry Muskrat, Reddy Fox, and Bowser the Hound opened the world of story and made me eager to learn to read on my own.

ADVENTURES ON THE CHICKEN FARM

Life on the farm was never dull. There were always opportunities to watch trucks and tractors in action. Each year, old hens were loaded onto trucks and disappeared as new laying hens were moved into the barn. As part of this annual process, cleaning the roosts, whitewashing the inside of the barn, and worming the chickens were important events. Sometimes they provided more entertainment than even my curious mind wanted.

Each of these processes required a team of workers and I loved to see my dad working with the other men, joking, and enjoying the company. Dad was a natural entertainer and storyteller. I marvelled as he entertained the men by balancing an egg on top of his bent arm near his elbow, and then quickly straightening his arm catching the egg in midair before it fell. This led to hilarious competitions with inevitable smashed eggs. During another break, egg-sucking became the topic, with demonstrations by Dad, and more hilarity.

As the roosts were opened to be cleaned out, the men wore their large red or blue handkerchiefs over their lower faces to block out some of the detritus and the smell. As the men removed the wire coverings on the roosts, they looked like a gang of outlaws about to rob a stagecoach. Armed with pitchforks and wheelbarrows, the straw and droppings were removed to a large door and dumped into a waiting manure spreader below. Shortly after the forks started disturbing the manure, large rats would emerge, and the men would scramble trying to impale them with a manure fork. What a show. There were three large floors in the main barn and this process would last several days. Then, the interior of the barn would be whitewashed with a mix of limestone and water that brightened and disinfected at the same time.

It was during this cleaning process that I learned that what is entertaining for a six-year-old could be terrifying for a four-year-old. One night I awoke from my sleep to see a ghostly figure standing on the dresser just beyond my side of the bed. He was screaming, "Don't let them get me! Don't let them get me!" About the time I awoke enough to realize my brother was missing from his usual location in our bed, my mother arrived and began to deescalate the situation. As she talked him down from the perch and reinserted him into the bed two things became clear—brother, Larry, was still sound asleep, and, he had left the bed and climbed onto the dresser to escape the whitewashers, or was it the rats? The next morning, he claimed the incident had never happened. Fortunately for my sanity that was his only midnight delirium.

Once the new flock was ready to fill the coop, the chickens were corralled with red snow fence and one by one, each hen was handed to Dad to be wormed. It was a simple enough procedure. The chicken's mouth was forced open and a jellybean-looking pill was pushed to the back of its throat. The bird swallowed and was then released into its new home. I was in the house with my mother the day that this went horribly wrong.

Little brother had been playing on the barn stairs as the men worked. When Dad checked on his four-year-old son, Larry had a black ring around his lips and Dad realized he had been popping worm capsules into his mouth. The men quickly placed Larry into a car. They stopped at the house to inform and pick up my mother. I was handed off to our neighbour Ruby and, as they drove wildly out the driveway toward the hospital, I watched out the window wondering if I would have a brother the next day. After what seemed like hours, Mom, Dad, and little brother arrived back home. The hospital staff had emptied his stomach and, after checking him thoroughly, had decided he would be okay.

Now that the new flock was safely in the coops, the dangers were still not over. If a storm shut down the hydro, the terrified rookie leghorns, raised on an open range, would panic and pile into the corners of the barn seeking safety. If Dad didn't get to the barn and pull them off the huge pile quickly, the ones on the bottom would suffocate. I was thrilled to be considered big enough to help, and I was soon quite adept at heaving chickens off the pile as we struggled to limit the death toll. Fortunately, such crises were infrequent, but the fragility of life was a constant reality on the farm.

THE RHYTHM OF LIFE

As I would be reminded years later when, as a grown man, I went to visit my parents at a summer cottage on Colpoy's Bay, my mother was never one to waste a day. Every day was filled with purpose and activity.

Dad worked six days a week from 7:00 a.m. to 6:00 p.m. Our household accepted that reality as the rhythm of our lives, with all meals as a family at the kitchen table.

As I settled into the routines of school life, my weekday routine meant that I carried a lunch pail with a Thermos. All the students ate lunch sitting on the floor around the auditorium. My lunch would include sandwiches, fruit or vegetables, and homemade cookies. School lunchtime was thirty minutes, and then we were locked outside from 12:30 p.m. until the bell rang at 1:30 p.m. At 4:30 p.m. I would head home, where I would join my brother in an hour of adventures before being called to supper.

We didn't have a refrigerator until I was eleven, or television until I was fourteen. We filled most of our hours with outdoor activities, and the farm was filled with possibilities. New barns were being built. There were cats with litters of new kittens. There were Bonnie and Rex, the police dogs that guarded the gate. Then we had a collie we named Lassie. My friend, Hugh, had rabbits at his home in town and, when they began to multiply and ravage the neighbours' gardens, they were brought to the farm and released to live feral under and around the farm buildings. White, brown, and grey rabbits and their new young bunnies entertained us as they tried to coexist with dogs and cats who prowled and chased.

We were dog people, or at least Dad and the boys were, but our dogs were never invited inside. Ruby, our neighbour, was a cat person, and she and her girls usually had at least one cat, and often kittens, living in their home. Ruby soon convinced our dog that leaving her cats alone was in his best interest. Hugh and I took a little more convincing. I remember well the day we experimented with one of Ruby's cats by putting clothes pins on its ears and tail and then turning it loose behind the house. The cat meowed loudly and raced in circles trying to escape the pain and the creatures that were tormenting it. However, the entertainment was short-lived as Ruby grabbed us, and with a shake and a swat sent us to rescue the cat and return it to her as she emphasized her anger with more tongue lashing. Ruby was a force and we decided to restrict our animal experiments to the barns and fields far from her territory.

Banished from Ruby's area, we did conduct a few more experiments with the abundant supply of barn cats—mostly to determine their ability to always land on their feet when dropped from a height. Our intent was never meanness, just boredom and insatiable curiosity. Not wanting to create enemies with our feline subjects, we were careful to prepare them well for their adventure and soothe them after their successful landings.

Monday was laundry day. Mother had a wringer washer in the basement and each Monday she would fill the outdoor clothesline with our laundry. Wednesday night was Prayer Meeting at the church. Thursday night was grocery night at the Loblaws store in town. Friday night was often a town night. With little money and no particular need, like most rural families, we would drive to town, park on Broadway, and perhaps wander through the Chainway or Woolworth's, but mostly just sit in our vehicle and watch people walk by, with frequent waves or open window conversations with people Mom and Dad knew from church or farm life.

Saturdays were filled with adventures as Larry and I had a long driveway and a variety of buildings to explore. One day we used a large red truck parked behind the barns as a slide and had a delightful morning climbing onto the roof and sliding down the windshield and off the hood. By the time Mert McClintock discovered us, we had unfortunately created a dent in the hood. Lucky for us, Mert opened the hood and gave a thump with his large hand and our damage was undone. However, that was one more activity added to our growing list of future restrictions.

Late Saturday afternoon, we would be summoned to the house to do our part in preparing for Sunday. Larry and I would polish Dad's and our Sunday shoes. We would have our Saturday bath and our wandering outdoors was curtailed. We would have to content ourselves with listening to the radio or playing with toys. Saturday was often an early bedtime because Dad's following day of "rest" was the busiest day of the week.

SUNDAY ADVENTURES

Sundays began with Sunday School and church. Then after lunch, we usually had some sort of outing. We would visit Dad's brothers Alex or Fred, or his Aunt Aida. On Mom's side, we would visit Aunt Mabel or Uncles Lloyd, Joe, Alan, or Art. Then we would stop at home, get changed and get ready to go to church from 7:00 to 8:00 p.m. Often, the day still wasn't finished as the evenings usually involved visits with Aunt Ruth, Uncle Ernie, or Grampa and Gramma Chipps. Each visit had its own challenges and charms.

Uncle Lloyd and Aunt Fleda's family were quite proper on Sundays, and the same was true at Uncle Joe and Aunt Hazel's. Here we had to be polite and sit quietly. At Aunt Mabel's and Uncle Art's, there were age mates and all kinds of adventures in the barn or fields.

Aunt Ruth's husband was a police officer who loved to captivate us with stories of crime and punishment, so when at their place, Uncle Ray smoked and laughed while telling us about incidents like the woman who was robbed at the bowling alley, or the fight at the hotel. Meanwhile, Aunt Ruth was an endless source of local gossip. She knew the details of every divorce, illness, or scandal in town. Most visits ended with cookies and Kool-Aid. The cookies were bargain brands and Aunt Ruth kept the sugar added to the Kool-Aid to such a minimum that Larry and I would make subtle faces at each other as we struggled with the contrast between cookies and the watered-down Kool-Aid, trying to make the other one giggle.

Uncle Ernie was a mechanic who worked at a wrecking yard on the edge of town. He not only knew all the gossip that Aunt Ruth provided, but he also had strong opinions about politics, religion, and science. He stated his opinions with such confidence that I was a teenager before I realized that bluster baffles brains and many of Ernie's theories were more noise than news.

On the evenings when we visited Grampa and Gramma Chipps' place they would be seated at the kitchen table with a Bible and hymn book atop the vinyl tablecloth. Often, they were sitting without any lights on as the last rays of sunlight allowed Grampa to read while saving electricity costs. After updates from Grampa on who had dropped in, and updates from Mom on whom we had visited, Larry and I would sing some Sunday School songs as our grandparents smiled their approval. This ritual continued for years, and as we learned to read, we would often spend an hour singing from Grampa's hymnal. Unlike my aunt, Grampa didn't scrimp on his store-bought cookies, and as the grown-ups enjoyed tea, Larry and I enjoyed milk and generous helpings of Grampa's favourite brand of crunchy treats, "Dad's Cookies."

On the drive home, my brother would quickly fall asleep and be carried into bed. I never gave in to the Sandman, afraid I might miss something if I closed my eyes. It wasn't uncommon for us to tumble into bed at 11:00 p.m. on a Sunday night.

OUR TOWN

The town and the people that shaped my early understanding of the world were typical of many parts of southern Ontario at that time. Almost everyone I met during my early school years had European roots, most from England and elsewhere in the British Isles. Our Baptist church pulpit and pews were filled with British names like Ross, Beattie, Nurse, Graves, Mackenzie, Mason, Johnson, and Jones. My teachers were also British descendants, with names like Alabastine, Bissett, Mackenzie, Collins, Andrews, and Currie. Like my Lester and Chipps ancestors, many families had come first to the northern U.S. in the 1700s, then moved north into Ontario in the early 1800s as tensions between the Colonies and Britain simmered and exploded in the 1770s and again in 1812. Anxious to populate the remaining British colonies in North America, Britain made it easy for settlers to move into what would become Canada. With opportunities to own a farm or property, as fields were cleared and farms and businesses began to develop, these early and late Loyalists moved north and created towns and villages wherever a river could power a mill.

Our town began in the 1820s as Dereham Forge, with a sawmill on the banks of the Big Otter River just twenty-five miles north of Lake Erie. In 1836, the village was renamed Tillsonburg in honour of its founder, George Tillson. It was also in this year that the main street, Broadway, was laid out to its full one-hundred-foot (thirty metres) width. Because the village started as a predominantly logging and wood product centre, the street was built as one of the widest in Ontario, to accommodate the turning of three-team logging wagons. By the time I was born, Tillsonburg was the centre of several vibrant industries—Borden's Milk Products, Keewadin Dairy, Beaver Foundry, Welland Vale, Tillsonburg Shoe Factory, Warwick Lumber, Newman's Flowers, Hawkins Feed, and the largest employer, Livingston Industries. The town also had two hotels, two bowling alleys, two movie theatres, pool halls, drugs stores, jewelry stores, a Chainway, Woolworth's, and Metropolitan store, as well as an A&P and Loblaws grocery store.

It was my good luck to be born in the Tillsonburg area at a time of growth and transition. With most people having family and friends living on the surrounding farms, the hard times of the Depression in the 1930s and the challenges of the war years had been just a bit of an inconvenience while progress continued in both farming and manufacturing. The end of World War II was a time of optimism and change. Many war-weary families began to arrive in our area from Europe, eager to start a new life.

Tillsonburg had several successful factories, and this, along with a rapid increase in tobacco farming, created a need for labourers. The newcomers settled quickly and did well. Our town thrived. Building trades flourished as small bungalows were pushing into what had been fields on the east side of town. As I was learning to walk, Tillsonburg added a new public school on Tillson Avenue to accommodate the increasing number of students on the east side of town. As I was beginning kindergarten, a large modern high school was being built.

FATHER AND SON

My father had smoked either a pipe or cigarettes since I was born so it wasn't something I noticed—until he quit. One Monday morning, my father headed to the barn with something new in his shirt pocket—a package of Dentyne gum. He had decided to give up smoking, and each time he had the urge, he unwrapped a stick of gum. As a six-year-old, I didn't pay much attention, until much later in life as I faced my own addiction to nicotine. Then recalling my father's quiet victory, his example inspired me.

My father also influenced my work ethic. He was a hardworking man who found something interesting in everything he did. He allowed me to follow him on Sunday afternoons as he gathered eggs in the large coops, and I was soon helping to remove the eggs from the nesting boxes along the wall. It wasn't long before I met a setting hen. There weren't many, but these birds, instead of laying their daily egg and then socializing and foraging on the floor, stayed put in the nesting box with the intent of hatching their egg. When I stuck my hand into the nesting box, the hen pecked me hard to let me know I wasn't allowed to touch her egg. Dad laughed as I winced and looked confused. He demonstrated his technique of distracting, then quickly removing the egg from under the reluctant donor. Soon it was my turn, and with a shaking hand, I slowly gained the necessary confidence and finesse to outwit the wary setting hens.

One Saturday, as I lingered around the barn, Dad offered me my first paid work. He would pay me a nickel to sweep the three floors of stairs and landings in the barn. My chest swelled as I found the broom and climbed to the third floor to begin my first real job. Slowly and carefully, I worked my way down the steps until I reached the cement floor at the entrance to the barn. Here Dad taught me how to use a flat shovel as a dustpan so that I could sweep up the dirt and straw and remove it one scoop at a time. As I struggled to manipulate the broom and shovel, I felt a sense of accomplishment. I was the oldest son. I was learning to make my way in the world.

This growing sense of maturity was further developed as the first snow fell and, for the first time, my father invited me to accompany him on a Saturday afternoon rabbit hunt in the woods at the back of the farm. Our quarry was a cottontail rabbit. Although I had a soft spot for Thornton Burgess' Peter Cottontail, I saw no contradiction in us killing and eating a rabbit. Farm life had taught me that people lived by eating animals and vegetables. That was the way of life. Dad had a single-shot sixteen-gauge shotgun. My job was to jump on brush piles and walk-through tall grass at the edge of fence lines. When we scared a rabbit out of hiding, and it began to run, Dad would take aim and shoot. On the third Saturday, after Dad fired, a rabbit fell in the snow, and we carried it home. As with the chickens we had killed in the yard, once again I saw death close up. As we walked to the shed where Dad skinned and prepared the rabbit meat for cooking, he told me how the Indigenous people thanked the animal and the Creator for sharing life so that they might live. As I was allowed to give the entrails and body parts to the police dogs, Bonnie and Rex, I marvelled at the fierceness of life. I was thankful to have my father as a guide on this challenging life journey in what the preacher called "the valley of the shadow of death."

CHRISTMAS CONCERT

Every Sunday we went to Sunday School before church. My early Sunday School teachers were kind and gentle older women, and I soaked up the grandmotherly love I never knew from my own grandparents. Mrs. Shepherd was especially kind and caring with cookies often accompanying her lessons about God's love. The little group of eight students was also a stark contrast to the thirty competing for attention at school. As Christmas approached, we began to practice a group presentation based on the word C-H-RI-S-T-M-A-S, with each letter reminding us of one aspect of the Christmas story. I certainly didn't know what an acrostic was, but our presentation felt very grown-up compared to the short recitations we had memorized in previous years. On top of that, we were going to sing two verses of *Silent Night*, my first chance to perform on stage. I quickly discovered that I loved drama and music and the applause from the crowd. After the concert, Mrs. Shepherd gave each of us a gift. My gift was a leather belt, hand-embossed by our teacher. I wore it with pride for a few years until it would no longer reach around my waist. Looking back, I realize that it was probably in Mrs. Shepherd's Sunday School class that the first seeds of my future career were sown.

TONSILLITIS

During my first year in school as the days grew colder, I started to experience a sore throat. Soon it hurt to swallow, and I felt hot and woozy. I missed school for the first time and my mother took me to the doctor's office. Doctors MacLeod and Alexander shared an office on Brock Street that opened every afternoon at 1:00 p.m. There were no appointments. People lined up and, after speaking to the receptionist, we sat, sometimes for hours, in a huge room full of people in varying stages of sickness, until our name was called. In the examining room, Dr. MacLeod would listen with his stethoscope and then get out his tongue suppressor and I would say *ahhh* as he shone his light into my mouth and nodded his head. I had a nasty case of tonsillitis. We left the doctor's office with the first of many brown bottles of "yellow medicine." The medicine was chalky and had a *mediciny* smell, but I had no choice but to be wrapped in flannelette and sweat it out.

I was not a good patient. I wanted attention and to be left alone at the same time. I tried to get going again too soon and ended up sicker for longer. My mother was caring and, with a hot water bottle for comfort and a mix of Raleigh's salve and chicken noodle soup, she would nurse me back to health. Until the next time.

My bouts of tonsillitis were a part of winter life for the next four years. When other children would get a cold, I would start with sniffles and a cough and then descend into tonsillitis hell. This went on each winter until, mercifully, a tonsillectomy ended the cycle.

CHRISTMAS MAGIC

My mother loved special events. No matter how meagre the budget, she managed to make every Christmas a joyous and festive time. Dad put up a pine tree in the corner of the living room just outside our bedroom door. One Monday, just before Christmas, Dad returned from the Sales Arena in Tillsonburg with three strings of Christmas lights and, to make it even more special, they came with silver reflectors. Dad's treasure box also contained our first tree ornaments. By the time my mother had added some strings of popcorn and silver tinsel called angel hair, our tree looked magical as it lit the darkened rooms.

Each year, as Christmas approached, we would spend hours looking through the Simpsons-Sears and Eaton's catalogues dreaming of Roy Rogers holsters and six guns, Daniel Boone coonskin hats, Tinker Toys, trucks and cars, Meccano sets, shirts and coats, sleighs, and skates. Mom would help us write our letters to Santa. We would send them off and then wait. On Christmas Eve we would set out cookies or Rice Krispies squares and a glass of milk for Santa and restlessly try to sleep in the bedroom right next to the empty tree. I was fairly confident gifts would show up since they had for five Christmases already, but I was a bit concerned based on the preacher's sermons about "the wages of sin," and that song "you better watch out, you better not pout," because I did pout, and I had behaved meanly toward my little brother on several occasions.

As we anxiously waited for Christmas morning, my brother or I would awaken partway through the night. We would then quietly wake the other, and together, creep to the door, hesitantly peeking under the tree. Sure enough, the milk glass would be empty, and the plate contained only crumbs. Under the tree were several boxes and packages wrapped with ribbons and bows. After some pinching and shaking, we reluctantly crawled back into bed and waited for the first rays of sun to reach our window so that we could go and share the news of Santa's arrival with Mom and Dad. Our parents were good sports and great actors as they quickly stumbled from bed and came to discover the surprises with us. Most of the gifts were practical items like pajamas, socks, and maybe even a set of Stanford's flannel long johns with a backside trap door. Then there were toys—trucks, cars, guns, puzzles, and once, a small train set. I loved the mystery and excitement of the Christmas morning, even if we soon had to leave our cozy home and travel to Grampa and Gramma Chipps' place for a huge family gathering.

Shortly after the Christmas of grade one, a disturbing debate erupted with some classmates. They started with questions about houses with no chimneys and soon they debated tooth fairies, Santa Claus, and flying reindeer. I could feel the magic fading and I realized that Christmas might not be quite as mysterious as I had believed. Two of them said they saw their parents eat Santa's food and put the presents under the tree. Another girl said her religious parents said there is no such thing as Santa Claus. As a nearly seven-year-old, I withheld this dangerous knowledge from my brother and my parents, but I would be watching and listening much more carefully as the next tooth was placed under a pillow, and as the next Christmas approached.

ICE SKATING

Our opportunity to learn how to skate came in an interesting way. As a Christmas gift, Dad's boss, Roger, invited our family to his home for a visit and a photoshoot. As an amateur photographer, Roger Hawkins had a very good camera and a darkroom. He posed us and took photos of our family and then of brother Larry and me together. I wore a clip-on bow tie for the event. Mother wore her best dress and a cameo broach. After the photos, we enjoyed snacks and conversation with Roger, Dorothy, and their children, Hugh and his older sister Margaret. During the conversation, the topic of Saturday skating at the local arena came up. We were asked if we liked to skate. When it was revealed that we lacked both skates and skills, Margie, as we called her, offered to teach us how. Somehow the next Saturday, we arrived at the Tillsonburg Arena at 1:00 p.m. and were equipped with skates and began our first tottery strides with Margie holding our hands. My wobbly ankles flopped in, then out, and I had to concentrate more on keeping my skates upright than keeping myself upright. Soon I was at least able to balance on the blades and start to glide a bit. The first afternoon was a blur, and we went home cheerfully exhausted. Over the winter we visited the arena a few more times, and by the end of the season, we were skating on our own. Our instructor, Margie, disappeared from our lives and my classmates Alan Tilton and Dave Kennedy became my skating buddies. What a wonderful gift from the Hawkins family. A few years later I walked to town every Saturday to ice skate and then, as I entered high school, I added roller skating to my recreation and spent many afternoons and evenings at the Tillsonburg arena skating as the latest popular songs played on the huge arena speakers.

BIRTHDAY TRADITIONS

My seventh birthday was a pleasant contrast to my kindergarten birthday party. There were four of us at the table—my father, mother, brother Larry, and me. We had roast beef and potatoes and a Devil's Food chocolate cake. Mother placed and lit seven candles. Dad and Larry sang "Happy Birthday" as my mother mouthed the words. I made a wish and blew out the candles. As I enjoyed my second piece of cake with vanilla ice cream, I was content.

Over the years, the family group has expanded and there have been larger groups for some significant birthdays along the way, but a simple meal with people I love, and chocolate cake, is still my favourite way to celebrate another year.

BLOSSOMING MIND

As a seven-year-old, I was growing in confidence. The long walk to school was no longer an expedition. Eating lunch in a large room with a hundred others was not so overwhelming. The hallways and washrooms seemed to have gotten smaller and the principal I had once feared was just another person who was part of my life. Although I had some concerns about moving on, I knew I was ready for the next grade. I was excited because in September my brother would start kindergarten.

Each day, the roadside and ditches between the edge of town and our farm were a never-ending source of interest. I had been paying attention but, up until now, my focus had been very narrow. I had been looking for pop bottles, which were worth two cents each. These treasures were collected at home until I had enough to purchase an ice cream cone or a Hires root beer.

As spring arrived in grade one, I was suddenly much more aware of the variety of wildflowers growing along the way. I picked samples and brought them home. My mother, ever the teacher, welcomed my botanical interests, and soon I could identify blue, dog-toothed, yellow, and white violets, adder's tongue, bloodroot, buttercup, mayapple, and of course, dandelions. As I walked in the woods, or along a river, Dad helped me discover skunk cabbage, marsh marigolds, jack-in-the-pulpits, and trilliums.

The human mind is a beautiful thing. One of the most important gifts my mother gave me was an insatiable intellectual curiosity. Something had blossomed that spring in my developing awareness and, as I started to discover the natural wonders, the universe opened up with dazzling beauty and endless discovery.

As I looked more closely, I began to discover not only the variety of plants but also the different kinds of ants, bees, bugs, and beetles. Then I discovered caterpillars, and my mother said that they would later become moths and butterflies. The cycle of life became even more fascinating. Each day became an adventure as I learned about the plants and animals around me, and everything from a blade of grass to the distant stars making up the Big Dipper became irresistible invitations to continue learning.

SETTLING IN

As my grade one year came to an end, I had settled into the school routines, and I realized that the rules and discipline were mostly necessary. I didn't like it when I, or one of my classmates, was sent to the corner or to stand in the hall, yet I accepted these punishments as just another adventure and I looked forward to each new day.

In the classroom, I was surprised to find that I was a good student despite my restlessness. I was quickly learning to read and I was developing a love for books. My curiosity and work habits led to A's in class—even in conduct. Recess and noon hour were filled with play and adventure. Hugh Hawkins was my constant companion at school, but Ron Bates, who walked on the same route home with me, also became a dependable friend. I had a short romance with a beautiful girl named Patsy who lived beside Ron on Tillson Avenue, but we soon quarreled, and when she pushed me into a puddle, I decided I wasn't quite ready for such relationship dynamics.

At home, my brother Larry had become a delightful companion and we spent endless hours together playing and exploring. Sometimes, like the time when we experimented with hiding in the trunk of our Dodge sedan, the results were unexpected, and it took time and hollering to get rescued. One of our most dangerous experiments occurred when I convinced Larry to climb into an empty forty-gallon steel drum, found conveniently located just behind the barn. The problem came when I placed the steel lid on the drum and flipped the latch. As I struggled to release the latch, my only brother was running out of air and patience. As he pounded, I hollered, and fortunately, one of the farmhands came to our rescue.

BETWEEN A FLOCK AND A HARD FACE

During my grade one year Roger decided to raise a large flock of turkeys at the farm. One sunny day I went strolling through the barnyard and into the large field which had previously been populated by timid young laying hens. To my surprise, there were now hundreds of large young turkeys strutting and jousting. As soon as I arrived a group of them immediately moved into attack mode. Gobbling and flexing their pecs, they began their assault. Soon I was surrounded by a surly group of teenage turkeys who began to whack me with their wings.

Thinking quickly, I climbed a chain-link fence near the front of the barn, proudly believing I had outwitted my new foes. My sense of safety quickly ended when I realized I was now caught between two nasty fates. On the other side of the fence baring her teeth and daring me to jump was Bonnie—the meanest German Shepherd I have ever met. So, there I was, between a flock and a hard face, with a tough decision to make. The turkeys were free-range, Bonnie was chained to her doghouse and limited by the length of her chain. This left a slim margin of opportunity for me.

With my nerve and my balance failing fast, I decided that *with a little bit of luck* I could escape with a nip rather than a beating. I took a deep breath and leapt. Bonnie lunged. I fell backwards just beyond her jaws. I quickly scrambled away and never entered the area again until the turkeys had gone to market.

For a while I choose safer adventures like dressing our dog in a sweater and pants and trying to convince him to pull us in the wagon or performing a pretend wedding between brother Larry and Heather Jordan under the spirea bushes on the front lawn using flower petals as confetti. However, it wouldn't be long before I would once again be pursuing more dangerous exploits.

NEW CHALLENGES

As I headed back to school in the fall of 1953 to begin grade two, I faced a couple of new challenges. First, my little brother would now be attending kindergarten, and I would be responsible for walking him home each afternoon. Second, instead of working my way down the primary hall as I had planned, I was placed in what had been known as the Auditorium at the centre of the school, in an improvised grade one/two class, with desks that had been brought in from one of the rural schools in the area.

Usually, walking home with brother Larry was not a problem, except when he decided he needed a washroom break when there was no option other than a ditch at the side of the road. As country boys that shouldn't have posed a problem, but when brother's bladder called, little brother suddenly became very aware of passing cars. After unsuccessful negotiations my brother trudged home with soggy underwear. We both learned from that experience. I asked better questions before leaving the school, and he realized that a tree-lined ditch could provide the privacy he needed in an emergency.

My new classroom was huge, with high ceilings and a stage at what became the back of our classroom. Unlike the tables of four students, we had enjoyed in kindergarten and grade one, everyone, including our grade one classmates, sat in rows of desks. Our desks were wood and metal, with sets of three attached to wooden ski-like bases. Mrs. McKenzie was wonderful. She was always well dressed, complete with sparkling jewelry and a ready smile. However, I quickly learned she was serious about decorum and brooked little foolishness. Sometimes that proved a problem for me and some of the other rambunctious boys.

My first experience of failing to meet expectations came one day in the first month. The boy at the front of our set of three desks tipped his desk, giving me and the surprised girl in the centre desk an unexpected jolt. Sitting at the stern of our little desk boat, I then realized we could push and lean our set of desks, giving the girl in the middle an unexpected break from the tedium of classwork.

My co-conspirator and I were cautious on the first few tilts, and a giggle from our captive in the middle was all the reward we required. However, one thing I have discovered about the male ego is that we often don't know when enough is enough. A few days into our new entertainment, disaster struck. As we leaned our set of desks, we lost our balance and over we went with a loud crash, spilling books and three students. Fortunately, no one was injured, but by the time the teacher had identified the culprits and dealt with the issue, our days of rocking the boat, at least in that fashion, were over.

The next adventure was the result of our newfound literacy. Some of my classmates began to pass notes. One day I saw one that a girl beside me received. It said, "I love you. Do you love me?" Not only was I intrigued, but I was also inspired because a beautiful grade one student had caught my eye. I loved everything about her—her frilly dresses, her smile, and especially her name, Phyllis. Before I could write my first love note I would have to learn to spell her name.

The spelling seemed to break all the rules I had learned in grade one. At home, I tricked my mother into spelling this difficult name by offering her an opportunity to teach. Questions like "How could 'ph' make an 'f' sound?" and "Why wouldn't the next letter be an 'i'?" and "Would that be one 'l' or two?" got me what I needed. Once I learned to spell her name, I found a pencil and a scrap of paper and a place to hide as I printed, "Dear Phyllis, I love you. Doug."

At school, I asked a girl in my class to deliver the note, and then for the next few days, I would smile at Phyllis every time she would look my way. When I received no reply, I decided that it was probably because of her lack of reading skills.

GENERAL CONDUCT

I was enjoying school, and by the second term had begun to feel very comfortable in my grade two classroom. I was so comfortable that the repeated reminders not to chat during class were ignored, so Mrs. McKenzie decided to help me pay attention by having me stand in the hall for a while. When she came to speak to me, I was repentant and, for a few days, refrained from chatting. Then I relapsed, and this time she really got my attention. She said, "Douglas, go to the Principal's Office." I was mortified. I hesitated, hoping she would relent, but as she moved toward my desk with a menacing look, I knew she was serious. Like a condemned man heading toward the gallows, I slowly walked toward the office, certain that I was about to be strapped. When I got to the door it was shut. Not wanting to disturb anyone, I decided that I needed to spend some time in the boy's washroom, conveniently located right across the hall. After a very long time, I peeked out. The principal's door was still shut, and I decided to try a return to my class. I quietly entered and the teacher asked, "Did you go to the Office?" I answered, "Yes," with a rueful look, and quietly moved toward my desk. To my surprise, my evasive, but technically correct answer, was accepted, and I was allowed to resume my studies. That morning, I became older and wiser. Mrs. McKenzie did get the final word, though—my straight A's on my second and third reports were marred by a B in General Conduct.

Part of the rationale for Mrs. McKenzie's concern about my conduct came as a total surprise to me and to my co-genius in what I considered an intellectual breakthrough that should have been celebrated. Our classroom also served as the meeting space for the Home and School Association, and after every meeting their agenda and key topics were still on a portable blackboard on the stage at the back of the class when we arrived the next day. Sometimes this handwriting would be there for several days. Jimmy, across the aisle, and I began to brag that we could read the words, and soon we could point out "Tuesday" or "December" and simple words like "the." Once we were convinced that we had cracked the code, we decided to surprise and delight our teacher with a demonstration of our intellectual breakthrough. We chose to write our Friday spelling test of ten words in cursive style rather than the mundane printing of grade two. When we were handed our papers for the quiz, we proudly wrote "James" and "Douglas" at the top and proceeded to use handwriting for words like "wagon" and "open." We smiled at each other as we handed in our papers for marking. As we prepared for afternoon recess, Mrs. McKenzie invited Jimmy and me to stay. I was certain she wanted to congratulate us without making the less advanced students feel bad. Instead, she placed our unmarked lists on our desks and angrily said, "What is this?" Before we could answer, she reminded us that we were in grade two and that in grade two you print. She then took the papers and destroyed our work without giving either one of us the satisfaction of knowing if we had any of it right. Then she quickly dictated the ten words as we dutifully printed. Jimmy and I never talked about it, but I know that I pouted internally for a long time after that experience.

As I learned to cope in the classroom with the teacher's expectations, increasingly my attention was devoted to the playground and its never-ending drama.

THE WIDER WORLD

As I began my eighth year, my curiosity about life continued to grow.

Since we now knew how to skate, we noticed that Mr. Rankin, who lived just across the road, had built a rink by his garage. We saw him spray the ice with a hose and then watched his sons and their friends skate and play hockey. I realized one of the sons must be about my age. When I asked my parents about our lack of interaction, I was told the neighbours were Catholics so they went to a different school, ate fish on Fridays, and probably weren't interested in Baptist friends. That spring, as the weather warmed and I made my daily walks to school or visited our mailbox in front of the Rankin house, I made a point of waving at my age mate. Soon, we just happened to be at the mailboxes at the same time, and I learned his name was C. B. As spring blossomed, C. B. sometimes invited me to play catch with a baseball or football on their large front lawn. Mother gave me permission to visit, but I was not to go into their house. As it turned out, Mother's caution was not needed for, although we did play together in our front lawns, there was an invisible boundary that separated us. C.B.'s parents and older siblings kept their distance. I learned that the Rankins went to the Roman Catholic Church and their children attended Separate School where nuns were the teachers. I wondered why God's children were separated this way.

My curiosity about religious divisions was increased one Friday night in the spring as our family was walking the streets of Tillsonburg. I saw one of my classmates standing on a corner handing out copies of a magazine called *The Watchtower*. I noticed my mother suddenly held my hand a little tighter as she steered us away. Curious, on Monday at school, I asked my friend David what he was doing. He said he was a Jehovah's Witness and he had to stand on a street corner every Friday to tell people about the real God. Later, I learned that he also came late to school each morning in order to avoid the opening exercises, and that he couldn't have the class sing "Happy Birthday" to him because his family didn't celebrate birthdays. I felt sorry for David, and I was surprised and disappointed that Christians in our town could have so many different kinds of churches with rules that kept us apart.

MOTHER TO THE RESCUE

In the fall and spring, the tarmac at the back of the school was filled with games of skipping, hopscotch, and marbles. My fascination was with marbles. The local stores sold marbles by the bagful, but some of the students had bigger marbles or large ball bearings that were not easy to find, and these became prized items. Some of the glass marbles were especially beautiful with names like "cat's eye" and "bumblebee." One of the most popular games among the younger students was rolling small marbles at a big marble or "alley" placed fifteen or twenty feet away. It was like a midway at the fair as ten or more barkers would place a "big alley" in front of them as they sat V-legged on the Tarvia and chanted, "Hit it you get it, a big alley!" We would line up for our turn and roll our little marbles at the target. I was often close, but I had soon exhausted my Chainway store supply of marbles, and after I had been through two bags of purchased marbles, my mother suggested I try a different game.

She helped me take a shoebox and wrap it with brown paper. Then we cut three round holes in the top, one just a bit bigger than a small marble, one about twice as big as a small marble and one about three times the size of a small marble. Then I printed the number one by the biggest opening, a three by the middle-sized hole, and five by the smallest hole. Before taking it to school I practiced dropping a marble from my waist until I could hit the large hole most of the time. Now I was ready.

On Monday morning I headed to school with a new bag of marbles and my new game of chance. I set up my box and invited others to try their luck at winning marbles—one if they hit the larger hole, five if they could drop their marble through the smallest opening. I soon had several takers and, although I had to pay out some of the time, by the end of the week I had to ask my mother to make me a larger marble bag. By the end of the second week, I had a stash of marbles at home, as well as in my school marble bag. Then two things happened. Some of my regular customers got more accurate and a few others made boxes that were more attractive and with bigger holes. My mother had given me a start and I had gained confidence. By the end of the school year, I had traded small marbles for large ones, and I was sitting V-legged on the Tarvia chanting, "Hit it you get it, a big alley!"

Soon, baseball would win my attention, but for now I had become a tycoon in the marble world—thanks to the help and encouragement of my mother.

SUMMERTIME

Summer has always been my favourite time of the year. For me, summer began with the bonfire and the twenty-fourth of May celebrations and ended at Thanksgiving with our annual visit to the Norfolk County Fair in Simcoe.

Our parents allowed us to experience life with its bumps, cuts, burns, and scrapes, and I am forever thankful for the freedoms we had during those childhood summers. We spent much of the summer barefooted. A cut or burn from stepping on yesterday's fire pit was never serious and we learned from each other's mistakes. Canvas sneakers and rubber boots were also essential equipment for our adventures. We wore the standard black farm boots with orange-red trim much of the time, but somehow learned they were much more stylish in warm weather with the tops folded over. With felt insoles, at the creek or in the woods, they were a perfect complement to bare feet, and we often wore them even on the hottest days.

After I demonstrated the ability to whittle without cutting myself, my dad gave me my first pocketknife, which I always carried. Soon I was cutting a kite string or an apple and feeling very grown-up. In the summer of

1954, Larry and I got fishing rods with reels and as we enjoyed our week in Midland, we caught good-sized perch that we began to learn how to clean and fillet.

Neither one of us had a two-wheel bicycle, but I had watched C. B. Rankin enough across the road that my tricycle seemed outdated, and I wanted to learn how to ride so fast and free. One Saturday, while he went to the show in town, C. B. allowed me to borrow his little red bicycle. By the time he returned at 5:00 p.m., I was riding the bicycle up and down our driveway. As I reluctantly returned his bike, I hoped by the next summer to have one of my own.

We were comfortable in the water from an early age, but now Mom decided it was time to really learn how to swim. Each summer, for the next three years, we spent many mornings at the Tillsonburg outdoor pool learning not only how to survive in the water but how to dive and swim with different strokes. A couple of times a week Mom would take us back to the pool in the afternoon so we could spend two or three hours as part of the public swim. At this stage, we were still restricted to the shallow end, but we got to see older boys and girls swimming well and doing amazing dives off the low and high diving boards.

Partway through the summer, my curiosity got me into another unfortunate situation. One morning, as I wandered through the barnyard, I noticed that the little Ford tractor used on the farm was parked at the edge of the field with the key in the ignition. Like Goldilocks, I climbed up and sat on the seat, and it felt just right. I reached out and grasped the steering wheel. It too, felt just right. I sat for a while practicing steering. I began to wonder what would happen if I turned the key just a little bit. I turned the key, and I immediately knew it had been a bad idea. The engine fired, and the tractor began to move. I grasped the steering wheel and managed to steer in a large circle, but I didn't know what to do next and was too terrified to let go of the steering wheel to touch the key. Once again, one of my dad's co-workers saw what was happening, and quickly intervened. After I was lectured and removed from the seat, I thanked my rescuer and meekly left the area. Previous experience had taught me that after an "incident" it was best to avoid that part of the farm for at least a week before returning.

Toward the end of the summer, I attended the most amazing food event of my life. At his backyard in Tillsonburg, my father's employer had the men construct barbecue pits using cement blocks and huge grills. Late in the afternoon as we arrived, billows of grey-blue smoke and the sweet aroma of barbecue sauce filled the yard as dozens of half chickens sizzled on the grill. Most amazing to me were the tubs of bottled pop of all the best varieties. The staff, and their families, filled several tables, and soon the food was served. As part of the celebration, everyone was allowed to have as much food and refreshment as they wanted. As Hugh, Larry, and I opened our second bottles of soft drinks we delighted in the abundance. I washed down part of my half-chicken with Hires Root Beer and then finished with an Orange Crush. There was ice cream and cake for dessert, and no one cared if we took seconds. I was thrilled that my dad worked for such a generous man, and that, as a bonus, the boss's son was my best friend. I rode home with a very full stomach and a very thankful heart.

ONE OF THE GUYS

As I returned to school to begin grade three, I was very comfortable in the classroom. I was skilled in reading and arithmetic. On my first report, I got ninety-one in English and one hundred in Arithmetic, yet my only focus was on recess and noon hour. I had become good at rolling marbles but lost interest. Now when I played marbles, I played a game called "tossies," where we placed a desirable big alley on the ground and then tossed marbles at it from a distance, and if you hit it, you got it. The stakes were high, and I won and lost some amazing fancy marbles in the process. I was good at the tossies game and only the best challenged me to play.

Meanwhile, I was learning how to play baseball. The town boys had already been playing on organized teams, so they knew the rules and most had baseball gloves, and a few even had a ball or a bat. We would watch the older boys play "Scrub" and "500" and then we would practice hitting and throwing. Slowly, my skill at hitting and catching barehanded improved. When I was allowed to join in a game of scrub, I knew I had become one of the guys and I loved every minute of playtime in the schoolyard.

MY HERO HUGH

Hugh Hawkins had a confidence that I lacked, and I admired him for his courage and style. At Christmas of our grade three year, he did something that changed my life.

As Christmas approached at school, we sang carols each morning. On the last day before our Christmas holidays, all the classes went to the Auditorium and sat in groups on the floor. We sang Christmas songs and some of the older children recited a poem. One of the classes did a skit. Another group formed a small choir that sang a few songs. I had seen all this at church, and I was not overly impressed—at least not until a boy stepped forward and began to sing, all by himself. The boy was Hugh Hawkins, and I learned later that he had sung a "solo." He was only eight years old. I was amazed. I was jealous and proud at the same time. I had no idea someone so young could sing by themselves and have people clap after they finished. Hugh was a good singer, but I was sure I had a better voice, and I decided right then and there that one day I wanted to sing on stage. Hugh had taught me another lesson and given me a special Christmas gift.

It didn't happen immediately but, because of Hugh's example, by age ten I sang my first solo in church. I have been singing on stage ever since. Hugh's performance in grade three gave me the self-confidence to sing in music festivals, choirs, and concerts.

Through Hugh's example, I learned that confidence and courage are often more important than raw talent.

THE TOE RUBBERS ESCAPADE

As another spring arrived, my mother decided it was time for us to join the men at church with protection for our Sunday shoes. Mother bought my younger brother and me our first set of toe rubbers. Now we could slip these on over our Sunday shoes and be just like the businessmen in our community—little gentlemen. I'm sure it seemed like a good idea at the time. However, my mother forgot to take into account the need for field testing—an oversight my brother and I were only too happy to remedy.

Now for those who may have lived on sand, you need to understand our testing environment. We were on dark heavy clay—the kind that makes walking across a plowed field in April an act of heroism. Despite our age, we were not totally without thought as we approached our study of the usefulness of toe rubbers in pursuit of outdoor adventure. We began our exploration with small puddles on the gravel driveway. With care and awareness regarding depth and traction, the toe rubbers proved quite successful.

Intoxicated with the success of our early experiments, we headed to the biggest and muddiest puddle we could find. Dare led to dare, and giggle led to laugh, and soon we found ourselves standing at mid-puddle with wet feet and goofy smiles. As we felt the mud grasping our feet, we simultaneously lost our nerve and bolted for higher ground. As we scrambled to safety there was a strange sucking sound. It was our new toe rubbers disappearing into the earth, never to be seen again.

Sixty plus years later, I still delight in seeing young children in April with boots and puddles getting that look in their eyes as they head for the depths to test their footwear and the limits of possibility.

THE CHICK DISASTER

On a sunny afternoon shortly after Easter, Hugh and I were wandering the farm looking for adventure. After experimenting with some young barn cats regarding their ability to land on their feet when dropped from the second story, we moved on to one of the brooder pens to check in on the latest group of young chicks from the hatchery in Tillsonburg.

The brooder pens had a heater in the centre and floor-mounted water sources on the floor. The pen we were exploring probably had two or three hundred three-week-old chicks. By removing the brass top of the water sources, we discovered a spring-loaded device capable of spraying across the room. Soon, each of us had our own water cannon and we had a small water war while the chicks danced around in the spray. Before leaving the area, we replaced the fountain tops and headed off to new adventures.

Unfortunately, one of the fountains tops was not properly replaced and when one of the men opened the door to check in the morning, three hundred dead chicks floated out the door. As soon as Roger Hawkins was informed, he and Hugh showed up at the farm. I was summoned with Hugh to the main farm gate and, with a group of farm men as witnesses, we were castigated and banned from the barns and any area beyond the gates. Suddenly my world had gotten much smaller. This punishment lasted a couple of weeks until one day I saw Hugh on the other side of the gate laughing with his father. I cautiously approached the boundary and, when I was greeted with a smile, I realized we had been forgiven. I was once again able to visit my father and the fields as long as I acted responsibly.

THE BICYCLE

As a nine-year-old, I had two dreams—to own a baseball glove and a bicycle. On a warm spring evening, we went to visit my Gramma and Grampa Chipps at their home in Courtland. Somehow, I ended up telling Grampa that I had learned to ride a two-wheeler. Grampa looked at my mother with a conspiratorial smile and said that he might have something that I could use. He led Mom, Dad, Larry, and me to his small barn and there, high on the inside wall at the end of the barn, hung an old blue bicycle. Mother smiled as she recognized it and she and Grampa reminisced about Uncle John and Uncle Alan putting it together from two or three old bicycles before they moved on to motorcycles. The history of the bicycle meant that in 1955 my "new" bicycle was at least thirty years old.

I was asked if I was interested. My goofy smile was answer enough, and soon my father had wrestled it from the wall, and I stood beside this huge dusty blue bicycle with two flat tires. The top tube of the frame was above my waist and the handlebars were up to my chin. I clutched my prize and pushed it toward our car trunk as the back wheel made a squeaky scratchy sound that I interpreted as joy.

At the farm, there was a garage where delivery trucks and tractors were serviced and repaired. With Dad's help, we got the tires patched and inflated and added some lubrication to the crank and wheels. After tightening the rear spokes and attempting to get the wheel to turn smoothly the men decided that, at some point in the past, the bicycle had been run over by a vehicle and thus had a permanent wobble. With a bit of adjustment, the wheel would just miss the frame on each side of its rotation. After a good cleaning and some fresh paint Dad handed the bike over to me. It was a proud moment. For the next ten years this was my only bicycle, and the quirky wheel was part of its charm as it took me on many adventures.

Getting onto the huge bicycle was very much like mounting the plow horse on my uncle's farm. The seat had been lowered as far as it could go, and I still had to stretch to touch the pedals. This was a totally different experience than the smaller bicycle I had learned on where I could touch the ground anytime I chose. On Big Blue, I couldn't touch the ground straddling the crossbar and the seat was even higher. At first, I used a fence to get up, and then pushed off, peddling wildly. Stopping was accomplished by reversing the pedal and then quickly dismounting before the bike came crashing down. That first summer, I never rode anywhere except on the grass and farm laneways. When it all came together, and I rode well, it was magical. When I crashed, the crashes were spectacular, often leading to a bandaged elbow or knee. I never complained, and I was soon riding my bicycle every day.

By the end of August, just before his seventh birthday, brother Larry got a small red bicycle, much more suited to his size, and we were soon riding the farm laneways together, reveling in our newfound freedom and mobility.

THE DAY THE MUSIC DIED

In the summer of 1955, my life was shattered.

As our grade three school year was coming to an end, my friend Hugh Hawkins was invited on a family outing with us. As we sat in the back seat of our family's Dodge sedan, I couldn't have been happier. Hugh and I talked about our future. After exploring several ideas, we decided that someday we would own a hardware store together. Then, with brother Larry, we sang a few of our favourite songs. As I remember that joy filled car ride, I recall us singing, "Row, row, row your boat, gently down the stream, merrily, merrily, merrily, merrily, life is but a dream."

Two weeks later, on Tuesday, July 5, Hugh and I spent the morning together with swimming lessons at the Tillsonburg outdoor pool. In the afternoon Hugh went on a road trip with his father. Late that afternoon my mother called me aside from my playmates. Tearfully, she informed me that Hugh had been in an accident. When I asked if he was hurt, she nodded sadly and then told me that he and his father had hit a large truck. Hugh struck his head and died immediately.

I don't know what happened next. Grief clouded my awareness and has blurred my memory. I don't know how any of us coped during the next few days. I now know that my father was at a Poultry Course in Charles City, Iowa the day that Hugh died. My mother had to carry the incredible burden of dealing with my grief and confusion and comforting her friend, Dorothy Hawkins, while my father was far away during his only absence in ten years of marriage.

I never went to the funeral home or funeral which made the disappearance of my friend even more unreal. I spent the afternoon of Hugh's funeral wandering the farm laneway with my dog. I didn't understand grief or the impact Hugh's death would have in my life.

None of this was ever spoken of in our home, and even when I was older, I never asked, and my parents never shared the impact of Hugh's death in their lives. I know that when my father arrived back at the farm, it had become a different place. Roger was no longer the happy-go-lucky boss. Hugh's mom and dad avoided me at church, and I was never in their home again. Our trips to Midland ended. It was a long, lonely summer.

I still laughed and played with my brother and our friends, but deep inside some of the music had died. It would take a long time to feel fully alive again.

DOC LESTER

We had arrived at the farm at a time of prosperity. Since our arrival, Hawkins Poultry Farm continued to expand with the addition of more brooder pens and a second barn for layers. In the five years Dad had been there, the number of laying hens had doubled, yet my father was still responsible for gathering all the eggs and attending to the health of the flock and paid the same fifty dollars a week. As Dad's responsibility grew, so did his esteem among the other workers. His status took another boost as he became known as Doc.

In July of 1955, Dad had travelled by train to a week-long training session in Charles City, Iowa and returned with a diploma from Doctor Salisbury's Laboratory. Dad was now a local expert in diagnosing and dealing with common poultry ailments such as worms and the dreaded coccidiosis, an intestinal parasite disease that can spread rapidly in hot weather. This, combined with Dad's ability to quickly cull a flock by carefully examining each bird made him a valuable asset. Soon it wasn't uncommon for one of the workers dealing with the young birds to ask "Doc" to help diagnose a concern. Dad enjoyed his status, but the demands were high, especially in the fall when new layers came from the range. Then, the shorter days, fall thunderstorms, and power outages would often create chaos.

With Hugh's death my carefree days of adventure on the farm were over. Now when I visited Dad to assist with collecting eggs, or to help deal with a panicked flock during a power outage, I had an increased admiration for my father's skill and hard work.

EMPTY DAYS

I returned to school in September of 1955 with a heavy heart and a new reality. I had been able to busy myself with my brother and the routines of the farm in the summer, but now my classroom lacked the joy I had known. The playground seemed empty without Hugh. Baseball and other games filled the schoolyard time and served as a distraction, but in the classroom, I was sad and had difficulty concentrating. I never talked to anybody about it, but I was internally confused. I didn't understand how the loving God I had been told about at Sunday School could allow the best boy I knew to die so easily. I didn't understand why Hugh's parents looked away when they saw me at church. I continued to do well in class, but I was lonely and filled with grief.

In the early spring of 1956, a classmate fell through the ice on Otter Creek and drowned on his way to school. Gene Armstrong's tragic death added to my sense of despair. The world was not as safe and carefree as I had once thought. I started to play with the rougher boys in the playground. I started to swear, cautiously at first, as I developed a "playground Doug" that I was careful not to bring into the classroom or my home. My new friends, the Harris brothers, who claimed their uncle was a professional wrestler who knew Whipper Billy Watson, began to teach me how to fight. When I wrestled, I could let my feelings go.

BASEBALL

The summer that Hugh died, I got a baseball glove and a hardball. I assume they came from the sales barn. Now I could practise catching and throwing with my father, and when I returned to school to start grade four, I was ready to really play baseball. With an aching heart, this pastime was a bright spot in a gloomy world.

At recess, we would run to the diamond and touch home plate to yell out our position in the "scrub" game we loved. Numbers one and two were batters, three was the pitcher, four catcher, five first base, six second base, seven third base, and after that we might go as high as twenty-five taking our places in the outfield, moving up one spot each time a runner got out. If a fielder at any position caught a fly ball, they were immediately up to bat, switching places with the batter, who then took their number in the process.

There were several baseball diamonds on the playground, and everyone knew that the older boys and older girls had their special diamonds with a fenced backstop behind home plate. The rest of us had a bare patch and three hollowed spaces, where years of players had created a worn base path and bases. We had no backstop, and when it rained our three bases became puddles. It was all part of the fun.

Baseball was not without its dangers. Unlike the Tarvia, where boys and girls could mix and mingle, the field was divided between boys and girls, and we weren't allowed to play together. For a while, my brother Larry was an exception. His curly hair and sweet smile had made him a favourite of some of the senior girls and, like a mascot, he was invited to watch them as they played baseball.

Larry's special status ended abruptly one sunny noon hour. Larry wandered toward home plate just as one of the girls swung her bat. It struck him in the middle of the forehead, and he went down with a sickening thud. By the time I was alerted and ran to help, Larry was sitting up with a large purple bump already showing on his forehead. The girls took him to the school where a cold towel and witch hazel were administered by one of the teachers. Larry managed to make it through the afternoon and was able to walk home with me after school. That was the end of his days as a mascot.

A HOUSE OF OUR OWN

Hugh's death affected us all, and my mother and father decided that, if they were ever going to get ahead, my mother would need to go back to work. My mother was hired to teach in a two-room school in Culloden. In the midst of my grief, this meant another loss as my mother was no longer waiting at home every day when we returned from school. In spite of the added workload Mom handled the new responsibility well and, after Christmas our parents announced that they had bought a piece of land from the Grimmets' farm just down the road for $300. They then found a retired farmer who would give them a mortgage and advance them the money to build a house that summer.

The timing of Mom and Dad's decision to build a house probably saved me from a continued descent into depression and despair. Dad found a builder named Merv Anger to frame and do most of the construction while allowing Dad and Mom to do some of the work themselves. As soon as spring arrived, a hole was dug, and a foundation and basement floor poured. Once the main beam floor joists were in place, Dad nailed the plywood subfloor down. Larry and I were invited to help nail the plywood in place.

My father's willingness to involve us has paid long-term dividends. Twenty years later, I helped Larry build his first home, and a few years after that he returned the favour. In both of those builds, Dad was a frequent helper. In 2013, at ages sixty-five and sixty-seven respectively, Larry and I were at it once again as we framed and finished his winter home in Lake Wales, Florida.

After the devastating loss of my dear friend, the excitement of a new home was good medicine. Throughout the summer of 1956 our new house took shape and, by late fall of my grade five school year, we moved to our new home. The two-bedroom bungalow had a large backyard and a full basement. Situated on the front corner of the Grimmet farm, we had open fields and woods behind us. Across from us, Wilford and Ola Beaman had a house and welding shop and two boys who were age mates for Larry and me. Soon we were spending many hours each week with Bob and Gerald and the Beaman family.

We were now two miles from Tillson Avenue Public School, and this presented new challenges. Since Hugh had died, and we had left the farm, Mr. Hawkins no longer offered to pay our town school fee. The boys across the road and all our neighbours went to a country school on a bus. There were some tense discussions at the kitchen table as I pleaded to stay at Tillson Avenue school even though I knew it was an extra cost for my parents. Part of the discussion had to do with our distance from the school. We would no longer be on the farm to ride with a delivery truck and the walk was now further. Eventually, my parents agreed to continue paying for us to attend the town school. We didn't know it then, but in a year our mother would be teaching at our school and we would have regular transportation.

DOGGIE TALES

From my earliest there had been at least one dog in my life. At Hawkins farm, I first made friends with the resident guard dog, Rex. Then we got our own dog Lassie, a beautiful collie. Lassie was a good-natured sport who allowed us to dress him in sweaters and pants and hook him up to a wagon. Unfortunately, at some point, Lassie decided that chasing the range hens was good sport, and he soon disappeared from the farm. Our next dog was a cross between a German Shepherd and a Collie. We named him Purp, and he was a constant companion. He loved to chase squirrels and rabbits, but chickens were beneath his dignity, which worked well on a poultry farm. As he grew older Purp developed two dangerous habits. The first was that he would wander far from the farm. One day he showed up at my schoolyard in the middle of the day. I spent an anxious noon hour walking him back to the farm. Purp's second habit proved to be his undoing. He began chasing cars and barking with delight as they fled from his attack. It started innocently enough as he chased the delivery van along the farm driveway, but when he started chasing cars and trucks on the highway his hobby became increasingly dangerous.

GROWING PAINS

Although I was very happy with our new home, at least part of me was no longer the good little boy Mommy and Daddy saw on Sunday. That summer, while visiting my Aunt Mabel's, cousin Val had introduced me to smoking. On a trip to Springfield, while his father was busy with other errands, Val bought a pack of Black Cat cork tip cigarettes. Back at the farm, Val and I sat in a remote spot in the barn and smoked the whole pack. I have spoken with people who turned green and were sick with one cigarette, but I found the nicotine rush delightful. Val and I leisurely talked and smoked for a whole afternoon with no noxious effects.

Back at school, I continued to get excellent grades, though effort and conduct were now consistent B's. On my first report Miss McFarlane commented, "I have to draw Doug's attention to his own desk quite frequently." By the second term she wrote, "Doug doesn't seem quite himself the last while." My teacher's comment was quite accurate. I wasn't the Doug I had been before Hugh died, and I knew I never would be. I was now two or three Dougs. I was comfortable with the roughest boys on the playground, and I swore and wrestled with them. I was also interested in sports, and I played baseball and skated with growing skill and confidence. There was still the good Doug who loved everything about Sunday School and church. I joined the youth group and memorized scripture and did my best to be a good Christian—at least when I was in the church.

In the playground, I was drawn to the wild boys and, more than once, I came very close to accompanying them to the office for a strapping. On one adventure, a young "wild thing" and I spent the noon hour hiding out at the nearby Jackson's Bakery after invoking the ire of some older hooligans. My companion, Bob, who would later die in a fiery car crash before he was twenty, was well versed in schoolyard wars and office consequences. I was a willing apprentice but knew little about the ins and outs of playground dynamics. On this early adventure into the underworld, we arrived back at the school guilty of two crimes—leaving the school grounds without permission, and being late for the lineup to return to class in the afternoon. As a first-time offender, I was chastised, and then both of us were dismissed without the application of the strap, which Bob had been preparing me for as we waited.

Just when it seemed I might permanently settle into the "dark side," fate intervened and changed my path. After the Christmas break, my mother was transferred to teach grade three at my school. This meant a ride to and from the school, usually with a long wait in the afternoon. It also meant a jolt to my abandoned conscience. Mother didn't need to know everything I did or said at the back of the playground, but she certainly would know if I was sent to visit the principal. My wild days in the playground came to a sudden end.

As I finished grade five, our move to a new home away from the farm with its constant reminders of Hugh and life before his death, something began to shift deep within me. I was no longer so angry and lost. I was becoming more aware of my responsibilities to others and appreciating my parents, brother, and the wider world. I was beginning to feel a joy and confidence that had been missing for a long time.

THE GOOD LIFE

As I turned eleven, life was good. Our new home was warm and comfortable with a modern kitchen and our first refrigerator. Larry and I shared a double bed that had a new mattress with no sag and no broken springs. We no longer had to share a bathroom with neighbours so long soaks in the tub became a new luxury. Our back yard had room for a large garden with a wide lawn behind the house where Larry and I spent hour after hour playing catch with a baseball or a football.

My Mom and Dad were content. My mother taught school, cooked, sewed, and gardened. Dad set up a workshop in the basement and enjoyed gardening with Mom and hunting. At the back of the garden by an old apple tree, Dad set up my rabbit pen, where I kept a variety of pet rabbits and, in the other corner of the garden Dad built a dog run and a doghouse where he soon kept his new beagle, Mike. Mike replaced me as Dad's hunting companion, and his ability to follow a rabbit by scent and alert Dad with his bark meant an immediate improvement in Dad's hunting success.

The Beamans, directly across the road, were wonderful neighbours. Beaman's Welding Shop was a hub of activity from morning to night, especially during the summer when farmers were waiting for Wilford when he opened at 8:00 a.m. The Beaman family welcomed us from the start. Before our house was finished Wilford remodeled his mailbox post so that the Lester and Beaman mailboxes could sit side by side on an immovable steel base. Bob Beaman was Larry's age, and they became lifelong friends, even attending university together. Gerald was my age, and although our academic interests were very different, he was a dependable friend and my companion as we sought our first tobacco jobs. Bob became a secondary school mathematics teacher. Gerald became an industrial electrician. As boys, we spent many hours playing together. When winter came, Wilford loaded our toboggan and sleighs in his truck and drove us to the Tillsonburg Golf Course where we joined a large group of others spending the afternoon on the hills. We were left to walk the three miles home. I never remember any complaints about an hour-long walk to get to the skating rink, swimming pool, or toboggan hill. In those youthful discoveries everything was an adventure. After that first tobogganing experience we would make the trek several times each winter.

Both families assigned Saturday chores. Often, we made that more fun by working together. Bob and Gerald would help us sweep our garage, and then all four of us would take on their Saturday cleaning duties. The Beamans had a TV years before we did, and we often found an excuse to go across the road for a visit. Their grampa taught us how to play euchre, and their older sister allowed me to learn basic piano skills. For several years, instead of going to Aunt Mabel's for Victoria Day, we had a bonfire and fireworks in the Beaman's spacious backyard.

Once we moved to our new home, I spent little time at Hawkins farm. We might stop in to see Dad on the way home from school, but the farm had lost its luster. Now our adventures took us across the fields to Grimmet's woods, or beyond the Beaman's property and across the railway tracks to a frozen pond or the Otter River. As summer came, the four of us rode our bikes to the Tillsonburg Pool most afternoons.

COMFORTABLE IN THE KITCHEN

My mother was an amazing cook and, with a new kitchen, new stove, refrigerator, and a chest freezer in the basement, she took her culinary arts to a whole new level. Washing and drying the supper dishes was a daily responsibility for brother Larry and me while Mother joined our dad in the living room for tea. If my brother and I squabbled, the offender would be assigned sole responsibility for the kitchen duties. Usually, I was the deemed guilty one and would end up washing and drying the dishes by myself. I may be experiencing selective memory, but from my retrospective view, there were times when my brother exaggerated his *ouch* to get excused from the task. Rather than developing a hate for kitchen duty, I found a comfort in the hot bubbly water and the act of drying and stacking dishes. I still enjoy helping with kitchen clean up at group events and at home.

As the older child I became interested in baking and cooking. My first success was a Sunshine Cake made from scratch, meaning that I measured and mixed from a recipe and baked it following the cookbook directions. I still remember adding the vanilla extract to the icing as I prepared my first product for suppertime adjudication.

As with many of the skills I tinkered with, I was more interested in proving I could do something than in making it a regular part of my life. After my baking apprenticeship I was content to enjoy my mother's cooking until, shortly after this, my mother had a medical emergency that meant a two-week hospital stay. Suddenly my kitchen skills were needed. My father was helpless in the kitchen, even though he and his father had been bachelors for a few years during the war. My father really couldn't boil a potato without having it boil over or burn in the pot. On his own Dad relied on scrambled eggs, toast, and cornflakes to survive.

During Mom' absence I stepped into the gap and created meals of meat and potatoes, fish sticks and veggies. That allowed us to survive until Mom was back at the stove. As insurance I decided I needed to learn as much as I could by helping and observing my mother's techniques in case of future emergencies. I had no aspirations to be a chef, but I was comfortable enough in the kitchen that over the years I have come to enjoy cooking and baking.

ICE HOCKEY

My ice hockey career was very limited. One year as winter came, we were visiting our cousin Val and he had a small patch of ice near his house. After showing us how he could skate and shoot a puck, he took us into the back entry to show us his pads—two Eaton's catalogues that he attached to his legs with heavy elastics. It all sounded good to us so, the first Saturday that was clear and cold, we packaged up our gear, two hockey sticks, a puck, four catalogues, and jar rubbers to hold our pads in place. By the time we added skates to our loads we looked like winterized hobos.

We set off across the fields toward a pond we had visited in warmer weather. After crossing several fences, a railway, snow-covered fields, and travelling the mile or more to our destination, we found our pond frozen but covered with snow. This was not unexpected as we had discussed bringing a shovel but decided we could not carry one more thing. So, we used our boots and hockey sticks to clear a space for our game. By the time we got our pads and skates on we were nearing exhaustion. We skated around shooting the puck back and forth. Neither one of us had the skill to lift the puck high enough to require shin guards and before long the jar rubbers had cut off the circulation to our frosty feet. We looked at each other the way only experienced adventurers can, and without a word we started to remove our gear and prepare for the long trek to warmth and safety. That was the end of my ice hockey career.

SPRING FEVER

Although we had only moved a short distance down the road, the fences and woods, ponds and rivers beckoned in a way that had never been possible in the fenced-in world of Hawkins' farm.

As the spring sun begins to warm the northern climes, strange stirrings begin beneath the earth and within the hearts and minds of birds, rodents, and young boys. On a sunny day in March a woodchuck might be seen sunning itself with eyes squinting to cope with the sun. Geese and ducks begin to move across the morning skies honking and quacking their way into a new season. We loved everything about the great outdoors. As the winter snows retreated, this was the time for exploring the awakening world of ponds and woods. With our rubber boots, we would set off across the glistening furrows of the plowed fields near home in search of discovery and adventure. First, we would test the ice between the furrows and, *with a little bit of luck*, find enough frost to offer a safe passage.

Then the trek across a plowed field of dark brown clay would begin in earnest. As the Saturday sun warmed the naked clay furrows, the mud turned to goo. Soon our boots would be covered with huge heavy gobs of mud and my boots would begin to weigh more than my legs. Like a Frankensteinian monster, I would wobble toward the woods with feet bigger than my head. Once in the woods, the first task would be to find a stick and poke and scrape until some boot began to appear beneath the gooey gobs at the end of my legs. Then it would be off for an adventure of checking the first signs of spring along the creeks and ponds of the woods. We knew the first spring flower was skunk cabbage so we would search along the edges of the marsh to see if it had poked its leaves up through the frosty earth. As a boy, when the skunk cabbage sprouted, I never tired of breaking it open to check to see if it smelled as rank as I remembered from the previous year. After searching for marsh marigolds in vain, we realized that although the expedition had broken the monotony of winter, spring was still a few weeks away. Reluctantly, we set out across the plowed fields toward home knowing that, *with a little bit of luck,* spring would be coming soon.

SUMMERTIME

I love summer. I enjoy the long hot days. This January baby can never get too much sunshine and warmth.

Now that we were allowed to go fishing on our own, summer began as soon as the snow was gone, and the Otter River beckoned. We discovered a special place near an overhead train bridge where a sandy shore created the perfect site for fishing and lounging in the sun. We reached our destination by crossing fences and fields from the country, and we usually met several town kids who had come along back streets to end up at the fishing hole.

In the Otter River, where I perfected my fishing skills, the most common catches were not edible, or at least not for our family. We caught suckers, shiners, and sometimes catfish. With a good supply of dew worms, dug up at the edge of our garden, we often shared our bait as we enjoyed catching large white suckers. Earlier in my fishing career I had proudly carried a few home, only to be told that these bony bottom-feeders were never going into my mother's frying pan. Instead, they helped fertilize Mother's flower beds. After that, we usually threw our catch back into the creek.

My brother, Larry, was a willing companion in these adventures and, as I reminisce, I realize how amazing he was at eight or nine years of age tromping across fields, climbing fences, and fishing with the older guys. The river was never considered a swimming hole, but we usually took off our shoes and waded in with rolled-up pant legs. More times than not one of us would end up slipping or being pushed so that we took an icy splash into the edge of the stream. We would end our day drying in the sun as we watched the older boys fish, smoke, and walk across the railway bridge above us.

With our fishing poles over our shoulders, we slowly made our way back home over fields and fences with a style and contentment that only a Rockwell or Twain could properly capture.

LAST SCHOOLYARD FIGHT

During the early grades, schoolyard tussles were a regular part of playground life. We would disagree over a baseball game and soon two or three of us would be wrestling for our dignity. These scraps were not mean-spirited and usually ended quickly. During my time of grief and anger over Hugh's death, I welcomed conflict and was involved in a few more serious fights. However, as we got older, the ability to inflict serious injury and create long-term grudges became real—especially when some of the guys on the playground were fifteen years old. I made the mistake one day of befriending one of the tough guys in a schoolyard war and ended up spending several days hiding out at noon hour until tempers cooled. After that I decided to focus on baseball and soccer as much safer ways to compete and release my competitive energies.

One sunny day in May, as the bell rang to call us to the classroom, I bumped into a classmate and soon push led to shove and we grabbed each other. As the entire playground emptied, neither teachers nor students paid any attention as we grappled on the grass. As we wrestled for a decisive pin, neither one of us was able to prevail. After a couple more rolls attempting to gain victory, we both realized that the world had moved on. We released our grips, stood, took a good look at our opponent, dusted ourselves off, and headed for the school. As we hurried toward the school we started to chat. I think both of us had been surprised by the tenaciousness of the other. That day, Alan became a trusted friend, and I never had another serious playground fight.

CRAZYLAND

I was in a great mood as I walked into class to begin grade six. By the end of the first day, I was anxious and discouraged. I discovered that we had a split grade with eight grade seven students in our classroom. Our young teacher was in trouble before the end of the day as she tried to juggle the demands of a rude and rambunctious group of grade sevens and twenty-five grade sixes. Every teacher up until now had ruled with an iron hand, now this recruit was inexperienced and indecisive—I sensed an impending disaster.

The weeks blurred as our teacher struggled to control the talking and silliness in the classroom. I ached for the teacher and took it personally when she yelled or cried. The principal came and told us that we were being difficult, and this would not be tolerated. Nothing changed. I did my work and then read as much as possible. When I was lost in a book the chaos went away for a while. By November, the teacher noticed I was covering my right eye as I read, and her conversation with my mother led to an eye examination with our local optician who also happened to also be our local jeweler. After testing, he determined that I was far-sighted, with a lazy eye. I was prescribed eye exercises and got my first pair of eyeglasses. I hated the look and feel of the glasses and wore them only when doing schoolwork.

Although the chaos in the classroom was unsettling, there were many bright spots. Our teacher was a great art teacher and I discovered skills I didn't know I had. Outside the classroom, I continued to develop baseball and soccer skills, and recesses and noon hours were filled with activity. During the winter, I walked to town most Saturday afternoons and spent my afternoon with my friend, Alan Tilton, skating at the arena. A few times each winter, we would spend a Saturday tobogganing at the Tillsonburg Golf Course, where we were now able to act like chariot drivers by standing on our toboggan, or we would find a ramp to add danger and excitement.

As I returned to school in January, a clash with a classmate forced me to realize how fragile reality is. I had started humming in my mind to shut out the constant chatter around me. A happy tune allowed me to concentrate as I worked through arithmetic or grammar. One day, the girl in front of me turned around and angrily said, "Will you stop it! Your humming is so irritating!" I sat in shocked silence, suddenly aware that the humming had not just been in my head. The realization that my awareness and sanity were being eroded frightened me. I knew that I needed to grow up and take responsibility for my actions, but I didn't know how.

REDEMPTION

As Baptists, our church talked a lot about redemption. I loved the songs about rescuing the perishing and seeing the light, but the lost souls had always seemed far away. During my grade six year, the whole process of being lost and rescued became very real for me.

As I experienced a young teacher who was struggling, I was in transition from being an angry grieving child to a thoughtful, spiritual young man. The chaos in the classroom pushed me into deep introspection. I was shocked and saddened by the rudeness and disrespect of the older students. To cope I escaped into reading more than ever. When the girl in front of me challenged me to quit disturbing her, I realized that I needed to quit trying to escape and face the reality around me. I started listening to our new pastor with a heightened interest in how his Jesus could rescue me from sinking sand.

Up until that year, at our church, we had had a preacher who challenged and reprimanded us and spoke of the horrors of hell. The new man, a retired missionary who had spent many years in India, still challenged us to choose between heaven and hell, but, to my relief, he focused more on the hope and love aspects of this powerful sky God than the wages of sin. Reverend Wilton organized a boys' choir, and here I grasped my first understanding of sheet music and the difference between the tenor and soprano lines of notes. With our new pastor's guidance I discovered my tenor voice and sang harmony for the first time. I came to believe I was one of "the perishing" and I now saw a lighthouse shining through the fog. Church became the highlight of my week, and I began to relax and enjoy school again.

CHOOSING MY PATH

Although my parents placed very clear restrictions on my behaviour, especially toward my brother and other children, they regularly turned me loose to face life's dangers on my own. I now realize that much of that freedom was based on their religious DNA. As Protestants, my parents believed that each person had to find their own relationship with the God of Creation. The belief that a twelve-year-old could choose between the path to a blissful heaven or a fire-stoked hell made my previous adventures, like walking a busy highway on the way to school, or fishing by an icy river in the spring, seem like casual excursions.

As I paid closer attention to the church traditions, I became aware of the path to adult responsibility in our church. A few times each year, the minister would preach a sermon on being "born again," referencing a baptism by immersion in the River Jordan. As Reverend Wilton retold the story of Jesus coming to John the Baptist and requesting baptism, I felt a stirring deep within. At the end of his sermon, Pastor Wilton moved to the front of the church and said, "If you feel Jesus has been calling you today to follow him, come to the front of the church and accept the gift of new life." Out of the corner of my eye, I saw a man and then a woman make their way toward the front of the church as the organist quietly played "Just as I Am" on the organ. I began to stand looking to my parents for permission. They were calmly disengaged. I was on my own.

I stood and slowly walked to the front of First Baptist Church. I had accepted Jesus Christ as my personal Saviour. Soon I would be baptized by immersion in the big tank at the front of the church. Just a few weeks past my twelfth birthday I had been detoured from my path to hell. I had been redeemed.

Looking back, all that sounds incredibly dramatic. It wasn't. In my small world it was just another rite of passage. The day of my baptism was just another Sunday, and my parents didn't take photos or gush. They accepted that their boy was growing up, and this was one more step in the process.

BORN AGAIN

Although in our church the altar call and baptism was considered just another rite of passage, the promptings that led me to answer the call and get baptized were part of a genuine shift in my life. As I turned twelve and learned to survive in the chaos of my grade six classroom, I felt like I had gotten the joy of life back again.

When spring came with a warm rush, for me, the whole world was born again.

To a boy who had just spent three dark years in grief and loneliness, the sunny days of spring 1958 were more than just another change of season. The last week of March was unusually sunny. This was a time of rebirth for me. Although I had managed to function as a good son and perform adequately in school since the tragic death of my friend Hugh, I had been lost and lonely, disconnected from faith and others. Now once again, I became aware of my brother's potential as a friend and playmate and the outdoors took on the glow I had known earlier in carefree days at Hawkins Farm.

Our Huck Finn moment came on the Good Friday weekend at a place on the Big Otter called the Black Bridge. The C.P.R. railway trestle that crossed the Big Otter River on the east edge of Tillsonburg was a couple of hundred feet long and some sixty feet above the rocks and river below. The cement footings slowed the river and created a wide shallow area where fishing was easy. Our previous excursions had taught us the basics but now we were ready to be fully involved.

Good Friday was a workday for Dad and a school holiday for us. We collected dew worms the night before, readied our fishing poles and tackle, and made a lunch. With our parents' blessing, we set out in blue jeans and rubber boots across the fields to the fishing hole. With our bags of lunch and fishing gear and our poles over our shoulders, we headed out under the morning sun. As we crested the hill and came toward the river, there were already several boys fishing on the sandy shore.

Experienced fishermen, we were soon baited and casting into the lazy stream. Success came easily. Huge bottom-feeders called suckers were plentiful and provided an exciting battle as we hooked them and reeled them in. We waded into the shallow edges of the river, getting soaked feet as the water breached our boots. Soon we were barefooted even though it was still only about sixty degrees. As we fished and splashed, and shared bait and stories with other boys, I was happier than I had been for a long time.

After a leisurely lunch, one of the boys invited us to explore the Black Bridge. As we reached the railway tracks above us, we started to walk toward the bridge. Our guide told us that he often walked across the railway trestle as a shortcut. We asked about trains, and he told us the coal trains only came a few times a day, and that you could hear their whistle in time to hurry out of their way. With our intrepid friend leading the way, twelve-year-old Doug and nine-year-old Larry walked onto the trestle stepping carefully from one tie to the next. Suddenly the distance to the other side of the bridge seemed to increase, but the excitement and challenge were too good to pass up. We moved steadily across and, after a few minutes of basking in our accomplishment, it was time to walk back across the trestle. As we reached the other side and returned to our fishing, we both were still exhilarated by our adventure.

We spent a long lazy afternoon fishing and swapping stories with the other young anglers. As we headed home with two trophy fish to show to Dad and Mom knowing that they would end up in the flower bed rather than the frying pan, for that moment at least we were the best of friends. We looked forward to sharing our fishing adventures with Mom and Dad but, without saying a word, we both instinctively knew that the walk on the railway trestle and the cigarette I shared with Fritz Werner would never be mentioned.

LEADERSHIP DEVELOPMENT

First Baptist Church was a thriving congregation with services morning and evening on Sunday and a prayer meeting on Wednesday night. Almost every night had at least one activity. There was a Deacons Board and Mission Circle. There was a Couple's Club, Youth Groups, Choir, and regular meetings for the Sunday School teachers. In the early years, we went to church twice on Sunday and to prayer meeting every Wednesday night.

Mother was a Sunday School teacher and a faithful member of the Hilda Lindsay Mission Circle. Dad helped with work crews and became a Deacon.

In this well-organized community, we all developed leadership skills. For me, that really began with participation in the junior youth group for twelve to fifteen-year-olds. The group was called Baptist High Fellowship (B.H.F.) With adult mentors, we had a president and vice-president, a secretary and treasurer. We had a formal agenda for our meetings, and minutes were read at each session. It was amazing training for future roles in life. By the time I moved on to the senior youth group, B.Y.P.U. (Baptist Young People's Union), I had been the B.H.F. secretary and learned how to create minutes for a meeting. I had also gained confidence and skill in expressing an opinion, an ability that was not always appreciated by the status quo.

WORKING MAN

Toward the end of grade six, our new school janitor, Mr. Gerrow, saw me waiting each afternoon after school for my mother to take us home. He asked if I would like a job to fill the time. To my delight, I became his custodial assistant and each afternoon for the next two years I helped clean the halls and classrooms. When I moved on at the end of grade eight, my brother, Larry, had his first paid work experience in the same role.

Jim Gerrow was an amazing person. He never wasted a step. He was always dusting, polishing, cleaning, and organizing. He was cheerful and friendly, giving dignity and respect to everyone, and expecting the same for himself and his protégé. Early on, as I entered a classroom to empty the pencil sharpener, remove the garbage, and shift the desks, the teacher angrily sent me out of the room because she was engaged in a conversation with a student teacher. Mr. Gerrow saw me skulk out into the hall, and when I explained what had happened, he summoned me to follow as he re-entered the classroom and proceeded to empty the garbage and move desks with a great deal of percussion and emphasis. When the message had been delivered, he nodded to the teacher, and we moved on to the next classroom. The most amazing part of this lesson in relationships is that the next day, I saw Mr. Gerrow laughing with that same teacher, and when I returned to her classroom to clean the next day, our "little incident" seemed to be erased from her memory—just as clean as the blackboards and brushes I cleaned each afternoon.

Now that I was a working man earning three dollars a week, I opened my own bank account at the Bank of Montreal and proudly began to build my savings. With changes at school and church, I very much identified with a verse from the Bible in the Apostle Paul's first letter to the Corinthians. Paul wrote, "When I was a child, I spoke as a child, I understood as a child, I thought as a child; but when I became a man, I put away childish things."

Jim Gerrow was an excellent teacher and role model. He worked hard with pristine standards, but he also laughed often and enjoyed every moment. He was one of the men who helped me move from childhood without losing the twinkle in my eye.

THE LARGER WORLD

As I joined the church and began working as an assistant janitor at school, I began to pay more attention to the interests and conversations of adult society. As a small-town boy, I knew very little about the larger world. Except for our three summers in Midland, I had never travelled more than an hour's drive from our home, and I had never been to a city. Since we didn't have magazines, television, or newspapers in our home, what little news I heard was through adult conversations, the barbershop, the grocery store, and church. I had come to understand that the World War had been terrible and that we were now worried about the Russians and their missiles. I had started to hear of trouble in some far-off country called Vietnam.

I realized that politics and much of life seemed to be either conservative or liberal. As a twelve-year-old, I saw conservatives as portly males with dark, well-pressed suits, and liberals as a bit trimmer in grey suits with the tie slightly loosened. My early generalization may have stemmed from the fact that the Prime Minister of Canada for my entire life, up until 1957, had been the soft-spoken Liberal, Louis St. Laurent. In 1958, the first Prime Minister I became more aware of was the dramatic courtroom orator, Conservative John George Diefenbaker. As I listened, I realized my mother and father were on opposite sides of this political fence. Although they seldom discussed their views at the kitchen table, as election day drew near, they often joked whether it was worth the gas to drive to the polling station since their votes would cancel each other out. They never elaborated on their positions, and all I could gather was that Mom came from a Conservative family and Dad's father was a Liberal.

As soon as I could read my mother introduced me to the public library, and this became my window on the world. Often, on Thursday evening when Mom would go for groceries, I could spend a precious hour in the stacks of books. In the early years I read *Bambi* and *Robin Hood*, and stories about animals and early settlers. As I became interested in becoming an adult, my reading interests shifted. I read *Reach for the Sky*, the true-life story of legless war ace, Douglas Bader, from the Battle of Britain. I read *The Small Woman*, the story of a courageous woman missionary, Gladys Aylward, who was involved in the War as Japan invaded China. Books like these and the stories of courage and action from the Bible inspired and challenged me.

MY PARENTS AS PEOPLE

I continued to become more aware. As I began to focus beyond my own pain or comfort, I started to see the adults around me, and my parents, in new ways. Beyond providing my food and care, I realized that my parents had their own unique personalities and their own hopes and fears. As they walked through the church narthex, I began to look at my deceased friend Hugh's grief-weary parents with a new love and understanding.

Now that I was part of the Junior Youth Group at church, I attended my first Easter Sunrise Service. This early morning event centred around young people ages twelve to thirty from a few churches in our area. I knew my mother was involved in some way with our local youth, but I was astonished when she was introduced as the speaker, and confidently walked to the podium. This woman, who I usually saw cooking with an apron at the kitchen stove, now stood confidently in her Sunday best in front of nearly 200 young people. My mother held the audience's attention as she spoke effectively quoting poetry and scripture. When the youthful audience laughed and applauded, I felt like I had hatched into a new world, and this amazing woman was part of my team.

Something similar happened with my father. Up until then, I had known him as a farmer with an interest in carpentry and the outdoors. Now that I was a junior church member, I was allowed to attend communion and church meetings, and there, to my surprise, was my father in his suit standing confidently with the other men of the Deacons Board that was responsible for hiring and providing guidance to the pastor and other church leaders. The idea that my father was a colleague of local businesspeople and community leaders was a shock. My respect for my parents was growing.

ROLE MODEL

My grade seven teacher was the complete opposite to my grade six teacher. The young woman from the year before was in a constant struggle to maintain control. Mr. Andrews ruled with calm confidence. Ross Andrews was an amazing man. He was handsome and well over six feet tall. He drove a bus and then did all the yard duty at the school. During his lunch hour as he supervised our class, he was always reading. I was concerned about his expectations since there had been a famous incident near the end of the previous year when Mr. Andrews lined up a dozen or more homework shirkers in the hall, directly across from our classroom, and loudly applied a couple of strokes of the strap to each one. Our classroom door had been conveniently left open and, as we heard girls and boys acknowledging their pain and being ordered back into the classroom, the effect was not wasted on our unruly students.

However, once I was in Mr. Andrews' classroom, I found him fair and consistent. He never used the strap and seldom raised his voice—he didn't need to—his presence and intensity set a no-nonsense tone from the first day. My earlobes were sometimes used as a mechanism to refocus my attention to my desk, yet I was comfortable enough to enjoy an active social life in the classroom. The teaching was stimulating—especially literature and creative writing. I excelled in Literature, Mathematics, and Social Studies with marks of 100, 87, and 84 in my final term. After a year of chaos in grade six, my grade seven year shaped my academic success for years to come. A Viking who read poetry was a role model that inspired and challenged me.

By the end of grade seven, I felt like I had gotten my life back. I was enjoying my role as the Janitor's Assistant and looked forward to new work experiences during the coming summer. I liked having a bank account. I knew that my summers of leisure were coming to an end, and I looked forward to proving myself through work.

THE SUMMER OF '59

The summer of 1959 was a magic time for me. I had come out of my deep grief and anger at the loss of my friend Hugh, and I was becoming aware of the larger world. Elvis Presley was in his prime and rock and roll was gaining my interest. Some Saturdays we watched *American Bandstand* at the Beamans' home with wide-eyed wonder. With brother Larry, and often the Beaman boys, we rode our bikes to Tillsonburg to swim several times a week. Larry and I would frequently swim all afternoon and return for another couple hours in the evening. We had both become very competent swimmers and divers. We did flips and dives off the low diving board and admired and learned techniques from watching the older divers who did a variety of dives off the high board.

One day on our trip to town, we saw a pile of lumber at the town dump and convinced the Beaman boys to join us in a building project. With Wilford Beaman's permission, we tied a couple of wagons to our bicycles and, after several trips to town, salvaged enough wood to build a small cabin at the back of the Beaman property. With borrowed saws and hammers, we spent many happy hours cutting and hammering and by mid-summer had succeeded in erecting a small shack. We never did bother with a sleep-out, but we did convince Wilford to cut a door in a rusty forty-gallon barrel that we turned into a stove. We got a frying pan and some beans and wieners and one evening fired up our stove and sat near our cabin. The four of us had a pioneer supper, just like the good old days.

That summer I worked for a local farmer picking strawberries and raspberries and made more money to add to my savings. I also began providing childcare for a family across the road. Overseeing two small boys for a couple of hours was a new and exciting responsibility. I had been around my mother enough when she cared for cousins that diapers and tantrums didn't frighten me, and I discovered I was very good at entertaining my young charges.

Toward the end of summer, I discovered roller skating. One of my town friends invited me to come to the arena on Friday night. The spectacle was amazing. The latest music blasted on the speakers and hundreds of skaters, from ages twelve to thirty, skated, danced, and performed tricks in roller boots with wooden rollers that squeaked wonderfully when skilled skaters sped around the corners. They had a supply of rental skates, so I was able to try out the new skill. Many of the techniques were similar to ice skating, so I was soon able to get moving and even do the step-overs on the corners. However, stopping with roller skates is a special skill. My only technique on my first night was to crash into the boards with as little speed as possible and then hang on. I was hooked. I loved the challenge of moving quickly, and I also realized that most of the girls from ice skating were at the arena. By my second week, I had found a boy who had skates to sell and as I walked home under an August moon with memories of skating with Jill and my own roller skates over my shoulder, I couldn't imagine life getting any better.

GRADE EIGHT

Despite some apprehension, my last year of elementary school went well.

I had been concerned about life in the room attached to the principal's office—a place of dread and violent discipline. Mr. Alabastine was a dark-haired, bespectacled, pipe-smoking enigma. He ruled the school with a shroud of mystery. He usually stayed close to his classroom and office, with a visit to the office being the ultimate deterrent for any unacceptable behaviour. Every day, students, usually boys, who had fought, or broken school rules, stood at the office door waiting for their interrogation and punishment. Often the result would be several strokes of the strap on each hand. Several times I had stood outside the door but had managed to sneak off or be dismissed with a frown and a warning. Now I wondered how I would measure up in the classroom with a door at the back that opened into "THE OFFICE."

As it turned out, Mr. Alabastine was an effective teacher who actually *had* a sense of humour, and I continued to enjoy my studies. I was fortunate to have several bright capable classmates. Recognizing this, our teacher gave us advanced learning opportunities and, in the last term, a group of us were given special privileges. One morning each week, we went to the public library and did independent studies. We were assigned research and written reports. I remember the excitement of walking across town on our own, feeling very mature. Mr. Alabastine must have created positive expectations since I don't recall any foolishness, just academic freedom and confidence building.

As the year came to an end, my attention turned to work. My Uncle

Fred was working for the newly formed Ontario Flue-Cured Tobacco Growers' Marketing Board, and I had heard that they were hiring students to measure the fields each summer. I missed my grade eight graduation ceremony so I could go to the Marketing Board Head Office to apply for work. I had to go back several times before someone took me seriously. In the process, I learned that they had pin boys and plotters and that I was applying to be a pin boy. Then I discovered that they had hired earlier in June and that older students had already started work. However, my efforts were not in vain, my name was now on the list, and they promised to call me when they started hiring for the next summer.

LAZY HAZY DAYS OF SUMMER

Free from school responsibilities on the first sunny day of the summer, my brother and I, and the Beaman boys, prepared fishing gear and lunches and, with our parents' blessing, headed north to Spitler Creek for a day of summer adventure. Larry and I had collected dew worms by flashlight on our back lawn the night before, and we looked forward to a day of fishing and lounging on the bank of the small stream a couple of miles from our homes.

The day was one of the best days of my early life. I remember riding up Martin's Hill on the gravel road just past Five Points. We were strong and confident as we stood on our bike pedals and pumped our way up the hill. We hooted and fishtailed as we raced down the other side, sending plumes of dust into the morning air. At the creek, a short distance from the road, we found a flat area where the creek curled and danced over rocks and pebbles. We relaxed and removed our shoes and shirts. Our skin was winter white, and we knew that by day's end we would all be sunburnt. There was no sunscreen but, in the evening, some Noxzema would be applied to our necks and shoulders. A sunburn was the way summer always really began.

We fished, waded, ate our lunches, and by mid-afternoon, in a moment of wild ecstasy, decided a skinny dip was called for. We found a deep pool in a curved section of the creek and removed the last of our clothing. None of us had ever been so daring and the wildness of it made the swim even more invigorating. After an hour or two, we dressed and lounged on the shore watching the clouds float by.

The day was never repeated. Work, play, family, and responsibilities took us in separate directions. Perhaps part of the reason we didn't try to duplicate it was that we knew it was a once-in-a-lifetime jewel.

MOWING AWAY HAY

With the tobacco jobs on hold until the next summer, I looked for other employment possibilities.

Growing up at Hawkins farm, with my mother reading stories by Thornton Burgess about Reddy Fox and Farmer Brown, I was always fascinated to learn that our neighbour was a real-life Farmer Brown. Born before the turn of the century, Fred Brown was a unique character. He had seemed old ever since I first met him. He dressed in faded denim overalls and, like many farmers of the day, had a truck for weekdays, and a car for special occasions and his weekly trip to church with wife, Mamie. His farming practices were an interesting mix of old and new. He had switched from a team of horses to a steel-wheeled Case tractor long before most farmers in the area, yet rather than using a mechanical baler like most farmers in the mid-fifties, Fred still loaded loose hay and mowed it away in his barn.

Now, as a fourteen-year-old seeking work, I knocked on Farmer Brown's door and, after a short interrogation and some chin-scratching, he said he'd give me a try. He told me to come at nine o'clock the next Tuesday.

I arrived early and waited nervously on Mr. Brown's porch. Soon another man arrived to work with us. I recognized him as a local farmer's son who was probably about forty years old. George was intellectually challenged yet big and strong and a dependable worker. When Fred finally appeared, the three of us headed toward the barn. The orange Case tractor was already attached to the wagon. While George harnessed Mr. Brown's horse, I was taken up into the hayloft where I was given instructions about my job once we returned to the barn with our wagon load of hay. Mr. Brown showed me how to operate the hayfork, attached to a rail that ran along the peak of the barn. With the horse and a pulley it would bring mounds of fresh hay up from the wagon. My job was to quickly spread the hay into even layers.

We headed down the lane to the hayfield where long rows of winnowed hay lay sun-dried and waiting. We attached a hay conveyor to the back of the wagon, and, with Farmer Brown driving, George and I piled and organized the fresh hay as it was lifted and spewed unto the wagon. There were no racks on the sides of the wagon, so I quickly realized that in order to stack the loose hay more than a little skill was required. It was a slow methodical process, as we used our three-tined forks to create layers of hay from one end of the wagon to the other. As the load grew, we stayed safely in the middle and continued to pile and distribute the incoming hay until we were perched high above the tractor even with the top of the hay conveyor. Satisfied that the wagon was full, Farmer Brown disconnected the hay conveyor and we headed to the barn where he parked the wagon just below the hay mow.

At the barn, each of us had a task. I climbed into the haymow and helped guide the hay fork to the open door where the rail took it out over the wagon. Then, Farmer Brown and George guided the large hayfork down to the wagon of hay, where George placed it in the centre and, by jumping on it, pushed the fork deep into the load and closed the jaws with a lever. Then, Mr. Brown attached the lift rope to his horse and, as they walked away, the first large bundle slowly rose until it clicked into place on the rail at the peak of the haymow. Now, I pulled the load by a rope to the back of the mow. When I had maneuvered the load into the depths of the loft, I pulled the release lever and the huge load fell in a heap. I returned the fork to the haymow door and scrambled to throw and push the hay into the burgeoning mow before Fred and George lifted another load ready to be moved into the mow. When the wagon was empty Fred came to inspect my work. Satisfied, we headed back to the field for another load. Over the next two days we repeated the process many times until all that cutting was in the barn.

It was hot sweaty work and I loved it. I enjoyed earning money but even more than that I was excited to prove my worth to my parents and the people I worked for. I was a man helping to bring in the harvest.

PAINT CONTRACTOR

That same summer I became an entrepreneur and, for a few hours at least, I was an employer. A neighbour was in charge of maintenance for the community hall nearby, which had previously been a rural school. The entrance paint was flaking and needed to be scraped and repainted. I convinced my potential employer that I could do the job. He offered me fifty dollars, and he would supply the paint. With the enthusiasm of Tom Sawyer, I sold my brother and the Beaman boys on the opportunity and promised each of them five dollars a day. I was confident we could complete the project in two days.

On a sunny morning, the four of us set out on our bicycles with brushes, scrapers, paint rags, and snacks, and a great deal of comradery. This working for ourselves was heady stuff. Unfortunately, years of neglect had left the schoolhouse paint curled and cracked and I quickly realized my simple project was not so simple. We set to work with scrapers and wire brushes to remove the old paint. It was boring, repetitive work. I tried to keep the crew inspired but, by mid-morning, the first signs of mutiny came when Gerald said, "I thought you said we were gonna paint." Shortly after that, as the last of the snacks disappeared, the younger crew members decided they had had enough. I continued bravely on, and, for a few minutes, I thought I might keep at least one worker. I was wrong. By noon I stood alone on the community hall steps. My crew had deserted me.

It took two more long days to prepare and paint the entrance. I was pleased with the quality of the work and so was my employer. He paid me and, after I had settled with my employees three dollars each for their short-term commitment, I had forty-one dollars to add to my growing bank account.

THE BROTHERHOOD

As I matured and moved on to high school, I became less competitive with my brother and began to admire rather than resent his talents. He was more artistic and nimbler than I was. He was very musical and had a whimsical sense of humour. Perhaps it is also true that distance does make the heart grow fonder, since I was no longer at the same school and, as it turned out, we were on separate educational paths for the rest of our school experiences.

We had already enjoyed swimming, fishing, and exploring together, but now we often spent hours in our back yard throwing a baseball or football back and forth. Our household chores expanded as we took turns mowing the lawn and helping with harvesting the garden produce. In the winter, we shoveled the driveway.

We shared a bedroom, with each of us having a desk on our side of the bed. We shared the double bed until I married and moved out at age twenty. We learned to share the space without intruding on each other's thoughts. In fact, in retrospect, I think we became so good at it that we seldom discussed our deeper thoughts or feelings. Once in a while, we would have a territorial dispute and draw an imaginary line down the center of the bed, yet, mostly, the arrangement was mutually accepted, and we lived with a single closet and one dresser. Larry had his friends and activities, and I had mine.

THE OUTSIDER

During the winter of my grade eight year, I read a book that captivated me—*The Strange One*, written by Fred Bodsworth. The characters and plot are brilliantly tied together by the story of a wayward barnacle goose and its relationship with a Canada goose, paralleling the relationship of a Scottish Canadian biologist and a Cree girl—themes related to the environment, living close to the land, and being an outsider seeking to understand your relationship to self and others.

As the country kid attending a town school, I had always been an outsider. Now, as I began high school, my isolation was increased as school boundaries meant that almost all my Tillson Avenue schoolmates attended Annandale High School, which stood next door to their elementary school. Because I lived in the country my new school would be the newly constructed Glendale High School on the far side of town. As September began, a big yellow school bus stopped at the end of our driveway, and I climbed aboard. I knew no one, except Gerald Beaman and one of the Martin boys from down the road.

Like the players in a tournament, the grade nine classes had been seeded with those most likely to succeed and go on to university in Class 9A, with those with less chance of success scattered in three other groups. I was placed in 9D. Our homeroom teacher was an army veteran whose son was one of the questionable characters in our delinquent class. In assemblies, or the hall, our class soon became labeled as the troublemakers. This came to a crisis in November when one of the 9D class members set off a fire alarm. We were kept in detention with Mr. Murray at the front of the class waiting us out with the threat that no one was leaving until the guilty person had confessed. I watched the buses prepare to leave. Most of us knew that the teacher's son, Scott, was the culprit, but none of us were about to tie a snitch albatross around our neck. We remained silent. Finally, the teacher blinked and after a stern warning turned us loose. I don't know what happened at home that night between father and son but, after that, our class stumbled through the year with much less tension.

THE TEST

My personal survival test came the second week of grade nine. As I entered the Boys' Washroom one of the toughs from Springford, the village where I should have attended elementary school, decided to check me out. He grabbed a fistful of my shirt and said, "So you're the country kid that was too good to go to our school?" My schoolyard training at Tillson Ave. had prepared me well. I grabbed his shirt and looking him in the eye said, "I don't know who paid for your shirt, but I paid for mine, and if we keep going, we are both going to wreck our shirts." He released his grip. I did the same, and after a brief final glance, we went our separate ways. For the next four years I rode the bus every day with Jim and his buddies, and I never had another problem.

SETTLING IN

I liked high school. The excitement of seven hundred students and the variety of courses including French, Agriculture, Science, and Shop made every day an adventure. I did well in all my subjects, and I especially liked English and History. I watched the Junior Football and Basketball games with envy, but I lacked the skill or confidence that the Rolph Street town students had. At some point in the fall, I decided to practice long jumping in the backyard at home. I have no idea what possessed me. I was alone as I ran across the yard and leaped into the air keeping my knees and feet up as I landed with a thud on the hard clay lawn. The pain seared, and I couldn't feel or move my legs. For a few terrifying seconds I thought I was paralyzed. Then, as I managed to roll over and struggle to my feet, I realized I was only badly wounded. A trip to Dr. MacLeod confirmed that I had indeed broken my coccyx or tailbone. The remedy was six weeks out of gym and no rough play. The weeks went quickly, and I was soon back skating and enjoying winter activities. That was the end of my track and field aspirations.

At the start of the year, I had taken a job in the cafeteria to pay for my hot lunch each day. My assignment was scraping plates into a large garbage container and passing them on to the people who would place them in the industrial dishwashers. It has been said that it takes a lot of humiliation to gain a little humility. Facing a horde of high schoolers while wearing an apron and scraping their dirty plates was certainly a preparation for facing the tough stuff in life. I managed to keep my sense of humour but, by the time I had dealt with a couple of hundred decimated meals, I had little appetite. At Christmas break, I gave up the cafeteria job and decided a cold sandwich at noon would be preferable to the offerings of the cafeteria.

As the year went on, I grew in confidence. I also developed the courage to challenge the status quo in ways that surprised and frustrated me, as much as it did others. I wanted to be liked and just one of the guys, but I found that, when the words or behaviour of a person in power were hurtful or haughty, I became possessed by an inner self that demanded justice.

One of the first times that this happened we were in science class reviewing our exam results from the second term. In the 1960s, exams were returned in order of results. I was embarrassed to be singled out near the top of the class, and I was even more embarrassed for those who not only did poorly but had their exam returned with a public embarrassment attached. As we took up the answers, I realized Mr. Murray had missed marking one of my questions that was worth ten marks. I raised my hand and said I had the correct answer, and would he please revise my mark. He looked at me with an army stare that said, "Don't mess with me," and then replied, "I will be glad to review your exam, but I would have to remark the whole exam." As we stood facing each other across the classroom, I knew exactly what he was saying and refused the bait, arguing that all he needed to do was mark my one question right now. While we parried, the thirty-seven other classmates soon grew weary of my stubborn stand and, as I demanded justice for the fourth or fifth time, I could sense that my classmates had reached their limit. I accepted my mark, but I knew that I had made my point. I had also discovered an unexpected bold crusader within.

In grade nine, I got the first D of my school life—in Physical Education. As the year went on, and my tailbone healed, I managed to improve to a C+, but it was clear that my athletic abilities were not strong. Gymnastics and basketball required a level of coordination, speed, and finesse that I lacked. I loved it in the spring when we got to play soccer and baseball, and I enjoyed the few times we did longer endurance runs. For most other activities, I was willing but not very competent. As the year went on, I realized that there was only one thing I liked less than Physical Education—cadets.

CADETS

One afternoon early in October, the grade nine boys were assembled and introduced to a new part of Ontario school life in the 1960s—cadets. Led by Mr. Murray and a few other veterans from World War II, all high school students were to be introduced to army drill in preparation for future opportunities. I was assigned to a group, and we began to practice saluting, standing rigidly at attention, and marching around in circles. I disliked everything about the process. The drill officers were older students who loved lording it over us newbies. Any disrespect or rebellion was met with a well-rehearsed diatribe. It was like being cast as an extra in a badly made movie.

After a winter reprieve, the process became more intense in the spring as we prepared for a big parade in June. Soon we were issued army surplus wool uniforms. They were hot and picky, and we were told this would give us a new respect for the sacrifices of our fathers and uncles who had served. On one of the hottest days of June, we marched onto the football field. The highlight was a "march by" with every cadet saluting the teachers and army veterans assembled on a platform next to the field. Then, we stood at attention for what seemed like hours as we were inspected. One of the boys near me fainted, hitting the ground with a soft thud. Sweat ran down my legs as I endured the ongoing discomfort. As we left the field and were allowed to remove our uniforms, I resolved that my army days were over.

The next year, when cadets began, I walked quietly down the street. I had gone AWOL. I managed to avoid cadets for the next four years of high school. I don't remember much about where I spent the time. I didn't share my decision with anyone at home or at school, and fortunately, I was never challenged or missed. At first, my motivation was simple. I didn't like being bossed around and I hated parading around in a picky wool uniform. By grade twelve, I had discovered Bob Dylan and Phil Ochs, and read enough war novels and Vietnam news that my avoidance had become moral as well as personal.

In order to complete high school I would need to move across town for my final year. Evading the draft at Annandale High School in grade thirteen in unknown territory would be a new adventure.

AL'S BUS

My bus driver throughout my high school years was Al Rice. Al was as capable a driver as he was as a people manager, and I always felt safe even on the wildest winter days. Al was one of my role models with his calm presence and pleasant demeanor. Al had a small farm nearby and drove the school bus to supplement his income. He looked like he could have been a wrestler in a different life. His thick strong hands and brush cut made it clear that he had a no-nonsense approach to life, yet he wasn't harsh or offensive.

Our bus was filled with a mix of rural students, many of whom were destined to leave school without a diploma. They were rowdy and enjoyed a good fight. Several became legends in Saturday night showdowns at the Highland summer dance hall at Long Point or the Belgian Hall in Delhi. On the bus, these rowdies sometimes teased or shoved, but one look from Al was all it took. He was an uncle or distant relative to a few, and they knew he was a man of few words. When he did leave the driver's seat to address an issue, he solved the issue so quickly and quietly that everyone's dignity was intact. In the 1960s, there was no such thing as a fog delay or snow day. We never missed a day in my five years on the bus.

UNIVERSITY BOUND

For me, grade nine was a surprising affirmation that I was a very capable student. There were thirty-eight students in 9D at the beginning of the year. By the end of the year, we had lost two who had reached sixteen and left school for the world of work. In the Tillsonburg area in 1961, many jobs did not require a diploma, and those who left early often did very well in factories, farming, or construction.

Until grade nine I had never thought beyond the next grade. Now, in a class of thirty-eight, I placed first, and my guidance teacher encouraged me to sign up for French and Latin in grade ten. He said that if I continued to work hard, I could go on to university. At that time, no one in my family had attended university. I had no idea what I might study, but I liked school and the idea of working at something other than farming was intriguing. I followed the guidance teacher's encouragement and signed up for Latin. In my second year, I would be in 10A.

HEART ATTACK

Life was going well as I started the second term of grade nine. John F. Kennedy had been elected in November and I was excited about the positive energy he was bringing to North America. He was about to be sworn in as the thirty-fifth President on January 20, 1961, becoming the youngest candidate to become president. Two days before that event, January 18, 1961, was another ordinary day—except that it was my fifteenth birthday. I boarded the bus and headed for home, looking forward to a birthday supper with my favourite dessert of chocolate cake and vanilla ice cream.

As I entered the house, I was surprised to see our car in the garage. I was met at the door by my mother and brother. With a hushed tone and concerned look Mom told me Dad was in bed. He had had a heart issue at work and, after passing out in one of the chicken pens, managed to get back on his feet and get help. There were no 9-1-1 emergency phone calls in those days or even an ambulance. They had called Mom's school, and a couple of the Hawkins men brought Dad home where Doctor MacLeod made a house visit, checked him, and gave him a sedative. When I arrived home, my father was resting quietly. My mother was calm and in control. Her simple faith and deep love for our family was all she needed to get through this crisis. They weren't sure how serious it was, but it appeared my father had had a heart attack. He was forty-five.

Instead of a birthday celebration, we stood around my father's bed and spoke words of love and encouragement. I watched my father cry for the first time in my life. He told each of us how much he loved us and through his tears said, "I don't want to die yet."

The next morning, my brother and I were sent off to school as usual and, somehow, we got through the last two days of the week. On Saturday, my father felt worse, so I helped Dad get into the car and Mom took him to Tillsonburg Hospital to the Emergency Department. In a few hours, he was admitted. Dad ended up being in the hospital for six weeks. My mother went back to work, and my brother and I continued with school and helping Mom at home. My father had had a serious heart failure, but tests showed that the damage was localized, there was no blockage, and with time, he should make a complete recovery. My mother visited Dad every day, and Larry and I went often for short visits.

By early March, Dad was home and starting to convalesce. In April, my parents celebrated their sixteenth wedding anniversary. As he got stronger physically, we began to realize that Dad's health crisis was not the only issue. This dance with death had affected my father's confidence. Although he was able to work in the garden and tinker in his workshop, he now feared crowds and noisy places. Even church was too loud and busy. He became easily frightened with even the slightest physical ailment. We realized it would be some time before he could go back to work and, by June, it had been decided that he would not return to Hawkins Farm. Dad settled into new routines of lawn care and gardening. It would be nearly two years before he had steady work.

My parents had no sickness benefits so, as Dad recovered his health and confidence, our family depended on Mom's income. She shielded and supported her man, and never once leaned on her sons to be little men, nor did she guilt us about family finances. For me, at fifteen, Dad's illness was an inconvenience while at the same time it was a motivation to work hard and earn my own money for clothing and future education. My then twelve-year-old brother, Larry, was mostly left on his own to navigate the transition into his teens and high school. Looking back, it feels like I abandoned him until we joined forces at Steve VanQuaethem's farm two years later.

I never heard my mother worry or complain. She had absolute faith that God would provide. As summer came, I was excited to be able to start paying for my clothing and continue saving for future education.

TOBACCO WORK

In the summer of 1961, I officially became a tobacco worker, and tobacco work filled my summers for the next five years. In early June, I was contacted by the Marketing Board, and as soon as school was out, I was to report for work.

The Board had been established in 1959, with warehouses in Tillsonburg, Delhi, and Aylmer. Now all tobacco grown in Ontario had to be sold through this board. Those who had been growing tobacco were issued a quota dictating how many acres their farm was allowed to grow. Prices were stabilized and the tobacco industry became a major employer in our area. To make sure farmers didn't exceed their quota, teams of two were sent to every farm to measure every field. Totals were calculated, and farmers were required to cut down any excess.

I was excited to be part of this world of work.

MEASURING TOBACCO

I had managed to get my name on the list of potential workers for the Flue-Cured Marketing Board in 1960 as I finished grade eight and, in 1961, I was hired as a pin boy to assist the plotter who drove to the farms and diagrammed the farm and each field. This was my first real summer employment, and I was excited.

I arrived at the newly built marketing board early in the morning on the first Monday in July and nervously waited with a group of other young men, waiting to be assigned to a team. Our names were called out by one of the supervisors, and we were assigned to our plotter. My first partner was a friendly-looking man in his mid-twenties. He handed me a stick, a tape measure, and a clipboard, and directed me to his old Chevy in the parking lot. After looking at his clipboard, he studied a map, and away we went, off to find our first farm. After finding the farmer, and getting permission to measure his fields, my plotter drew a diagram showing all the fields and numbering them. The farmer left us, and I was about to learn how to measure a field.

I was told that the tape I carried was called a "chain." It was sixty-six feet long. Apparently, chains with one hundred links had been used to measure land since the 1600s. Each field had to be measured so that the length times the width could be multiplied to determine the acreage. My plotter's job was to get the measurements and create a diagram of each field. I was instructed to insert my stick through the wire loop at the end of the tape and head up the first row. The plotter held the other end and when I came to the end of the tape, we both hollered "one." I drew a line in the sand with the stick and marched on. When I reached the end of the field, our positions were reversed. I returned to the last mark, and then the plotter decided where he would average the ragged end of the field and write the length to the decimal.

Since few fields were squares or rectangles, we created a series of trapezoids. At the end of the first row, I was sent running along the end of the field until my plotter decided that would be the width of his first trapezoid. I was told to mark the sand with my foot and count the rows as I walked back. Then we measured across the field to that row. The tobacco plants were only about six inches high so walking without damaging the plants was easy. After measuring the width, we measured the length of that row. We had completed our first trapezoid.

Soon, we were walking faster and faster, as I understood my role. By noon, as we sat in the shade on our second farm, I was more tired than I had ever been in my life, and I still had hours to go. Fortunately for me, there was no set quitting time—other than we had to be back at the Main Office by 5:00 p.m. By 3:00 p.m., my plotter decided to call it a day, and as he organized his work for the day and transformed his rough notes into neat diagrams with a ruler I was allowed to pour the sand out of my shoes and relax.

By the end of the first week, I understood my role and I was able to walk and sometimes jog along the rows. I watched with admiration as my partner dealt with angry farmers who were concerned about the process. Several times we were met by the usual farm dog—a large German Shepherd. A few times, the only reason we weren't devoured was that the farmer chained the dog so that we could get safely by. I worked hard and paid close attention to every detail, hoping eventually to move to the other end of the tape. That first year I got fourteen days of work before I was told my services wouldn't be required until the next year.

As a pin boy, I made twelve dollars a day. To put that in perspective, in 1950 my father was paid fifty dollars a week for sixty hours of work. In 1954, my parents bought a building lot for three hundred dollars. In 1963, the minimum wage in Ontario was one dollar an hour. I was thrilled. I had a bank account and, from then on, I bought all my own clothing. I had a short break as the tobacco grew, and I waited for my chance to work as a part of the tobacco crew on Steve VanQuaethem's tobacco farm.

UNLOADING BOATS

My next adventure in the world of work took me to a tobacco farm two miles from home where I would join a harvest team. I had been hired in April when, on a sunny Saturday, Gerald Beaman and I had ridden our bikes to every farm in the area looking for a summer job. Gerald was hired by Ernie Toth, and I was offered a position by Steve VanQuaethem, a tobacco farmer's son growing his first crop on one of Charlie Thomas' farms. I didn't realize it at the time, but because of the formation of the Ontario Flue-Cured Tobacco Growers' Marketing Board, 1959 marked the beginning of a fifty-year flourishing of the tobacco industry in the Tillsonburg area that provided work for thousands of seasonal workers and turned many local farmworkers and war-weary immigrants, especially from Belgium and Hungary, into wealthy landowners.

My boss was only twenty-three as he and his wife, Nellie, took over the shareholder responsibilities of a large farm. In 1961, Steve had forty acres of tobacco. I learned that it usually took one day for each acre, meaning Steve would need forty days to harvest the crop. Prior to my first day, the tobacco had been planted in late May, fertilized, cultivated, and hoed. Then, during dry weather, the fields had been irrigated. In mid-July, Steve, and a few others, had broken off the top of each plant, leaving about twenty-two leaves, so that all the energy would go into producing large leaves. As the bottom leaves turned yellow, it was time to begin harvest.

When I showed up for work, shortly after 6:00 a.m. on the first Wednesday of August, I had no idea what was really involved in tobacco harvest. I didn't know what a boat was, let alone what I would be expected to do as the boat unloader. I wore a T-shirt, blue jeans, and running shoes. I had no clue how inadequate my clothing and previous experience would prove to be during the next few days. I soon learned that the harvest gang consisted of sixteen people—six primers in the field, a boat driver, a boat unloader, two tyers, four leaf handers, and a kiln hanger, and finally the essential cure man, who tended the tobacco as it cured, and who ensured that the leaves went from green to a consistent flue cured golden yellow.

When I arrived that first day, the tying table had already been dragged into place, the big doors in the side of the kiln had been opened, and a conveyor had been set up to carry the tobacco into the kiln. As the women, who would tie the tobacco and send it into the kiln, arrived, I was instructed to help set two metal stands in place between the table and the kiln. These were the tying "horses" where a tyer, assisted by two leaf handers, would tie thirty-two bundles of leaves to a stick. Next, I helped move bundles of tobacco sticks into a pile at each end of the table. The sticks were in bundles of fifty, and each pile had twelve bundles and thirty extras. Each tying team was responsible for six hundred and thirty sticks of tobacco.

As the tyers taped their fingers with black electrical tape and prepared their role of tying twine, the leaf handers smoked cigarettes, and my education had begun. They were all in their late twenties or beyond, with many years of experience. I quickly learned that we were not employed by the hour. We would be working until the last stick of tobacco was hung in the kiln. As I started to realize that I would be responsible for handling every leaf of tobacco, I began to wonder what I had gotten myself into.

THE TOBACCO WORKER'S HONEYMOON

For the first two days, everyone was helpful. As the first tobacco arrived from the field the boat driver pulled two boats of tobacco close to the table where I would place it. The "boat" was a large metal and plywood box, about thirty inches wide, eight feet long, and three feet high. It had metal runners so it could slide down the tobacco row, pulled by a horse. The six primers each had a row, and they always primed the same row. They picked three leaves off the bottom of each plant and stuffed them under their arm. When they got an armful, they placed the bundle in the boat. Ideally, they were careful to keep the bundle together with all the stems pointing the same way. Within the first hour, I realized that my success depended on how well the primers filled the boat. Jumbled leaves were a disaster for me.

The boat driver helped me place the first bundles on the tobacco table, exactly as the leaf handers instructed us. The table was eight feet long and four feet wide. I was to fill the far side closest to the tyer with leaves, with the stems pointing toward the kiln so that the handers could pick up leaves three at a time and quickly hand them to the tyer, who would loop each bundle with twine. As we got started, I was anxious to prove my worth and I piled the leaves on the table as fast as I could. Soon I was leaning over to remove the last leaves from the first boat. I was already sandy and wet. I now understood why the tying crew wore rubberized aprons. By the time I had emptied the second boat, the boat driver had arrived with two more from the primers and was waiting for me so that he could take the empties back to the field.

As the women, having the advantage of prior experience, began to find their rhythm, the leaves on the far side of the table disappeared faster and faster. Each leaf hander used both hands to pick up three leaves at a time and hand them to the tyer. Each stick required at least one hundred leaves, and when the handers and tyer were in sync their hands were a blur. Over two hundred leaves left the table every minute. I was responsible to ensure that there were always leaves pushed and piled neatly on the table so that they could continue without a pause. I scrambled to keep up. The hours passed in a blur and by 5:30 p.m., with rubbery legs, I was riding my bicycle toward home.

By the end of the second day, every muscle ached, and I looked forward to getting some rest on the weekend. When I was foolish enough to say something about our day off, the tying team laughed at my naiveté. They informed me that, in tobacco harvest, there would be no days off. It was a race against the fall frost and only a severe lightning storm would cause the primers to stop harvesting until the last leaf left the field.

These women were tough on themselves and each other. They passed the hours with constant banter filled with curses and obscenities. According to the chatter, most men, including our primers, were useless. The language wasn't new or shocking since I had heard it all in the schoolyard or the change rooms at the pool or ice rink. But these were women, mothers, and sisters, and that was hard for my Sunday School–educated naiveté to reconcile. On the third day, one of the leaf handers had no childcare so she brought her two young boys to work. I was astounded as the three- and four-year-olds spent most of the day playing under the tying table and finishing off the cigarettes the women discarded at their feet. When one of the women dared comment on the boys' behaviour, she was told, with crude emphasis, to mind her own @#$%&! business. Such heated exchanges between the women were frequent and continued through the harvest, while never missing a beat in lighting the next cigarette, handing the next leaves, or tying the next stick.

The nastiness and drama that filled the women's lives was intriguing at first as they focused on each other, but it soon became deadly venom as they turned their dagger-like tongues on me.

WOMEN AT WAR

Nothing in my life had prepared me for the wrath and scorn of four women who had a vocabulary that would make a sailor blush. The criticism started gradually, but soon it was constant, and, like tag-team wrestlers, the attack was relentless. They needed more leaves. I needed to be faster. The stems were a mess. There weren't enough leaves on their side of the table. There were too many leaves on their side of the table. They were scraping their fingers raw on the bare table. Their shoulder was sore because the leaves were piled too high. I was favouring one of the tying teams. I wasn't helping enough with cleanup during breaks. The barrage was relentless. I realized that if things didn't change soon, Steve would be forced to replace me. An incident on my first day had shown me how easy that would be.

On the first day of harvest, six men went to the field at 6:30 a.m. None of them had ever worked for Steve. We could see the field from the kiln yard and, at about 11:00 a.m., there was a commotion in the field, with shouting, and soon three of the men were escorted by Steve toward the bunkhouse where the workers stayed. The other men went back to work, and soon Steve's truck sped down the road toward town. In less than an hour he was back with three new workers to replace the three he had unceremoniously fired. That's how it worked in Tillsonburg, Aylmer, and Delhi throughout the 1960s. Hundreds more than were needed showed up for harvest work, and those that didn't get a job at the start waited along the main streets for the first week or two of harvest, hoping someone like me would need to be replaced.

I was very much on my own. I now realized that every leaf of tobacco on Steve's farm had to be handled by me if it was going to get into the kiln. I was physically and emotionally tired, and it was only the eighth day of a process that could last over thirty days. I was doubting my strength and courage, but I was not about to burden my father, who was still recovering from a heart attack a few months ago, or my mother, who was keeping our family afloat as my father recovered.

If I was going to survive the toughest test of my life, I would have to do it by myself.

MUSIC TO THE RESCUE

At first, I started humming as I had during the insanity of the sixth grade. This time, I was well aware of the tactic, and it had a double purpose. I hummed church songs to give me strength and remind me of my faith, and I hummed as a flippant response to the endless complaints. By mid-morning I could breathe more easily. By late afternoon I was whistling a happy tune. We finished at 4:00 p.m.—our earliest finish yet.

When I got home, I asked for a ride to town and I purchased a battery-powered Sony transistor radio which came with an aerial and a brown leather case and carrying strap. The radio could pick up all the top rock stations. The next morning, I rode my bicycle to work early, and when the women arrived, I had already attached the radio to the roof of the tying table, playing songs like, *Hit the Road Jack*, and *Itsy Bitsy Teenie Weenie Yellow Polka Dot Bikini*. It worked! The women still demanded speed and constant attention, but I was confident that, if I worked hard, they would tolerate me.

The music improved all our moods, and I did get better at my job, and none too soon because, by the third week, the horses, primers, and our tying teams were in sync. One day, we tied our last stick before 2:30 p.m. By then, I was a part of the team, and I was already thinking about next year's harvest.

LEADERSHIP LESSONS

As I mastered my role, I was able to appreciate the amazing process involved in growing and harvesting a crop. Steve and his young pregnant wife were up before 5:00 a.m. every morning. Just behind their house, a garage had been converted into a bunkhouse that housed eight or nine men. Nellie prepared meals and fed the whole gang three times a day. Steve slept a few hours at a time as he helped the cureman manage the kilns and then, on day seven, Steve's responsibility had an added feature. A new task was required. From then on, each morning he and the primers placed a wagon by the kiln at 5:30 a.m. and emptied the kiln, piling the sticks of cured tobacco on the wagon so they could be taken to the Strip Room and stored until the fall when the tobacco would be graded and prepared for market. By 6:30 a.m., the primers were in the field and the table gang that I was part of started to arrive so that we could begin by 7:00 a.m. As the harvest progressed, and everyone got better at their jobs, it became common practice for the primers to prime extra for the next day. I couldn't leave the tobacco in the boat, or it would overheat and spoil, so I would fill the table and place bundles under and beside the table ready for an early start the next day.

From the first day, Steve was constantly on the move. He was calm and confident. He laughed often and when he had to correct or fire someone, he did it without any waffling. He was determined, but always in control of his emotions. I watched and learned. On the first day, he replaced three primers. By the time he had a consistent and competent team of six primers and a kiln hanger, fourteen men had spent a night in the bunkhouse. Each time a man was replaced, he had to take his belongings and leave the farm. Often Steve drove them to town, but sometimes, right after a payday, one of the men would sneak away in the middle of the night. Near the end of the third week, a fight erupted amongst the women and, as tears and insults flew, one of the leaf handers quit. Nothing Steve could say mattered, so, as she walked down the laneway, Steve quickly summoned Nellie to fill in while he went in search of another woman. Soon, a new woman was handing leaves, and by the next morning the women acted as if nothing had happened. I was getting an education in people management that few jobs could offer.

Steve's challenges were not just with people. Steve didn't own horses so, like many other farmers, he rented two work horses for the summer. These big horses had spent the winter pulling logs through the northern Ontario bush. There was no question about their toughness. On the first day, Steve, and the primer with the most horse experience, harnessed the horses and hooked each one to a boat. On farms with well-trained horses, the two horses would pull the boats in the third row behind the lead primer. The primers would fill the front boat first and then send the lead horse to the end of the row while they filled the second boat. With Steve's rented horses, the two-horse plan worked for two days and then, just as Steve had dependable primers and thought his field gang was settled, the horse rebellion began.

The horses had spent the winter in a logging camp with constant action and wide-open spaces. The second horse got bored and competitive and decided he had followed long enough. He decided to make a right turn and pass the other horse, in the process tearing tobacco plants out by the roots.

The horse that had been in front was not about to be so easily bested, so he passed on the left, taking out many more valuable plants. When the alarmed primers tried to settle the horses, one of the horses panicked and headed across the field toward the barn with the boat flopping sideways and leaving a path of destruction. Finally, the runaway horse was stopped, and Steve unhooked it and returned it to the barn. In typical Steve VanQuaethem style, there was no big display of emotion. He decided that one horse would pull both boats in the morning and the other horse would pull both in the afternoon, with the horses alternating their shifts. Steve hoped this would solve the issue in two ways—avoiding competition between the horses, and ensuring their excess energy was used in pulling a heavier load. The solution worked and was used, without incident, for the rest of the season.

As August progressed, I asked Steve to find a replacement so I could return to school. By the first week in September, Steve had located a worker from another farm that was finished harvest, and I was able to return to school without leaving Steve with another problem to solve. I was offered work for the next season, and I rode home on my last day with a cheque in my pocket and a new sense of confidence.

ACADEMIC PATH

My new work ethic and confidence were certainly required as I started grade ten. Because I had chosen Latin instead of Industrial Arts, I was placed in 10A—the academic stream. I quickly discovered that my classmates were bright and hardworking. I would have to really apply myself to keep up. I loved the intellectual nimbleness of the teachers and my new classmates. I now had homework every night. I enjoyed Mathematics and History and found Geography and Physical Education the most challenging. In Physical Education I enjoyed some of the games, but in gymnastics and basketball, my balance, flexibility and jumping skills were weak. This flat-footed boy was strong with good endurance, but not built for speed and agility.

I finished the first term with an average of 85 percent, almost the same as grade nine, but now I was third in the class. I didn't have any idea what the academic path would lead to, but I knew what it would lead from—a lifetime of farm labour, like my father and the workers in tobacco. It wasn't that I disliked hard physical labour. In fact, as a healthy teen, I took pride in my endurance, but after Dad's heart attack and working with older tobacco workers, I knew that year after year of such work takes a toll. I also realized that, after thirty years of working as a labourer, you were usually still working as a labourer. My work as a janitor's assistant and as a tobacco worker made me determined to use education as a pathway to professional work which would depend more on knowledge and skill than on physical endurance.

MY BACK-ROW BUDDY

As I settled into grade ten, I developed my first real high school friendship. Jamie Vance and I had connected in grade nine shop class. We were the two who often went to the shop during lunch hours to work on projects. We had both been forced to leave our hands-on learning behind as we launched into the academic stream. Together, we found some outlets for our need for action. We learned chess together, playing often in the cafeteria. Then Jamie got a miniature magnetic chess set and, for the next three years, we found opportunities to play during the slower parts of science classes. We found this worked best when we were seated toward the back of the class.

Jamie and I also shared interests in hunting, fishing, and the outdoors. Jamie's father was a well-known supplier of fly-tying information, tools, and supplies. His shop was filled with feathers, fur, and all sorts of fishing poles, lines and hooks, much of his material sourced from his own outdoor adventures. Although Jamie showed me the basics of fly casting, I stuck with my baitcasting reel and line. Jamie and I were up at dawn each year on the first day of trout season. After two years of failure, we managed to discover a stocked pond, and for the first time ever I returned home with six small trout.

Jamie and I had our last great classroom adventure one day halfway through the final year of our science days at Glendale High School. The class was working with carbon disulfide, and, at one of the lab stations near the front of the classroom, a Bunsen burner caused a minor explosion in the pipes beneath the tables. Sitting near the back, as keen experimenters we added a small amount of the volatile compound to our drain. In a few moments, another impressive boom shook the room. Other than the consternation and confusion of the teacher, there seemed to be no other ill effects, so we were able to orchestrate one more anonymous demonstration of the combustible characteristics of CS_2 before the end of the session.

Jamie and I also saw the explosive possibilities of politics at my first political debate. I am not sure what prompted us, but one evening, in the lead-up to the 1963 federal election, we went to a union hall basement where the Conservative candidate and his Social Credit opponent were to discuss current issues. As the two candidates debated, the voices rose then anger grew, and neither candidate could remain seated. After a few angry exchanges and fist-shaking the two men abandoned all civility and the event started to shift from debate to donnybrook. As a crowd on each side of the aisle moved to join the melee, Jamie and I chose safety over valour, abandoned our back-row seats, and headed for the exit.

As I moved across town for my final year of secondary school, Jamie and I ended up on different paths. The last time I heard of him, he was a commercial geologist exploring mining possibilities in Northern Ontario.

CHURCH ROUTINES

During my high school years, church was still an important part of our family life. I was now a member of the adult choir. A neighbour, Meta Avey, picked me up every Thursday night for choir practice and I sang in the tenor section on Sunday morning. Dad was now able to attend church again, enjoying the music and interactions with others. My mother taught Sunday School and was a leader in the Mission Circle. Both Larry and I faithfully attended Sunday School. Once a month, Mom and Dad would attend Couples Club, where church couples would enjoy a meal and a guest musician or speaker. It was one of the few times my parents went on a date.

I had now moved up to B.Y.P.U., the senior youth group. They met every week and had social events like skating and tobogganing in the winter and fastball, bonfires, and hayrides in the summer. The group went from high school to young adult, with some of the leaders being in their late twenties. This wide range of ages had three advantages for me—friendships, transportation, and leadership examples. The young men and women set positive examples of playfulness and ethical behaviour that helped me as I made important life choices. Throughout the year we had social and sporting events with other area youth groups.

As I grew older, Sunday remained an important family day. Once Mom and Dad settled into their new home, one of the first appliances they bought was a chest freezer for the basement. This allowed them to purchase a half of beef each year which was prepared as steaks, hamburg, and roasts. Each Sunday morning Mom would put a roast and potatoes in a roasting pan and place it in the oven. When we arrived home from church the smell of beef and potatoes greeted us at the door. Our Sunday meal was a feast. As well as salads, jellos, potatoes, meat, and gravy, there was always a delicious dessert. My mother loved to bake, so the meal was accompanied by several choices of pie.

By the fall of 1961, my father was recuperating well, but his illness had had an unexpected effect on years of faithful Sunday night church attendance. During my father's recovery, Sunday night had become a special family time as we watched *Bonanza* and *Ed Sullivan*. As Dad recovered, his Sunday night church attendance waned, which suited my brother and me quite well.

SWEET SIXTEEN

As I approached my sixteenth birthday, life was good. I was enjoying school, and my father was getting healthier every day. I was excited about the work and social possibilities having a driver's license would bring.

Preparing for my driver's licence was easy. I had been driving tractors and farm trucks for a couple of years. All I needed was a practice session to master parallel parking and I was ready for my driver's test. I passed my on-road test with one small problem—I was too cautious at intersections.

After a brief pep talk on being decisive, the Ministry official gave me a pass. Shortly after getting my licence, I was in London, Ontario, trying to make a left-hand turn on the main street with no advanced green. A police officer was assisting with traffic flow, and, after I had sat through two green lights waiting for an opening, the officer approached my window and said, "Look son, if you are ever going to turn you have to get out in there!" This was great advice for driving and life. I pulled into the intersection and turned on the amber light.

Now that I could drive, I told myself that there was no rush to get romantically involved since my parents had been in their late twenties when they found a life partner. However, I did like the thought of having a special girlfriend so that I could attend dances without spending most of the night standing by the gym wall watching from the sidelines. To complicate my social backwardness, my mother's church background had prohibited dancing and movies so, as the oldest in our family, I had to negotiate with her to even go to a dance. I finally wore her down as Dad pleaded neutrality and avoided any conflict. I had watched enough *American Bandstand* at our neighbours' house to bounce around to the faster songs, but I was in serious trouble with a slow ballad. High school Physical Education was supposed to help with this by having a few dance classes each year. That certainly didn't work for me. My assigned dance partner was either one of the "untouchables" in our grade and both she and I endured the forced process trying not to create further pain for either of us, or I was paired with one of the "beauties" and I was so hypnotized by perfume and softness that I couldn't tell my left foot from my right.

The truth was that, at sixteen, I had about as much confidence and charm as Forrest Gump. Although I'd had a few early romances when I was passing notes in the primary grades, my romantic life up to now had been limited to daydreaming and a few hand-holding sessions as I skated with one of the girls at the arena. At school, I had a smile and nod relationship with several of the popular girls, but I knew I was not in their social orbit and having access to our 1959 Ford Galaxie was not going to change that.

Flirting and interacting with girls was fun, but for now, I was not in a hurry. For the time being, my romantic interactions would be limited to the girls on my bus, skating encounters, or the church youth groups where we had hayrides and bonfires.

MISSIONARY CALLING

In May of 1962, I was invited to travel to Ottawa for a huge youth convention sponsored by the Baptist Conference of Ontario and Quebec that our church was associated with. Most of the "youth" I travelled with were already in their twenties. I was awed by the big city and the adventure of staying in a motel. At the conference, there were sing-alongs with rousing songs, like, "It Only Takes a Spark To Get a Fire Going," and presentations by men and women who had travelled the world sharing hope and love, and the good news of Jesus. I was mesmerized by stories from missionaries who had lived in rural villages teaching about God and helping the local people with health and education. When there was a call to action on Saturday afternoon, I stood to indicate my commitment to making the world a saner, safer place.

As we travelled home, in a car filled with enthused young men and women, the warm glow of community kept my newfound calling shining in my heart. On Sunday afternoon I sat in our living room with Mom and Dad and announced that I had decided to devote my life to missions. I had expected at least my mother, who had been a faithful member of the Mission Circle for my whole life, to be delighted. Instead, the room filled with an icy silence. As my parents tried not to show their fear and disappointment, I felt my enthusiasm for my new calling seep out of my heart like the air out of a punctured tire.

The pained look on my mother's face was one that I would see several times in the next few years as I made choices that frightened her. At the time, I considered the look to be one of disappointment, and I felt guilt and shame, yet over the years I realized that this mother hen struggled all her life to allow the chicks to really leave the nest. Mother's default to judge and disapprove was based on her own insecurities and her fierce love for her family. Choosing to pause my actions because of my mother's concern probably saved me from several disasters along the way.

A SUMMER OF POSSIBILITIES

I soon left any thoughts of a missionary calling behind and focused on finishing grade ten well and having a summer full of work experiences and a growing bank account. I finished the year maintaining my third-place position in the class of thirty-five, with an average of eighty-five percent.

I had been hired as a pin boy again, and I started work on the first day of the summer holidays. This year, I got two very different plotters. The first was a wild young man who had already left school, and for him measuring tobacco was one of many jobs during the year. His car was an old Chevy that had rust holes that I could see the road through. He worked hard and had a sense of humour that kept me laughing, even when the door on my side of the car flew open on a curve and I clung to the handle while the pavement and my life sped before my eyes. As I scrambled back to safety, I expressed my concern that he hadn't slowed down, and his laconic reply was that I seemed to have the situation under control. After two weeks with "wild thing" I was assigned to work with another plotter. He couldn't have been more different. This university student's car was clean and well cared for. He was athletic and precise. I learned how to excel as a plotter with his coaching. On the third day, we got into a swarm of bees, and during the process, I had a few bees tangled in my hair. I didn't have Beatles' long hair, but an Elvis-inspired crew cut with a Brylcreem-enhanced ducktail pompadour. Later in the day, as sweat poured down my face, "Mr. Clean" challenged me to get my hair cut short. I didn't wait. That night, I went to the barber and asked him to cut it short. It wasn't quite a buzz cut, but it was very short. He charged me four dollars. I decided that the price of haircuts had gotten too high and walked directly to Woolworth's and purchased a Dahl Home Barber Kit. From then on, for the rest of my high school years, Larry and I gave each other our summer haircuts. My efficient plotter was right. The shorter hair was an advantage during the hot days of summer. I finished my Flue-Cured Marketing Board work during the third week in July and applied to be a plotter the next year.

As I finished at the Marketing Board, I heard of a nearby farmer who needed help with irrigating his tobacco crop. This was a new experience for me. The farmer had a spring-fed irrigation pond about the size of a large swimming pool. When I arrived for work, he had already set up a large diesel-run pump at the edge of the pond with an intake pipe reaching deep into the water. We then headed to the kiln yard where large aluminum pipes were piled. We loaded these thirty-foot-long pipes onto a wagon with side rails. Like a huge Meccano set, there were elbows, shut-offs, end caps, and sprinkler pipes. I was intrigued as I learned how to hook these together starting at the pump and connecting large pipes from the pond all the way to the field. At the field we placed four-inch pipes, with a sprinkler head every sixty feet, all the way down the row. Our first row of pipes was twenty rows from the edge of the field. After that we placed a row of sprinkler pipes every forty rows. At the end of the first row, we placed an elbow and shut off to take us forty rows over where we set up another set of pipes and sprinklers. We had enough piping to do three lines at a time. Despite the engineering involved, in a couple of hours we were ready to start up the pump. With a roar, the pump started pushing water to the field, and the sprinklers, which stood six feet high, began shooting life-giving water across the rows of tobacco. Now came the best part of my new job as an irrigation assistant—waiting. Each line had to run for two hours. Then, we would move over forty rows and set it all up again. Moving the field pipes meant walking through wet tobacco, carrying the sections of pipe with sprinklers above our heads, but it only took a short time, and then we waited again. During the waits, I was sometimes assigned some cleanup of the grass in the kiln yard, or other tasks to prepare for harvest, but there was usually lots of time to sit in the shade and snooze. Late in the afternoon, after another set-up, I was sent home for the night while the farmer kept irrigating all night long, getting up every two hours to move pipes. I arrived early in the morning, and we repeated the moves until all the fields had been irrigated. By the time we loaded all the pipe and moved it back to the kiln yard, my work there was done, and my next job was about to begin back at Steve VanQuaethem's farm.

SUCKER BUSTERS

When I arrived at Steve's for my second year of harvest there was a buzz of activity in the yard. Several other workers were waiting for instructions. As we helped prepare the new equipment, I learned that the thirty-five acres of tobacco were nearly ready for harvest. The bottom leaves were already turning yellow, and these "sand leaves" needed to be harvested within a week. I learned that Steve, and a few experienced tobacco workers, had already finished "topping" the plants, and we were about to try a new process that was intended to keep suckers from growing at every leaf junction on the tobacco plants.

Over the next few days, I learned that "topping" tobacco is an important part of getting large ripe leaves. Left alone, the tobacco plants would continue to grow taller with smaller and smaller leaves leading to a flower on the very top. From the plant's perspective, the whole purpose of the leaves was to supply food to the flowers and seeds. From the tobacco farmer's perspective, since he was paid for weight and quality, the whole purpose of the leaves was to produce heavy, well-cured tobacco, with a high nicotine content. Breaking off the top caused the plant to produce large leaves and to begin to ripen, from the bottom to the top.

Steve explained that once the plant is topped, determined attempts to produce flowers and seeds would cause little plants or "suckers" to grow at the junctions of its stem and leaves. Left alone, these suckers would take the energy from the plant and make harvesting the leaves difficult. In 1962, experts had decided that a special mix of chemicals applied to the stem would prevent sucker growth. When I arrived at the farm, a group of us were each given a red plastic tank which we strapped to our back. The tank was equipped with a "gun" comprised of a hose, a handle, and an application head that, when placed over the plant stem, released a stream of sucker control down each plant as we squeezed our trigger. Looking like Ghostbusters, we each had a row, and at every plant, we placed the application cylinder on the top of the plant and shot a dose of white liquid down the stem. Once we mastered the process, seven of us moved quickly and methodically through the fields. We worked long hours. The work wasn't difficult, but my gun arm and hand were very tired by the end of a ten-hour day. On the fourth day, we completed the sucker control process. An average acre has about 5,000 plants. That means, that to sucker-bust thirty-five acres, each of us had applied about 25,000 doses of sucker control.

There was no rest. The next morning, the harvest gang would arrive, and harvest would begin.

COMING OF AGE

As I worked in the fields that summer, I felt strong and competent. I was becoming a man. I wasn't the fastest at many of the tasks, but I made up for my lack of speed with optimism and endurance. I looked forward to work each day and never struggled with getting up to go to work or grumbled about working late. I loved being outside in the sun. Often, we worked barefooted, with short sleeves, my skin turning brown and my feet becoming calloused. I felt like each new learning experience was an adventure, and the best part of all was that I got paid every week by cheque. I received one dollar and forty cents per hour for oiling and suckering and I received fourteen dollars per day for unloading boats.

Steve was a hard-working, decisive leader and I felt privileged to learn from him. He faced the challenges of broken machinery and changing weather with calm competence, and he handled the diverse group of harvest workers with clear instructions and a sense of humour. At the same time, I had seen how quickly indolent workers disappeared and I had no illusions about what would happen if I didn't follow his expectations and continue to work hard.

THE TYING MACHINE

When I arrived in the kiln yard early the first morning of tobacco harvest in 1962, I discovered that I would still be unloading boats as I had the previous year, but this time there would be no leaf handers and tyers. Instead of the tobacco table from the year before, there was a shiny new green machine with a conveyor belt and some sort of tying mechanism. Along with an older woman and her thirtyish daughter, I was to unload the tobacco and help operate this new tying machine.

The conveyor, which was long enough to hold four sticks of tobacco, ran from right to left, with a rubber belt and posts to help us position the sticks. We were to spread fifty leaves between the posts, place a stick on top of them, and then add another layer of fifty leaves as the conveyor constantly moved the process toward a large sewing machine, which sewed above the tobacco stick and cut the string. The finished stick then moved unto a second conveyor which carried the sticks of tobacco into the kiln where the kiln hanger was waiting to hang the 1260 sticks in the kiln. It sounded very complicated, but the company that sold the machinery to Steve had assured him all would go well once we got used to the process.

Our first task was to help move the bundles of sticks into place. As we prepared to begin our day, we had twenty-six bundles of sticks, each containing fifty sticks. None of us had ever even seen a tying machine, and I was the only one who had ever unloaded a boat. The initial plan was that I would unload most of the tobacco while the women scrambled to spread it evenly, place a stick on top and then spread another layer of tobacco before the stick reached the sewing machine that ran continuously. As my anxiety increased, Steve showed us that we did have control of the speed and that we could stop the machine in case of an emergency. My moment of calm ended immediately as Steve pointed out the dangers of getting caught in the mechanism or punctured by the huge tying needle. I was able to breathe again when Steve assured us that he had already been trained and would work with us until we mastered the new skills.

The theory was that we would complete each stick in less than thirty seconds, and that the sticks would move smoothly from the tying machine to the kiln conveyor and that, by noon, half of the kiln would be full. By 7:00 a.m. tobacco arrived at the kiln yard, and we began to assemble our first sticks. The conveyor was an unforgiving taskmaster, and, at the beginning, it seemed to be moving incredibly fast. By the time we had emptied the first two boats and had a short break as we waited for more tobacco from the field, we were all exhausted, and it was only 7:45 a.m. Our rest time was interrupted as Steve yelled from inside the kiln. We rushed in to see what was wrong and discovered a huge pile of tobacco on the floor of the kiln. The machine's tying process was allowing many of the leaves to come loose as they were placed on the rafters high in the kiln. We had a problem.

We picked up the leaves, and Steve tightened the sewing tension and anxiously assembled a few more sticks. He was one of the few farmers trying this new technology and, if he was going to succeed, this problem had to be solved quickly. We took extra care as we processed the next boat of tobacco. Instead of sending the sticks directly to the kiln hanger, Steve shook each stick as it came off the conveyor to check for "fall-out" from the stick. Another hour proved that no matter how careful we were the process would never hold the leaves as well as the old hand-tying technique. By 10 a.m. it had been determined that we needed one more member on our team, a "stick shaker," who would take the stick from the machine, shake it to remove loose leaves, and then place it on the conveyor to the kiln hanger. As Steve discussed the qualifications for this new role, I suggested my thirteen-year-old brother. Steve liked the idea, and soon we were in the truck, headed the short distance to my house. Larry was home and, after a brief discussion, he said he would give it a try.

Soon, brother Larry was an important part of our team. His humour and hard work made him an instant favourite with Steve and the women, and as the days went by, he not only shook sticks and helped us at the tying machine, he also learned how to untangle and re-thread the tying mechanism when it was jammed.

Despite the challenges at the beginning, by the end of the first week we were sometimes finishing our day by 4:30 p.m. As we got better at the process, there were days when we finished by 3:00 p.m. Larry became Steve's technical expert, and I enjoyed having my brother accompany me to work. When we got home, we would head to the basement to scrub off the tobacco gum in the laundry sink. As September came, Larry left to begin high school at Annandale, and I stayed on for another three weeks until the last leaf was hung.

I had earned Steve's trust, and I was promised a job as a Boat Driver for the next year's harvest.

QUIET COURAGE

While I was proving myself in tobacco harvest, my father was quietly finding his way back to health and employment.

My father was never loud or flashy. He took life as it came and cherished his wife and family. After his heart attack and hospitalization in 1961, he recovered slowly. Dad never complained as he gradually regained his strength and confidence. I don't know what conversations he had with his friend and employer, Roger Hawkins, but soon after his heart attack, it was accepted that his days as an employee with Hawkins Poultry were over. As his second summer after the illness approached, Dad was still unemployed. He helped Mom with gardening, and gradually took on lawn mowing, cleaning the car, and a bit of carpentry. He filled some of the summer of 1962 with an old passion for raising fancy pigeons. Dad took over my old rabbit pen and rebuilt it so he could house several pigeons. Dad had fantails, tumblers, and rollers.

Throughout Dad's illness, he and Mom never let us boys know about any of their financial struggles. Neither of them ever whined or complained. My mother's teacher salary and her unwavering faith in God and her man carried them through the lean years.

As fall came, Dad took on some part-time work—first with a used car dealer across the road, and then at a television store in town owned by one of the church members. By the beginning of 1963, shortly after I turned seventeen, Dad took on full-time work as a night cleaner at the Tillsonburg Shoe Factory. Dad and one co-worker cleaned from 9:00 p.m. until 5:00 a.m. It was dirty, demeaning work, but, once again, my father never complained, even when the harsh cleaning chemicals made his hands dry and cracked. I remember him putting salve on his hands and wearing plastic gloves to bed. In the fall of 1963, Dad was hired by a carpenter, Merv Anger, and started framing houses and doing building repairs. I was amazed and knew my father had regained both his strength and confidence when

I learned he and Merv were re-shingling one of the buildings on our main street, three stories above the sidewalk in the middle of the winter.

My father was forty-seven years old when he reinvented himself. He would work with Merv for five years before taking a job with Livingston Industries, where he worked until he retired at the age of sixty-two.

My dad's quiet courage continues to inspire and challenge me.

ROMANCE

Ever since I wandered to the next farm to visit Mary Rutherford when I was four, I have been a romantic. I have always admired the beauty and grace of the girls in my life. After having been in and out of love a few times in the early years of school, I realized how challenging romance can be. I learned that feelings are easily hurt, and that until I was older, it would be safer to focus on academics and sports, a bit of flirting, and skating with girls at the arena.

Now that I was a working man with a driver's licence and access to my parent's car, I was ready to find a girlfriend. I had already had my first rehearsal one night early in the summer when my cousin Val invited me on a double date to a drive-in movie. Val had arranged a date for me through his girlfriend and, as Val and his girlfriend cuddled and kissed in the front seat, my date and I awkwardly held hands in the back seat. At the intermission, I strode to the concession booth and bought footlongs and fries. I was feeling cool until I bumped into another guy and spilled half my tray onto the floor. Out of money, I salvaged what I could of my pride and the meal, and then shared the battered remains with my date. As Val delivered the girls to their homes, I did manage to have my first good night kiss.

With this very limited experience, I set out to find a girlfriend. I started by flirting with a girl that sat in front of me on the bus. I soon discovered her name was Sharon, and that she lived just down the road from the farm where I worked. She invited me to her birthday party. She was celebrating her sixteenth birthday, which was on October 1. On Saturday night, I arrived at the Williams' farm, parked in the huge farm driveway, and nervously joined Sharon and a few of her friends. I didn't know anybody there. Sharon's parents stayed out of sight and allowed us to take over the large kitchen, where we danced to vinyl records and ate snacks. It was a Pepsi night. Most of the dancing was imitating the gyrations we saw on

American Bandstand in lines or a circle. During the few slow songs, I danced with Sharon or one of her friends. At the door, I thanked Sharon for the evening and left without any sense that this might be the beginning of something special.

Back at school, I was scrambling to catch up after missing the first three weeks of classes. It took me most of the fall term to get my notes and assignments up to my expectations. I finished the term eighth in my class, the lowest ranking of my academic life. Even though during the winter I continued to flirt with Sharon on the bus, my primary focus was on schoolwork, and by the end of the second term I was second in my class with an average of eighty-six percent. I decided that the next year I would have to leave tobacco harvest earlier, even though I enjoyed the work, and loved watching my bank account grow.

By winter, I began dating Katie, a Baptist girl from Ingersoll, and, as we ended our evenings, I learned how to kiss without embarrassing nose collisions. It was the first real dating experience for each of us and neither of us had any illusions of this being a lifetime romance. It was fun to go skating or tobogganing and be invited back to her house for hot chocolate. I remember walking into her home in January of 1963 to be greeted by a current hit from the Rooftop Singers of "Walk Right In," sung by Katie's parents. We had a few more dates during the winter and early spring, and then the romance faded as I became more serious about the girl on the bus.

Sharon's parents, Norm and Gladys, couldn't have been more different from Katie's. On my first experience with Sharon's mom and dad, they took us fishing on Lake Erie. As Sharon and I sat in the back seat, her parents lit up cigarettes and played country music on the radio. With a playful smile, Norm said, "Do you smoke? Do you chew? Do you associate with those who do?" I quickly realized I was stepping into a new world of hard work and quick wits with no pretence of sophistication. I realized Norm was challenging me to prove I was willing to accept his daughter with all the reality of her family. I immediately liked Norm and recognized his strength and courage. I didn't realize it at the time, but this was the beginning of the romance that would shape my life for the next twenty-five years.

As the school year came to an end my romance with Sharon became a weekly event with dances, movies, moonlight walks, and long mushy good night kissing. Soon our goodbyes lasted longer and longer as we sat parked in the farm driveway. At first, I feared Sharon's father, but about the second time that I brought Sharon home and we snuggled in the car, her father, Norm, found a reason to check the barn and, as he passed the car with its open window, he smiled and said, "Now don't you two stay up too late now." By summer holidays, Sharon was wearing my Glendale school ring, and we were "going steady."

THE BIGGER WORLD

I had a curiosity and a yearning to understand the big issues in life but no one in my world seemed to want to talk about them. Our church leaders never addressed any of the political or social issues of the day. My history teachers taught dates and places from the sanitized version of the First and Second World Wars, but I never learned about colonialism, slavery, the Great Depression, anti-Semitism, racism, Hiroshima, or the real horrors of war.

I filled the gap in my education first through reading and then, as I discovered Pete Seeger, Phil Ochs, Bob Dylan, and Woody Guthrie, through folk music. My early understanding of the horrors of war came through *All Quiet on the Western Front* and *The Rise and Fall of the Third Reich*. My social service sentiments and interest in other cultures came through books like *The Small Woman*, *The Invisible Man*, and *Black Like Me*. Fortunately, I also discovered Stephen Leacock's *Sunshine Sketches of a Small Town*, and, in his flippancy and humour, I found an antidote for my tendency toward melancholy. I never discussed my thoughts about war and social issues with anyone. I was the outsider, passionate enough about Jesus and the social gospel to be accepted at church, and successful enough academically to be accepted at school. For our annual compulsory five-minute speech in English class, I chose to entertain my classmates with Leacock-inspired humour, rather than choosing a more serious subject.

In August of 1962, as Martin Luther King marched with 250,000 people to Washington and made his famous *I Have a Dream* speech, I was working as many hours as I could in the tobacco fields. The U.S. civil unrest was of little concern as Tillsonburg finished up another tobacco harvest.

International politics heated up in the fall of 1962, as President Kennedy and the U.S. had a showdown with the Soviet Union over Russian missiles based in Cuba, and Prime Minister Diefenbaker infuriated the U.S.

military by refusing to put our troops on high alert. I was only vaguely aware of these issues as our family depended on TV news and the local paper to keep us informed.

Then, early in 1963, the Canadian government went further by refusing to allow Canada to become a base for nuclear warheads. Again, our teachers and church leaders had little to say about sending young men off to war. As a quiet deserter from high school cadets, I remained silent the few times when such issues were discussed. As I edged toward conscription age, I had an opinion, but I was smart enough to keep it to myself.

AS GOOD AS IT GETS

As grade eleven came to an end, I was thriving in every area of my life. I was going steady with my sweetheart. I was doing well in school. My father was working and enjoying life. My bank account was growing. I had been granted permission to drop Geography in grade twelve and replace it with grade thirteen Botany and Zoology. I was going to be a plotter and Boat Driver during the summer.

Looking back, I am amazed how our family coped with four drivers and one car, yet I never recall a dispute over a need for a vehicle. For me to be a plotter, measuring tobacco fields for the Marketing Board, I had to arrive each morning before 8:00 a.m. with a vehicle, pick up a pin boy to assist me, and drive to my assigned farms. My father gave me permission to use the car, as long as I drove him to Delmer to his workplace and picked him up each day during the weeks I would measure tobacco.

As I began my first summer as a plotter, I was fortunate to be assigned a cheerful pin boy with an unusual gift with animals. Each morning the Tobacco Marketing Board staff gave us the address, the farmer's name, and the assigned acreage of the farms we were to measure. First, we had to find the farm. Then, we had to find the farmer. As I learned as a pin boy, most of the farms had a dog—usually a large one with German Shepherd or Doberman lineage. I liked dogs, but I had been bitten enough times to be cautious as I went to the farmhouse door. Pin Boy Pete was not only fearless, but he also had some kind of mojo working that allowed him to calm and befriend even the wildest beast. At one farm, the huge German Shepherd was chained with a beware sign posted nearby. As I met the farmer, the dog was lunging at the end of a heavy chain. By the time the farmer had agreed to let us measure his fields, the dog was lying on his back, with Pete stroking his belly.

The job went well. I had enough farm experience to win the trust of the farmers, and my previous summers had taught me how to diagram the farm and transform each field into a set of trapezoids that I carefully finalized each night and handed in the following morning. When I met with the farmer, he would help me create a map of his farm laying out the fields—usually four or five. Large fields with straight ends were a dream. Small irregular fields in mosquito-infested wooded areas were torture. I knew that if I measured one hundred acres a day I was doing well. On the days when I had large open fields, I would sometimes finish my farms by 3:00 p.m. and then park in the shade and prepare my final drawings to hand in to my bosses. On the days when the fields were small and irregular, we would work as long as we could and still report in by 5:00 p.m. Those days I would have to finish up my drawings at home. That summer, I got twelve days work as a plotter before the tasks were handed over to more experienced employees who then returned to the farms for the more demanding work of cut-downs.

A STRANGE ADVENTURE

That summer a chance encounter with two high school friends led to a strange and exciting holiday weekend in Huntsville. Gord Humphrey and Stu Gregson were farm boys from Straffordville. Gord and I were classmates, and he knew Stu. It turned out that all of us had a few days before we were to begin work in harvest. As we sat at the Glen Mur Drive-In Restaurant eating footlongs and fries, we began dreaming up a plan. I was able to borrow our car. Gord said he could get an army tent, and Stu said he could supply sleeping bags. Gord knew a pastor from his Brethren denomination who had a summer home in Bracebridge where we could spend our first night. Here, we would check out our gear and then, on the weekend, we would find a campsite near Huntsville to stay at until Monday.

On Thursday afternoon, we loaded up my parents' car and headed north. After wandering the streets of Bracebridge where Stu and I bought corncob pipes and some cheap pipe tobacco, we had a burger feast and then searched out Gord's preacher friend's cottage. After introductions we were led to the spacious backyard where we were to camp for the night.

After setting up the tent and lots of silliness, we finally settled in for a night's sleep. Almost immediately, thunder roared, and the skies opened. Gord's borrowed army tent leaked everywhere and since we had set it up close to the house at the base of a backyard hill, we were soon flooded from above and below. We tried to endure the hardship, but by midnight our optimism had drowned. We woke the preacher and his wife and straggled in the back door carrying our soggy belongings. Our hosts placed our dripping sleeping bags and weekend clothing in the entry until morning. The gracious wife, who probably had nothing to do with inviting us to camp there, now helped us find sufficient blankets and corners to sleep in. In the morning, we laid our wet sleeping bags and soaked belongings on the car and clothesline to begin to dry. After a delicious home-cooked breakfast, we thanked our hosts again and again, packed our still soggy belongings in the trunk of the car and headed further north.

When we got to Huntsville we parked and wandered the streets admiring the swarms of teenage tourist girls and checking out the restaurants. We learned that the best campgrounds were on Ferry Lake, just south of town, and we set out to find a campsite. Determined to be on the water, we stopped at every campground around the lake. After the fourth or fifth location with still no spaces available, we started to realize that arriving without reservations on a Friday late in July in one of Ontario's most popular summer destinations wasn't likely to get us a camping spot. By late afternoon we had circled the entire lake without success. As we passed a farm bordering the lake, there was a sign advertising fresh bread and baked goods. We wound our way up a long driveway and, as we crested a hill and reached the farmhouse, we saw beautiful fields that went all the way to the edge of the lake.

Under the guise of purchasing bread we set out to charm our potential hosts. After discussing haying and sharing a bit about our own farm experiences, we asked if we might rent a spot near the lake to set up our tent for a couple of days. To our surprise, the farmer and his wife not only agreed, but they also refused any payment, other than our bread purchase. With Cheshire Cat smiles, we drove along the farm laneway to the edge of the lake and found a spot to set up our tent. Although our lakeside location was ideal, we quickly discovered that every bit of level ground was used for fields. Under a gnarled old tree near the edge of the lake we found a spot with only a few tree roots and stones where we could erect our soggy covering. Quite pleased with ourselves, we hung clothing and sleeping bags on tree branches to dry while we headed back to town to admire the scenery and find our supper. On the road to Huntsville, we discovered a canoe rental site and made arrangements to pick up a canoe early the next morning.

Early Saturday morning, after a campfire breakfast, we arrived at the canoe rental place. Stu and I were to paddle the canoe to our campsite while Gord drove the car back to meet us there. Both Stu and I had boating experience, so we loaded up life jackets and paddles for three and set off along the shore east toward our tent. We soon realized that lake edges are not a straight line. Next, as we detoured around a rocky section, we unwittingly drifted into open water where the morning fog was so thick, we had no idea which direction we should go. We had no choice but to drift along waiting for the sun to lift the fog and for the shore to reappear. Gord probably thought we had deserted him, but by late morning we arrived at the campsite. We felt like real campers as we built a fire and feasted on wieners and beans.

We were just finishing lunch when we saw three canoe loads of teenage girls paddling right past our campsite. We watched as they passed by and started toward the far side of the lake. We decided to give chase. We placed Gord in the front of the canoe, I was in the middle, and Stu took the stern. We started well and were soon halfway across the lake, gaining on the young women as they headed to some location on the opposite shore. Later discussions were inconclusive, but either Stu or I said, "Faster," which proved to be a serious mistake. Farm boy Gord summoned his strength, dug his paddle deep into the water, and flipped our canoe in a flash. We were confident swimmers so none of us were wearing the life jackets. As we surfaced, Gord had somehow managed to save his glasses and, as he put those back on, we collected paddles and life jackets and prepared to right our canoe. When we flipped the canoe right side up, it was filled with water and we realized that, if we tried to get in, we might lose the canoe. So, Gord, our weakest swimmer, put on a life jacket, while we loaded the other jackets and the paddles into the canoe, pointed it toward the distant shore where our tent was, and began to swim while pushing our water-filled canoe along.

Soon, a powerboat zoomed up to check on us. The man and woman were quite concerned, but we assured them we had everything under control and continued to swim. A few minutes later, another boat arrived, this time with a man and woman, and a shapely teenage daughter. They pointed to their cottage just a short way along the shore from our campsite. This time we accepted their help. We loaded Gord, and our paddles and life preservers, into their boat, and Stu and I insisted that we would pilot our craft back to shore and then come to collect Gord and our equipment. It was a beautiful sunny afternoon, and Stu and I enjoyed our swim, emptied the water from the canoe, and placed it safely on shore. We put on dry shirts and shorts and went to the cottage to retrieve Gord and our equipment and to thank our helpers. The mother and daughter welcomed us, and, after a chat, we began to say our goodbyes. As we collected our paddles, they asked how long we were staying and if we had time for some waterskiing. By the time we left, it had been arranged for us to come back the next afternoon to waterski.

As we headed back to our campsite, we argued whether our young host's name was Bri-ann or Brianna, soon deciding it didn't matter since we would call her Bri. We grilled Gord to learn more about the family and the cottage. Gord said the family obviously had money since the cottage was only for weekends. Their big house was in Huntsville. Gord thought the father was in gas or oil.

We decided we were finished canoeing, so we figured out that, if we protected the car roof with a couple of life jackets, and Gord and Stu held on out opposite side windows I could carefully transport the canoe back to the rental place as we headed to town. Our plan worked and we were all relieved to leave the canoe behind and head to Huntsville for generous helpings of tourist food and an opportunity to experience a Saturday night in a tourist mecca. After eating until we hurt, we wandered the streets. We discovered that the most exciting option that night was a big lacrosse game at the Huntsville arena.

None of us had seen a lacrosse game. The team names have long since left my memory, but the rancour and violence we witnessed have certainly endured. During team introductions we learned that these men were experienced warriors. The opposing teams obviously had a history and they seemed ready to do battle from the first bounce of the hard rubber ball.

One team seemed to be the "Homeboys" and the other the "Outsiders." The players wore team jerseys and had shoulder pads and heavy gloves. The goalie was the only one with face or head protection. The game moved at a dizzying speed, and we loved it. The way the players attacked the ball carrier's stick soon led to whacks on the arms and shoulders with occasional errant blows to the head. It wasn't long before the first fight erupted. As bodies rolled on the cement arena floor the referees struggled to restore order. Several players were sent off to the penalty box. We had chosen seats high in the stands and that proved to be wise as the ball often ended up bouncing off spectators.

As the game went on, the violence escalated. One of the "Homeboys" intentionally used his stick as a weapon and hit one of the "Outsiders" on the head, opening a wound that spewed blood and led to another fight that cleared the benches. This time spectators joined in and there were several fights in the bleachers. By the time a truce had been negotiated several players and one coach had been ejected from the game. The announcer warned that further violence in the stands could lead to arrests.

The players were skilled, and the game moved quickly. Late in the game the wounded warrior from the "Outsiders" returned with a bandaged head. As soon as he returned to the arena floor, he ran straight to the player who had injured him and knocked him senseless with a whack to the head. This time, as fights erupted all around us, we left by the nearest exit. As we headed back to our campsite, we learned from CKAR 590 that the game was suspended because, after another round of ejections there weren't enough players or coaches to continue.

As we sat around our campfire swapping tales, eating marshmallows, and reminiscing about our day, we realized we had already had quite an adventure, and we still had an opportunity to water ski on Sunday afternoon.

FINISHING WITH A BANG

On Sunday morning we headed back to town, and after a huge breakfast and an hour or two wandering the main street, we went back to our campsite to get our bathing suits and made our way to Bri's cottage. When we arrived, we were greeted by Bri and her mother. Bri's mother apologized that her husband was away for a while so we might not be able to ski since there had to be a driver and a spotter at all times.

Stu assured her that he had extensive powerboat experience, and we all promised to wear life jackets and act responsibly. I noticed that the mother had her legs wrapped with some sort of elastic bandaging as we assembled skis, donned life jackets, and got into their twenty-plus foot powerboat. Finally, we headed out onto the lake, with Bri driving and Stu enjoying learning the details of gears and acceleration from Bri. I quickly realized that Stu really did know what he was talking about.

Neither Gord nor I had ever waterskied, so Stu was the first to take a turn with Bri driving and Gord and I as spotters. Soon, we were zipping around the lake in figure eights, laughing and enjoying the sunshine. Back in the boat, Stu practiced his acceleration until Bri was satisfied, and then she was ready to ski. Stu carefully accelerated until she was up, and then he showed off his driving skills as Bri dazzled us with her beauty and skiing excellence. With Bri and Stu coaching us, by the end of the afternoon, after several failed attempts and a great deal of laughter, both Gord and I had managed to ski.

As the time came for us to head back to the cottage, Stu was at the controls. Gord and I were chatting as Stu did a wide arc and swung toward the T-shaped dock. Then something went horribly wrong, and the next thing I knew, the boat had hit the dock and seemed about to launch right on top as Bri screamed, and her mother, with legs wrapped, edged toward the end of the dock, hoping not to be run over by a boat. Mercifully, the motor stopped, and the boat settled back into the water. As we climbed onto the dock, Stu examined the damage and promised to cover all the costs. Realizing the damage to the boat was minimal, and that her daughter and all of us were okay, Bri's mother regained her poise. I was beginning to relax when I saw the large father get out of his car and start toward us. Bri and Stu did the explaining, and Stu did another round of apologizing and promising to pay as Gord, and I looked on with biblical fear and trembling. With unexpected graciousness, Bri's father patted Stu on the shoulder saying things like, "We all make mistakes, It's no biggie," and "Glad everybody's okay." As he walked us toward our vehicle, we knew it was time for us to go. Quite relieved, we escaped back to our campsite.

Our trip north had certainly proved memorable, but it wasn't quite over yet. Gord wanted to go to church in Huntsville that night. He borrowed the car and headed to town, while Stu and I built a campfire and settled in for the evening. We relaxed by the lake until the mosquitoes drove us into the tent where we discovered, with our pipe smoke, we could keep the pests at bay. When Gord returned and opened the tent flap, he could hardly see us in the blue haze. Gord announced that he thought he was in love. After rolling in laughter, we heard all about the beauty he had met at the Brethren gathering. Knowing how strict the church members were, we had a great time teasing good-natured Gord about what his new friends would say if they knew about his weekend. With more laughter and a rehashing of the adventures, we eventually nodded off.

In the morning, we packed up and headed back to our more normal lives. I don't recall us swearing each other to silence, but I certainly knew that my parents would only hear a very sanitized version of the weekend. It was like a trip to Vegas—what happened in Huntsville would stay in Huntsville.

The next day, I was back at work at Steve's farm.

THE TEST

In the summer of 1963 as I worked at Steve VanQuaethem's farm I was a regular at the Williams farm just a mile down the road, since Norm and Gladys's youngest daughter and I had become sweethearts during the winter.

I learned Norm had started out with nothing and now, in his mid-fifties, owned a small tobacco farm. It had taken years as a tobacco worker and share grower to get his opportunity to own a farm, but now he was growing seventeen to twenty acres a year on his own. Because of his smaller acreage Norm had a half gang for harvest, with three primers and only one tyer and two leaf handers. As Norm prepared for harvest, I had a day off and he asked me if I'd like to do some odd jobs for the day. I saw this as a chance to demonstrate what a good worker I was to my potential father-in-law. I soon realized that Norm saw it as a chance to see what I was made of.

The morning assignments were straightforward—trimming the grass around the kilns and kiln yard and organizing the bundles of tobacco sticks that would soon be used for harvest. After lunch, it got interesting, and my efforts to impress were put to the test. I was taken to the old converted dairy barn that served as the space where the cured tobacco was stored, sorted, and baled before being shipped to the tobacco auction and sold to the big tobacco companies. I was asked to clean it out, load the tobacco scraps into the old red farm truck, and drive to a gully on the edge of the farm to dispose of the refuse. It was an awful job. Sweeping the old barn floor stirred up a cloud of tobacco bits and dust. I was on my own to figure out how to get the refuse into the back of the pickup. I found an old scoop shovel to use as my dustpan. It was hot stuffy work, but I persevered and by late afternoon was ready to take the load to the gully. I was feeling pretty good as I shifted the stick shift into gear and headed down the road. At the edge of Norm's farm, I found the roadway to the gully and drove to the dumping spot. I backed up, emptied the truck, and swept out the truck box. I prepared to make my triumphant return. I started the truck and went to shift from reverse to first gear. As the shift lever moved freely in my hand, I knew I was in trouble.

All I was familiar with under a vehicle hood was the oil stick and fan belt. Now I had wrecked Norm's truck. After some exploring, I managed to open the hood of the ancient Chevy. I looked in and immediately had to smile at Norm's parsimonious ingenuity. I didn't know how to correct the problem, but I sure knew where the issue was located. Up above the engine, wire and binder twine were woven together in some strange way. After some greasy exploration, I realized that to engage the transmission, the shifter rod had to be reconnected to a doohickey that went to the transmission. The wire and binder twine had somehow held that in place, and now it had gotten loose. If I didn't figure it out, I would have to walk back to the farm, covered in dust and grease, having failed the test.

After a few failed experiments and *a little bit of luck*, I finally managed to pop the shifter in place and rewrapped some of the wire to hold it together long enough to get me back to the farm. Sure enough, I was now able to find first gear and set the truck in motion. It was late in the afternoon as I drove into the farmyard.

As I handed the keys to Norm, he thanked me for my work and asked how it went. Trying to look like Paul Newman, I replied that there were no problems, but that he might want to check out the shifter — it seemed a little loose.

MANNING UP

At Steve's I had become one of his hired men working almost every day in July and August at a variety of jobs. I helped him irrigate. Then I loaded the aluminum irrigation pipes onto a wagon, took them to the farmyard and piled them beside the implement barn. I learned how to disc rye. I really knew I had arrived when Steve let me drive the farm truck home for the night so that I could be back at the farm early the next morning.

As Steve began to top the tobacco, his harvest crew began to arrive. Four men were from Spain and spoke little English. The Spaniards were wiry rough men who, I discovered were only in Canada for the summer. These newcomers joined me in the field as we applied sucker oil to the tobacco plants. Now at seventeen, I found myself the expert, pushing the pace as the men in their thirties learned the new skill and grumbled about going too fast.

As harvest began, Steve's southern cureman, Lonnie Abbott, had brought his two grandsons, Jerry and Billy, and who, although they were only sixteen and seventeen, both had a lifetime of tobacco experience. I loved hearing their relaxed southern drawl. I felt sorry for my age-mates as they were escorted to the bunkhouse, a converted garage that now had ten beds along one wall. The thoughts of spending a summer with their rough workmates seemed daunting to me, but I soon learned Jerry and Billy were more than capable of taking life's challenges as they came. Having grown up in rural North Carolina on a sharecropper's small farm, they had been working in the fields with rough older men most of their lives and were quite capable of handling the work and their safety.

None of the Spanish recruits had ever worked in tobacco, although they bragged that recent work on a mushroom farm had strengthened their backs. Somehow, Steve chose three to work in the fields and one to climb high into the kiln and hang the tobacco as instructed. Jerry, Billy, and a local guy in his twenties completed the priming team, while I was to drive boats, which meant I would pick up the primed tobacco in the field and bring it to the kiln yard to be tied and hung. I was nervously excited as I began my new role.

As harvest began, I found my boat driver role boringly easy. I sat comfortably on the seat of the big red International Harvester tractor as the horse and primers worked their way down the row. As they arrived at the end of the row, I would help lead the horse and the full boats to the roadway and help them hook up two empty boats and get started toward the other end of the field. Then, I would hook the boats to the back of the tractor and drag them to the kiln yard, parking them by the tying machine. As soon as possible, I would hook up two empty boats and head back to the field. This process would be repeated over and over for hours until the kiln was full. Even though I had now worked in tobacco for three years I didn't know anything about priming. Now, with my front-row seat I watched each primer and studied the techniques. During the first few days Steve was often in the field instructing the new primers, stressing the need to pick three leaves off each plant and to avoid breaking the stems. Next, he helped the primers learn how to create a large bundle of leaves under their arm and place these neatly in the boat. I watched and learned and began experimenting by priming partway down each row to help the primers. As my skill and confidence grew, I was placing armfuls of primed tobacco between plants at the end of most rows. Jerry and Billy Abbott were always the first to finish their rows and I began to look forward to my conversations with them. By the third day, they were encouraging me to forget about them and help that "poe boy" struggling at the back. They were convinced he wasn't going to survive. Soon our boss Steve shared their opinion. When I suggested I would trade roles with the straggler, both Steve and our struggling primer welcomed the switch. Now I had jumped into the deep end and would have to sink or swim as a primer.

That night I went to the hardware store and bought my primer's suit—yellow rubberized bib pants and a yellow rubberized jacket. In the suit, I looked like an east coast fisherman as I prepared to start my first full day of priming. We started priming by 7:00 a.m. As I joined the crew, we were finishing up sand leaves, the bottom three leaves on the tobacco plant. The tobacco was wet and, if you got the juice in your eyes, it stung. I wore rubber boots and my yellow suit and started down my row, picking with my right hand and creating a bundle under my left arm. I quickly realized that being bent over all day was going to be quite different than helping out from time to time.

For the first morning I struggled to keep up, feeling a huge sense of relief each time we reached the end of a row. Here I got a chance to stand tall and stretch as we got the horse and the empty boats ready for our next row. By mid-morning, the tobacco was dry and the boots and rain suit were too hot so I followed the example of the other primers, created a bundle, and placed it in one of the boats of tobacco headed to the kiln.

With each row my technique improved and by noon I was mostly keeping up with the others. I took comfort in the fact that the Spaniards were struggling as much as I was. I learned that they knew some French as well as Spanish, so I was able to make a bit of conversation. Jerry and Billy found the work easy, and they never quit talking. I was soon giggling as they commented on everything with an amazing sense of humour. One of the Spaniards had been assigned the responsibility of the horse, and he was not having fun. The northern logging horse would either be almost stepping on his heels or stubbornly lagging behind us. "Cabello, hie!" was the first Spanish phrase that I learned.

At lunchtime I was almost too tired to eat, and I knew I had several more hours in the field. I never felt sorry for myself, and I never complained. I was determined to succeed and to prove to Steve, the other men, and to myself, that I was strong and capable. During the afternoon, there were a few times where I primed on my knees, hoping to give my back a little respite. Mercifully, late in the afternoon, the newly appointed boat driver announced that we were on our last boats. What a welcome message. When we finished, I collected my boots and rain suit, helped the table gang finish up, and headed home for a basement scrub and a hot bath.

The next few days were a blur as we finished up the sand leaves and prepared to start back at the beginning of the fields on what was now called "seconds," brilliantly named because they were the next set of leaves to be removed. It had taken seven days to complete the first pulling. Steve had ten kilns. Lonnie, our cureman, had done his job well, and the first two kilns of tobacco were now golden and moist from bottom to top. After we finished priming our first kiln of seconds, Steve informed the primers that tomorrow our day would begin at 5:30 a.m. as we "took out" the first kiln. He told me that I could take the pick-up home and that I needn't bother with breakfast—I could join the other primers at the farmhouse breakfast table.

The scene was circus-like as I arrived at the VanQuaethem farm the next morning. Steve was waiting with the tractor and a farm wagon at the driveway by the bunkhouse. As I climbed on, one of the Spaniards was already aboard, and soon the rest of the Spaniards and our Southerners straggled out of the bunkhouse, pulling bits of clothing into place as they climbed onto the wagon. I was greeted with "Buenos Dias," and "How y'all doin," simultaneously. It was wonderful. With his usual wild humour,

Steve popped the clutch as the last man was trying to climb on, and we all watched with amusement as Jorge struggled onto the moving wagon. I sat with a goofy smile as we bounced our way to the awaiting task.

At the kiln, where Lonnie, our cureman, was waiting, the big side doors had been opened, and Steve parked the wagon next to the waiting sticks. Steve placed himself at one end of the wagon and Lonnie at the other as the rest of us removed the tobacco, stick by stick, from the rafters of the kiln. Steve and Lonnie made sure we treated the cured tobacco with proper respect as huge piles grew on each end of the wagon. Soon, we had guys perched on rafters high into the kiln as we removed the upper sticks, handing them from person to person while maintaining our precarious balance. When the kiln was empty, nine of us headed toward the farmhouse kitchen.

The scene at the kitchen table was delightful insanity. Steve's sister, Thelma, had helped Steve's wife, Nellie, prepare the meal of eggs, bacon, toast, and coffee. Steve was the master of ceremonies, as he sat at the end of the table telling tales of Jorge's struggle to get on the wagon and how scared Doug had been as he climbed up into the kiln. No one was spared, including Steve, as good-natured teasing and laughter filled the room. As we finished our meal and headed for the fields, I was amazed to realize it still wasn't 7:00 a.m.

Although I was not asked to help every morning, taking out the kiln was now a necessary part of every day to make space for the tobacco coming from the fields. Later in the day, Steve and Lonnie would take the wagon load of tobacco to the large storage barn and pile the sticks in huge stacks that, at the end of harvest, would be "stripped," graded, baled, weighed, and stored until the bales were shipped to the tobacco auction. My appreciation of the process, and the leadership it took to keep it all organized, grew each day.

In the field I had found my rhythm. Again, as I had discovered in earlier harvests, I enjoyed hard work, and what I lacked in speed, I made up with endurance. I was now able to keep up with Jerry and Billy, and they taught me every nuance of picking tobacco that they had learned in the south. I found the combination of a southern drawl and constant banter a never-ending source of amusement. A statement as simple as, "I think you all jus' build roads up here so's you kin tear them up," would have me giggling. They would tell me what a pretty girl I had, and then tell me that Sharon had stopped in for visit at the bunkhouse the night before. When I invited them to my place for supper they turned on the southern charm and had my mother blushing as she offered them seconds of everything. We pushed our Spanish co-workers hard, but we also helped them out, and we had days when we were out of the field by 3:00 p.m. I loved the camaraderie, the sunshine, and the work. Every day was an adventure.

TAKING THE LEAD

By the time we moved up to "thirds," the horse issue was becoming a problem. The man who had the horse in his row was sometimes too slow, and we had to walk back to get to the boat. Other times, when the horse was right on his heels, our horseman was frustrated and anything but gracious. When Miguel punched the horse in the nose, the boys and I intervened. At the end of the field, we switched the horse into my row and at noon I talked with Steve and the new arrangement was confirmed. Now the three of us could really push the pace. I liked the old work horses, and we got along well.

With the big leaves on the third pulling, a new issue had to be addressed. The third priming was easy to pick since we were now able to stand upright. The leaves were big and filled the boat and the kiln more quickly. However, for our cureman, Lonnie, these big leaves brought special challenges. The size of the leaves meant that, when they were packed on sticks and stuffed into the kiln, the air had a harder time circulating as the tobacco was heated to dry it out and hopefully, turn it flue-cured yellow. This meant that Steve now asked his primers to become connoisseurs of quality in the field. Steve spent time in the field with us, instructing us to know when a leaf was ready, and when it needed to be left on the stem to ripen. When leaves are ready to be harvested, they begin to turn a lighter shade of green and develop a pebbly surface. When they are too green, they are smooth and dark. Steve brought us a sample from the kiln of leaves that were too green that had turned black instead of yellow during curing. We were sternly admonished to avoid picking green tobacco. Usually, there were only a few patches near the edge of the field or in low spots where this was an issue. Soon I was saying, "Muy verde!" to the Spaniards as we went through a green patch and acting like a field boss.

As harvest progressed, the tobacco suckers that the "sucker oil" was supposed to have eradicated began to be an issue. At the junction of each leaf, a little tobacco plant was trying to grow, and by the fourth week of harvest these suckers were getting big and, at times, made it difficult to pick the leaf without getting a small tobacco plant as well. Steve was concerned because he said the food and energy that made good tobacco leaves was now being used by these unwelcome hitchhikers.

Our jobs got easier when Steve hired some people to "sucker" the crop, walking the rows and removing the little plants one by one, and pinching the little sprouts near the top. To get the job done faster, he offered an hourly wage to the primers if we wanted to "sucker" after we filled our kiln. I always said yes, and, during the last weeks of August I sometimes worked twelve hours a day.

As we came to the end of summer there were a few days when, because of the weather and the delayed curing process, Steve didn't have an available kiln to fill, so I was offered work at a neighbouring farm or at Steve's dad's farm in Tillsonburg. What an insight to experience different workers and different bosses!

At neighbour Maurice Tach's farm, there was one primer who was in his fifties. He kept up to the younger primers by never stopping to help with turning the boats and by not talking much to anyone. He primed well, but as I studied his work-worn body I was reminded once again that, for me, education was essential.

Working a day for Steve VanQuaethem's father was another opportunity for me to learn about different approaches to leadership. Steve's father, Joe, grew tobacco for a wealthy southerner named Hunter Floyd. Joe's farm was right in the middle of residential Tillsonburg, on Broadway just behind the Glen Mur Drive-In Restaurant.

As Steve drove me to his dad's farm, I learned the reason for my "work opportunity." I discovered that Joe pushed himself hard and expected excellence from his workers. When challenged, he was quick to lose his temper. Trouble had been brewing ever since the late summer mornings grew colder. Now mumblings had led to revolt. When Joe made his usual trip to the bunkhouse to call the men to breakfast, the mutiny leader proudly announced that the men had decided it was too cold to work.

When I arrived there to replace the missing primer, I learned that Joe had not only immediately fired the troublemaker but had added emphasis by chasing him up the main street of Tillsonburg with a pitchfork.

By the time I arrived the other primers were waiting, and the morning went well. At noon I was invited to join Joe's remaining primers for a hot meal at the kitchen table, and what a meal it was. Joe's wife, Adrienne, had taken a huge, ordinary pot roast, and with beer sauce and a long cook time, turned it into a culinary delight. I was amazed as the food kept coming.

As the afternoon progressed, I learned that Joe was very different from his son, Steve. Joe was old-school, still using tyers and leaf handers because he wanted to squeeze every leaf he could onto each stick, and as many sticks as possible into each kiln. Days at Joe's farm seldom ended early.

As August came to an end, I told Steve I had decided I couldn't work until the end of harvest like I had the year before, but I would continue working until another farm had finished and Steve could get a replacement for me. I was able to be back in school by the third week of September.

It had been a very good harvest. I had earned my boss's respect and had a job for the next summer. My bank account was growing. With each new skill I gained confidence. I headed back to grade twelve, tanned and more fit than I had ever been in my life.

MY SENIOR YEAR

As I finished up another summer in the tobacco fields, I pondered my learnings. As a plotter for the Tobacco Marketing Board, I had travelled the backroads of our area, working with farmers who were prosperous, fluent in English, with large farms and manicured lawns. I had met many other farmers who were new to Canada, struggling with a new language, small quotas, and marginal soil in order to eke out a living. I had discovered that prosperity had no correlation with hospitality. Each person I met was unique and unpredictable. In the fields, I had now worked with men from Europe, Quebec, and the U.S. of all ages and sizes and had discovered that each person is a mysterious mix of biases, hopes, and fears. I had learned that the man I was becoming enjoyed the challenge and physicality of working as part of a team. I also discovered that I was skilled at leadership and teaching.

MY FOOTBALL CAREER

As I began my last year at Glendale High School, I was invited to try out for the football team, and since I was back at school early in September, I decided to give it a try. Although I lacked speed, I was strong and fit, and I was soon part of the squad. Coach Wayne Coyle decided I would play on defence as either an end or a linebacker. Although I had enjoyed watching high school and professional football I quickly realized that it moved a lot faster when you were in the middle of a game with a two-hundred-pound runner coming straight at you. At the time I weighed one hundred and forty pounds.

I enjoyed the practices and the camaraderie in the locker room and on the bus as we travelled to and from our games. On game day, the players dressed in suits and ties, and during the morning, we strutted the school halls before being released early to board the bus while classmates wished us well. On the field, everything changed. I rode the bench most of the time. Our team tried hard, but our defensive line wore down as the game went on, and soon the opposing running backs found huge gaps that allowed long runs into our backfield. Leo Rouse was our deep safety, and he was often left on his own to make another saving tackle. Leo was amazing but couldn't stave off defeat by himself. By the time I was inserted into the lineup we were usually trailing the other team. Everything happened so much faster during a game than it did in practice that the plays were a blur as I attempted to stop the runners as they galloped by. I felt guilty as I watched Leo's heroics once again.

Practices ran late and I had to walk or hitchhike the three miles home. I took it in stride, and this inconvenience added to my determination and endurance. We lost every game that year, and as I stood shivering in snow and sleet during the last game of the season as wounded players sat on our bench or were attended to on the ground, I knew that the warm shower that awaited me after the game would mark the end of my football career. I had made some new friends and been part of a team while gaining a whole new appreciation for the training and skill it takes to excel at any team sport.

A HARD RAIN'S A-GONNA FALL

Just after lunch on the Friday afternoon of November 22, 1963, our Principal, Mr. MacPherson, signalled an announcement over the P.A. system. We all listened in stunned silence as he announced that the forty-six-year-old thirty-fifth president of the United States, John F. Kennedy, had just been shot and killed as his presidential motorcade travelled through the streets of Dallas, Texas. Girls gasped and cried while most of the guys sat in shocked silence. Fortunately, we were in Frank Kuhl's English class, and he provided the calm stability we needed to get through the next hour.

The weekend was filled with conversations about conspiracies, the Cold War, fear for the future, and lost potential. On Sunday, my family came home from church and immediately turned on the TV to learn of the latest developments. We watched in amazement on live TV as Jack Ruby fatally shot the suspected assassin, Lee Harvey Oswald. It felt like the safe little world I had known was becoming a much more dangerous place.

Although I had been too busy with school, romance, and hard work to pay much attention to Walter Cronkite, Peter Jennings, and Harvey Kirck on the TV news, I had been becoming increasingly aware of the Cold War and the United States' tensions at home and in Cuba, Iraq, and Vietnam.

I had recently discovered Bob Dylan and began listening to his folk-inspired sound on the record player I shared with my brother. Bob's first album, released in 1962 and simply titled *Bob Dylan,* introduced me to Woody Guthrie and other social activists who had used music as a way of expressing hope and raising awareness. Meanwhile, my brother had discovered Pete Seeger and began to learn the five-string banjo. Although we seldom talked about it, I think we both took comfort in the honesty and beauty of poetic expression shared through music.

Bob Dylan's lyrics led me to pay attention to the Freedom Riders and Protestors in the American South, and Martin Luther King's March on Washington, on August 28, 1963. I resonated with Bob Dylan's and Phil Ochs' lyrics, but I had no one to talk to about my growing social consciousness. I didn't believe for a moment that President Kennedy's assassination was some random act of a madman. Times were changing. As the lone deserter from cadets, I didn't talk with anyone about my tendency toward melancholy and a growing distrust of the establishment.

With most of the world we watched the president's brave widow, Jackie Kennedy, with her little children, John and Caroline, at the funeral. My loss of Hugh Hawkins made JFK's death all too real. Fortunately, Dylan and the folksingers I was discovering did more than talk about poverty and war, greed and injustice. They also had a joy amid struggle that gave me the hope and strength I needed. Rather than bring me down, songs like Dylan's version of Bukka White's *Fixin' to Die* proved to be a dose of blues reality that helped me see that struggle and grief are just part of life's journey.

As Lyndon B. Johnson took office as president of the United States, we all realized that life would go on. The sixties were filled with energy. It was an exciting time. Beatlemania was at its peak, and we were wowed by the Beatles' record-setting appearance on the *Ed Sullivan Show* on February 9, 1964. The Toronto Maple Leafs were also thriving as Frank Mahovlich, George Armstrong, Red Kelly, and Johnny Bower led the team to victory over the Detroit Red Wings to win the Stanley Cup. Aside from helping win the Stanley Cup in 1964, one of the Toronto defencemen, Tim Horton, opened a little coffee shop bearing his name.

As the 1960s took off like a rocket I found comfort in family and church and treasured the simple things. Sharon and I bought a scrapbook, and on snowy nights we would go through magazines and catalogues and cut out pictures of house plans and furniture that we liked, as we discussed our hopes and dreams for the life we might soon have together.

SOLITARY JOY

As winter came, I spent most Saturday afternoons in the woods alone. I would dress warmly, take my twelve-gauge double-barrel shotgun, and head across the frozen fields to a network of woods and streams at the back of the neighbouring farms. Ostensibly, I was hunting cottontails and partridge in the great pioneer tradition of my childhood heroes, Davy Crocket, Daniel Boone, and my father. The truth is, I was not trying very hard to chase rabbits because my real need was not physical sustenance as much as the solitude and beauty of the wild that restored my connection with an essence of life that was unaffected by politics and human affairs. Here, in the evergreen stillness, I would lose myself in the beauty of nature as chickadees, juncos, and nuthatches sang and flitted from tree to tree.

As the snow crunched beneath my feet and my muscles strained after miles of walking, the woods and fields became my cathedral, and here I lost all fear and concern. Nature was "red in tooth and claw" but that was no reason for despair. Life and death, darkness and light, decay and renewal were all part of the mysterious cycle I was beginning to appreciate.

At the end of the afternoon, I would return from the woods renewed and refreshed. I didn't realize it then, but my need for time alone would be misinterpreted as aloofness by others, and melancholy by me. Often in social situations, I felt more like an observer than an active participant. When I discovered William Shakespeare's words in *As You Like It*—"All the world's a stage, / And all the men and women merely players; / They have their exits and their entrances; / And one man in his time plays many parts"—it resonated deeply. Increasingly, I saw myself choosing my costume for the role I played as a son, student, labourer, and lover.

President Kennedy's death was just one more reminder of how fragile and fleeting life is for all of us. Having lost two close friends by age ten and then having watched my father's near-death experience with a heart attack, I knew that there was no guarantee that I would have a long and leisurely life. In these moments, the closest literary quote to capture my profound thoughts and feelings was a verse from the Bible in Luke 2:19, "But Mary kept all these things and pondered them in her heart."

FINISHING WELL

Glendale High School ended at grade twelve with the commercial and industrial classes graduating and heading off to work or community college. For those of us in 12A and 12B who wanted to go on to university, that meant we would be finished at Glendale and have to go across town to Annandale High School for grade thirteen. This made the last year at Glendale extra special and allowed those of us going on to university an extra opportunity to strut the halls as seniors. My classmates and I made the most of it.

Aside from playing football, I was on Student Council, the Yearbook Cub, the School Choir, and the Prom Committee. I also practiced for Church Choir every Thursday night and attended Sunday School, Church, and Youth Group every week. I spent most Friday and Saturday nights with my sweetheart, Sharon. Looking back, I don't know how I did it all, but I was in the flow of life and enjoying every experience.

For my oral composition that year, I did a five-minute comedy piece on the challenges of being a teenager. It was well received by my classmates and teacher, and I was chosen to be one of the speakers at a town-wide speak-off in the auditorium. Speakers from our school and Annandale presented to a full auditorium of students, and a panel of judges. Again, I did well. Bill Beattie from Annandale and I were selected as finalists and had ten minutes to prepare a second speech. I chose to keep it light and lively, talking about the humorous side of getting up at dawn to stumble off to work in tobacco and pretending that I had found several ways to try to escape the job. Meanwhile, Bill Beattie gave a formal presentation with historical significance. I wowed the crowd but not the judges—Bill was declared the speaking champion. I enjoyed every bit of the notoriety and challenge.

As the year came to an end, the School Prom was a major event. Jamie Vance and I were assigned the task of decorating a corner of the gym as part of the "Night in Paradise" theme. I don't know how much notice we had, but we didn't start our assignment until the day of the prom. We drove around town assembling the materials for our scenic corner of the gym. We borrowed grass mats from the funeral home and flowers and a water pump from a nursery. We bought a kiddie pool for our pond and then built a tall trough for our waterfall. The green paint was still drying as we filled our pool and inserted the pump and hose. Just in time, it all came together, and with mood lights, our waterfall gurgled happily as we rushed home to get ready for our dates. My date, Sharon Williams, looked stunning, and, as I pinned on her corsage, we glowed with joy.

In June, Sharon graduated from the Commercial Program and got a job at Hamilton Trust. As a graduation gift, and to compensate for years of unpaid tobacco labour, Norm bought his daughter, Sharon, a low-mileage 1960 white Ford Falcon.

As I finished the year, second in my class of forty with an eighty-two percent average, I looked forward to another summer of tobacco work and a new school experience at Annandale High School in the fall.

A SUMMER IN THE SUN

As I began my fourth year of tobacco labour, I looked forward to a summer of fun and hard work outdoors. I was returning to familiar roles, and I had confidence in my skills. I worked three weeks for the Tobacco Marketing Board as a plotter and, in the last week, I was entrusted with my first cut-down orders. This involved a whole new level of diplomacy and skill. Each year, based on market needs, every Flue-Cured quota owner was assigned a very specific quota for the year. It would be as precise as 34.45 acres. Up until this year, all I had done was carefully diagram the location of the fields and measure each field, handing in my results to the staff.

Now I was considered ready for the next level of responsibility. I learned that, after the numbers had been calculated, results were sent to each farmer, and those who were over their quota were told that they would have to cut down the excess. I was given the information on a few farms and coached on the safest and most helpful approach. I was to be calm and patient. If the farmer refused to comply, I was to remind him of the rules. I would have to come back three times. If he refused each time, then supervisors would come to enforce the cut-down.

I was nervous as I approached my first farmer. Fortunately, he was willing to co-operate, but he was questioning the measurements of his largest field. I had the detailed drawings and all the measurements, so we walked the field with the farmer. While the farmer watched closely, my pin boy and I checked the measurements. The plotter who had measured the crop had given the farmer generous margins. After we had re-measured half the field, the farmer realized he wasn't being cheated and agreed to cut down the required 0.65 acres. Now the negotiations took a new twist. The farmer had some poor spots on a couple of hills and in a low wet spot. However, the rules stated that each cutdown had to be at least 0.10 acres in size. We measured a possible section and then I calculated that it was 0.25 acres. The farmer said he would have the discs ready in the morning when we came back. The next day we finished his cut-down and one other. By the end of my tenure in 1964, I had completed three cut-downs and hadn't been chased or threatened, as some of my co-workers were. I had gained new skills and confidence and was ready to go back to work with Steve VanQuaethem.

As soon as I was done with the Marketing Board, Steve put me to work and he kept me busy acting as a hired man. Every day was a new adventure. We worked hard and laughed often. I enjoyed working long hours as I took on many different tasks—discing rye, doing underwater repairs to the irrigation control gate, setting up the pump and pipes, irrigating, and organizing sticks and harvest supplies. As I bounced around the farm in Steve's old pickup, I was a contented cowboy riding the open range.

As the workers arrived for harvest, I was delighted to reunite with Jerry and Billy Smith who had returned from North Carolina for another harvest with their grampa, Lonnie, who would be Steve's cureman again. My Carolina buddies had grown bigger, and Jerry now towered over both Billy and me. We were joined in the field by two mature Spaniards who had worked for Steve's dad and proven to be good primers in the past.

The last member of the crew was a young Quebecois, Maurice, whom I almost immediately lost a bet with. Proud of my high school French, I greeted Maurice with a mix of French and English, and he then asked me to pick up some cigarettes for him the next time I was in town. He said he wanted "Mactan" brand. I assured him there was no such brand in Ontario as he handed me a ten-dollar bill. Confidently, I replied that if I found such a brand, I would buy two packs and pay for them myself. A few days later, I delivered two packs of "Mark Ten" cigarettes and the ten-dollar bill to Maurice.

We were all anxious to get started in the field. I took the horse row from the start, and with Jerry and Billy on either side, we set a challenging pace. The Spaniards proved to be up for the task as we all bent low to take the bottom three sand leaves from each plant. Poor Maurice scrambled to keep up. By the third day, all of us had aching backs but we tried to out-psych each other by minimizing our complaints.

The previous harvest, during a visit to my Grampa Chipps in Courtland, as I talked about my aches from priming, he suggested Absorbine Senior. Grampa, who had struggled with arthritis for years, was an expert on pain management. He stressed that I seek out Absorbine *Senior*, not the more common Absorbine Junior. I immediately bought a bottle and applied it to my back, legs, and ankles. At first, I was disappointed as I prepared for a much-needed night's sleep. Then, just as I was about to doze off my back and legs felt like they were on fire. After a night of intermittent sleep, I returned to the early morning field, thankful for the cool wet leaves against my face. Then, as I started to sweat under my wet suit and rubber boots, the liniment came alive again. Soon I was priming without boots or wet suit and my aching back was no longer my first concern. I left the liniment on the shelf and never used it again. But when Jerry, who was now well over six feet tall, began to complain about his back, I felt it my duty to offer him some relief.

As soon as I got home and cleaned up from our day's work, I took the Absorbine Senior to the bunkhouse and offered the cure to Jerry, which he accepted with the usual southern hospitality. The next morning, as I arrived for work, Jerry met me with his tale of woe. He had me laughing hysterically as he told how at 2:00 a.m. he had been rolling on the dew-covered grass seeking relief from the liniment. I reluctantly admitted that I had experienced some discomfort myself, but I reminded him that he hadn't thought much about his aches recently. We started our day's work, and about an hour later Jerry started to howl as the liniment began phase two. As Jerry scrambled to strip while spewing curses, Billy and I laughed until we cried. Once we regained our senses and returned to priming, none of us ever complained about our aching backs again.

By the second week of harvest, our muscles had adapted, and we were now on the second pulling which was cleaner and easier to reach. Poor Maurice was a nice guy, but he struggled to keep up to our blistering pace. We now had times when we had to wait for boats because the table gang couldn't keep up. One day, we finished priming before 2:00 p.m. We helped Maurice as much as we could, but, by the third week, Maurice had had enough. He decided to move on and seek a different job on another farm. He was good enough to tell Steve and offer to work until Steve could find a replacement. When we discovered he was leaving, the remaining primers begged Steve not to replace him. The five of us would prime and split the sixth man's wages. Steve agreed, and with no need to help Maurice, we soon were doing as well with five primers as we had before with six. Everyone did their part, and the days flew by. We even started priming extra tobacco for the next day. This meant following the extra boats to the kiln yard and spreading out the tobacco so it wouldn't overheat and spoil. In the morning our table gang could start work as soon as they arrived rather than waiting for the first priming of the day. Soon, we were finishing before 3:00 p.m. with five primers, and having fun in the field.

GRAMPA CHIPPS COMES TO STAY

In the summer of 1964, we became a multigenerational household. My mom's mother had died in February 1963, and shortly after her death Mom's father, Grampa Frank Chipps, went to the hospital at age eighty-six for a long overdue operation for a perforated ulcer of the stomach. The anesthesia and the operation weakened him enough that he was forced to give up his home in Courtland and accept assistance. It was agreed that the three daughters would provide this care until a suitable nursing home became available.

Since my mother was still working as a teacher, it was decided that, after a stay at Aunt Mabel's, we would welcome Grampa for the summer of 1964, and then he would move in with my Aunt Ruth in Tillsonburg. Our home was a two-bedroom bungalow, with a single bathroom. To accommodate Grampa, Larry and I were assigned a mattress on the floor of Mom and Dad's bedroom for the summer, while Grampa took over our bedroom. It was certainly a challenge to navigate clothing and bodies with early morning preparations for work. Fortunately, Larry and I were so tired after our workdays that we fell into a deep sleep each night.

Aside from the crowded sleeping and bathroom conditions, what I remember most about Grampa's stay is his dogged determination and resilience. He had turned eighty-seven in April and had no intention of sitting patiently waiting for the "sweet chariot" to carry him home. His time in the hospital had allowed his arthritis to seize up his knees and back, and each day getting out of bed and walking was a challenge. Grampa never asked for help. Using a cane, Grampa made his way to the bathroom and kitchen on his own. On sunny afternoons, when I would arrive home from work, I would sometimes witness his afternoon workout. Grampa would make his way down the steps into the garage, by descending backwards. Then, using a wooden chair as a walker, he would do loops around the garage pushing the chair. Often, he hummed or sang a hymn. By the end of the summer, he and the chair were doing a circuit on the front yard, and by the time he left our home, he was slowly navigating with a single cane.

Grampa's courage and determination made it difficult to complain about my puny issues and left a lasting impression. Seeing him up close also gave me a better understanding of my mother. Grampa was caring, in his own way, but he was not a hugger or a person who showed emotion, not even when the love of his life, Minnie, had died the previous year after helping raise nine children and fifty-three years of marriage.

Grampa's Christian belief was faith and action in equal portions. He would welcome the Jehovah's Witnesses who came to our door, and they would discuss and debate with Grampa's well-worn King James Bible open on his lap. For a few days after such a visit, we could hear Grampa in his bedroom rehearsing for his next encounter. I would giggle to myself as he began his preparatory conversation with, "Look here, Mr. Man, the good Lord says…" As the summer came to an end, and my mother prepared to return to teaching her grade two class, Grampa packed his suitcase and moved to Aunt Ruth's. As Grampa said his thanks and farewell to my mother there was a tenderness that I had seldom seen in their interactions. I came to love and appreciate both my mother and my grandfather more that summer.

ENDING WITH A WHIMPER

My summer at Steve's had a disappointing end. On one of my last days before returning to school I arrived early to help take out a kiln, and the kiln yard was buzzing with activity. Steve was with Lonnie, Jerry, and Billy and something was seriously wrong. As I got closer, I realized Lonnie was drunk. He was weaving his way across the kiln yard toward his cureman's shack. With a great deal of protest Jerry took his grampa's prized bottle while Billy and Steve guided Lonnie toward his bed.

Steve was more upset than I had ever seen him. He had a strict rule against alcohol on the farm during harvest. Besides the anger, I think Steve was deeply disappointed. Lonnie's skill and sense of humour had helped Steve become a skilled cureman. Lonnie's debauchery spelled the end to the Carolina connection, and all of us had grown very fond of Jerry, Billie and their grampa. We learned that somehow Lonnie had gotten two twenty-sixers of Jack Daniel's. Lonnie was halfway through his second when Steve went to the kiln yard to discover Lonnie hadn't prepared the kiln for our morning take out. Worse than that, Lonnie's night of indulgence meant he hadn't managed the delicate curing process for over eight hours. Such negligence could seriously reduce the quality of a couple of the recently filled kilns.

Once Steve was convinced Lonnie was sleeping off his stupor, he hugged the shaken young grandsons and rallied us to take out the required kiln, and after a subdued breakfast, we headed to the fields to prime another kiln. I was only there for a few more days, and in typical Steve Van-Quaethem style, the workdays quickly returned to normal, but, as I said my goodbyes to Billy and Jerry, we all knew that it was unlikely they would be back the next summer.

I don't know how the summer ended with Steve and Lonnie, but I never saw Lonnie again. Twenty-five years later, I had a reunion with Billy and Jerry in Raleigh, North Carolina. Both were doing well. Their grampa had died several years before my visit. I stayed at Billie's home, and the three of us shared meals and stories, and I felt like we had finally brought a proper ending to our summers in the sun.

ANOTHER BEGINNING—ANOTHER ENDING

As I rode the bus to begin my new school experience at Annandale, it was a strange beginning. Here I was, starting at a new school where I would have to navigate hallways, washrooms, and classrooms, meet new classmates, learn from new teachers, while knowing that in ten months I would be moving on. These realities added to my tendency to feel like a witness to my own journey as a part of me watched this country boy navigate a new set of challenges and expectations.

As I settled into 13A, my homeroom teacher was our English teacher, Arn Stover. I could not have been luckier. Arn had a brilliant mind and an iron will. He had been an outstanding athlete and scholar, and after excelling in English studies and completing his master's degree, he chose to return to his hometown and live a simple life, coaching football, and raising his two boys with his wife, Becky, who also taught at Annandale High School. As I settled in, I discovered that with one notable exception in Chemistry class, all my teachers were at the peak of their careers and ready to engage and challenge their students every day.

I was glad I didn't return late from harvest because the courses were demanding from the very first day. My toughest subjects were three maths, English, and French. I had two or three hours of homework every night and often went to bed with one unsolved mathematics problem still intriguingly teasing my mind. We had been encouraged not to join school teams as we sprinted toward Provincial Exams and post-secondary education. For me it was good advice.

I was still active in our church and was now spending much of the weekends with Sharon and her family. Although Sharon and I enjoyed romance and dreaming of a home and family together, I now realize that from the start, our relationship had a tragic flaw. Sharon saw education as a means to an end. I saw learning and ongoing discovery as an end in and of itself. At the time love was blind.

AND NOW I BECOME A MAN

In Norm Williams, I saw a hard-working, self-made man who, in the words of Oscar and Hammerstein's song from the 1959 Broadway show *The Sound of Music*, inspired me to *"climb every mountain"* and *"ford every stream"* to find my dream. These lyrics were just the right mix of faith and works to inspire and challenge this Baptist farm boy. In Norm Williams, and his youngest daughter, Sharon, I saw the grounded practicality and determination that I needed to balance my tendency to idealism and missionary zeal.

Born in poverty and abandoned by an alcoholic father, Norm had left school at fourteen to provide for his family and had overcome the odds to become a successful farmer, respected in his community. Norm was seventeen when he married Gladys, who was a year younger. Together, they worked in tobacco and eventually share-grew small tobacco crops until Norm managed to purchase a small tobacco farm. Although he left school early, Norm was self-educated. He read the *London Free Press* and other newspapers from cover to cover. As I met Norm's mother, who lived in a small house on the edge of the farm, and Norm's siblings, Harold and Edna, they showed themselves to be bright, capable people with warm loving families. I had fallen in love with Sharon. Now I found myself falling in love with her family.

As I continued to define myself and discover my career path, Norm was another role model in my quest. In my home, my mother was the driving force. Dad worked hard and certainly had opinions, often much stronger than he shared, but when it came to the big decisions in life Dad often deferred to my mother. When I would come home after curfew, it was my mother who was waiting up to challenge and rebuke me. I knew that, as a man, I wanted to be a leader in my home. Norm Williams had his flaws, but perhaps by learning from him, as well as Dad, Steve VanQuaethem, and my biblical role models, I could become the man, and eventually the husband and father, I dreamed of being. As I finished high school, I knew I wanted to be a man of courage and character willing to climb and ford the metaphorical mountains and streams of life.

THE DODGERS

Early in my year at Annandale, I faced a crisis. As we settled into our new classes and routines an announcement was made on a Wednesday afternoon that all the male students should report to the football field for the first cadet drill of the year. I hadn't been involved in cadets for three years and had no intention of participating. My problem was to find a safe place to hide out while I dodged the draft.

On the first day of cadets, I was in one of the remote boys' washrooms biding my time when another boy came in. He looked like Alfred E. Neuman from *Mad Magazine*. He asked me what I was doing—not the most appropriate way to start a bathroom conversation. After some ambiguous meanderings we realized we were on the same mission—to avoid the cadet parade outdoors. Jerry, as I soon came to know my new associate, said that we should find a more dignified place to spend our time. As he began to elaborate on his theory of human behaviour, I was fascinated. Jerry explained that skulking around and hiding in a washroom made us look guilty and ashamed. The only thing to do, he explained, was to stand tall and walk out the front doors as if we had a very important appointment uptown. And so, we did.

After an enjoyable afternoon at the local billiards parlour, we returned in time to catch our buses. The next week, we followed the same routine. On the third or fourth week, we encountered two other guys returning from the local convenience store with chips and pop. Suspicious, we followed as they entered the gym from a back entrance and climbed a set of stairs into a small loft. Soon, we were invited to join in, as a few other dodgers spent cadet afternoons chatting while our classmates learned to march and salute. We never discussed politics or war and, looking back, I surmise that we each had a mix of reasons why we had first deserted. So, for a few weeks in the fall, and again in the spring, Jerry DePlancke and I either played pool or visited with our fellow dodgers. Fortunately, we were never forced to enlist.

In Jerry, I found a unique intellect with an irreverent attitude toward the establishment that facilitated my exploration of my own disaffection with the Settler ambitions and Puritan work ethic that my mother's family and my early school and church experiences had etched into my psyche. Over the next two years, Jerry and I would spend many hours over billiard tables and chess boards trying to outwit each other while verbally we explored our hopes and dreams. For Jerry, it wasn't about some vague set of mores. Without the psychic baggage of church and state, for Jerry all of life was a strategic game filled with decisions like whether to sacrifice a knight for a bishop or attempt to bank the green ball into the side pocket. Jerry seemed to be more daring and direct while I tended to focus more on what I didn't want, while struggling to clearly define what would make my heart sing. Even though at times, I found Jerry's pragmatic nonconformity terrifying, it was a good antidote for my idealistic romanticism.

FINDING MY PATH

I had spent more time dreaming about the kind of house that Sharon and I would live in than I had thinking about how I would earn a living. One day early in 1965 our English teacher, Arn Stover, initiated a conversation with our graduating class that woke me from my dreams. With Arn's skilled facilitation, the discussion soon became much larger than the sum of the parts. I listened to myself and others with a profound detachment as it soon seemed we separated into two camps—a group who saw life as getting, and a group who saw life as giving. Several of the young men in our class knew exactly where they were headed as they planned their university paths to high-paying careers as lawyers, accountants, bankers, and businessmen. Some of the young women were very open in declaring their desire to attend college or university, to marry well, and then raise bright successful children.

As my friend, Dixie Esseltine, declared her decision to study medicine, I heard myself for the first time stating that I would dedicate myself to elementary education. The discussion continued with deep philosophy that ranged from science's concepts of survival of the fittest to Shakespeare's assertion that all of us are mere actors on life's stage, to the late President Kennedy's famous, "Ask not what your country can do for you—ask what you can do for the freedom of man."

My declaration that I would teach school was not deeply rooted. Though I had stated that I would help young children thrive educationally, and I was very self-satisfied with my humanitarian stance, I really had no clear plan of action.

As the end of the school year came, I focused on my present courses and the upcoming Provincial Exams. I knew that university was not an admission requirement for Teachers' College, but I had planned and saved for university for five years, and without any clear academic goals, I just kept moving forward.

One Sunday, shortly after our big discussion of career and contribution, I came home from church feeling very proud of my noble aspirations and wrote my thoughts in a poem. As a self-confident nineteen-year-old, I not only rationalized that a wife and family and local contributions were the best I could do, but I arrogantly criticized those I judged as being blinded by greed.

I chose to call my declaration *Numismania*.

Numismania

You rush on, you prurient godly men
Striving, struggling, and all for what? –
Riches and fame and their mundane pleasures,
Hoping always that money will bring happiness.
Is that all that this mad life has become? –
A merry-go-round ride to oblivion?
Please stop the world I'd like to get off,
And God and I will watch with saddened eyes
As we wonder why He gave man free choice.
I'm tired of watching people as they seem,
Searching blindly for some happiness
And they could find it too. It's such a shame,
Those blinkers of money hide it from them.
What can I say to them? What can I do?
They'd never hear; they're too busy figuring,
"If I take a course or two this summer.
And a couple more next winter
That would raise me up one category.
Why I'd make nearly three hundred more a year!
Man, oh man, with that kind of salary.
A guy could just about be satisfied."
Just about is right. They'll never give up
Killing themselves for "just another buck."
They have no time for God. "And anyway
How could He give us this happiness?"
I'd tell them, "by assuring more than this
Vain struggle which ends only at the grave."

But already, again they interrupt.
"Love can't bring you joy either, by itself.
You've gotta have money first; that's the thing.
Once you've got it you don't need to worry."
I'd ask them why happiness can't just be
Doing what you want to do, the best you can
And having enough money to get by,
With a wife and couple of kids to love.
And church on Sunday and God throughout the week,
Knowing always that you're going "somewhere."
But they're not listening to me again.
They look instead for a penny that fell.
So, I'll go and let them live their lives, their way.

Twenty years later a wiser Doug read these words with deep humility and contrition.

MY DARK NIGHT

Shortly after my grandiose condemnation of greed, and my confident declaration of my desire for a simple life, I became discouraged and overwhelmed by the social and military issues that dominated the news. Racial unrest had been simmering throughout my high school years with sit-ins in 1960 and Freedom Riders in 1961. Africa was beginning to shake off the fetters of colonialism. President Kennedy had been assassinated in 1963. In February 1965, as Martin Luther King, Jr., was leading violence-filled marches in Alabama, black leader Malcolm X was assassinated by rival Black activists. The United States' war against communism in Vietnam was no longer a secret. Something big was happening, and I realized it was about to get bigger.

On May 16, a Viet Cong bomb destroyed a major U.S. base at Biên Hòa, South Vietnam, and on May 30 the Viet Cong offensive against the U.S. base Da Nang began. Meanwhile, both Russia and the United States kept testing huge nuclear bombs, though ratification of the Partial Nuclear Test Ban Treaty in October 1963 had imposed a moratorium on above-ground tests. How big would these conflicts get?

I worried that the growing unrest in the United States and beyond would disrupt my plans. Although I felt no immediate threat, the racial tensions and the war drums in the distance made me less certain that all was well on planet earth. Though my little part of the world still seemed well insulated from the immediate impact, I sensed that even rural Ontario was about to change.

One sleepless night, as I lay in bed thinking of the chaos in the world, I pieced together an anguished doggerel rant that began like this:

> *Run in circles. Run and hide.*
> *Confusion rules with hate and pride*
> *If you're lucky you may die*
> *But not so fortunate am I*
> *Here I am these seventy years.*
> *In this dread land of hate and tears*
> *Where children cry out in the night*
> *Blindly searching for some light…*

The next morning, I scribbled the lines down, but as I looked at the sentiments in the cold light of day I knew that *this* was not how I wanted to face the challenges ahead.

The truth was that I was too excited and too optimistic about life to stay with the cynic's viewpoint for long. The scrawled poem soon disappeared, and instead, I focused on building a life with Sharon and moving toward a career where I could help make the world a safer, saner place. At school, I quickly shifted my creative energies from the wider world to a little class newspaper, *Peek … A Little Look,* that I published, filled with cartoons and fun writing from classmates, that we sold for ten cents a copy.

As I finished fourteen years of hometown education and prepared to venture into the larger world, my idealistic commitment to living a simple life helped me take the next steps in a journey that had, up to now, been focused on pleasing Mommy, Daddy, teachers, and preachers, with little thought about the future.

The last weeks of high school went by quickly. I had been accepted at the University of Western Ontario in London based on my marks, and I had reserved a place in the University Men's Residence. With those decisions made, I didn't have to think about university until later in the summer.

Throughout June, the focus was on the upcoming Ontario Provincial Exams. Our teachers prepared us by spending many of our final classes going over questions from past years. Soon I was sitting at a desk in the school auditorium with our teacher-proctors and nearly a hundred other nervous students. I checked and rechecked my exam schedule, more nervous about showing up at the wrong time than I was about the exam itself. Soon they were over. I was confident I had done well on all but mathematics. Some of the algebra and trigonometry questions had eluded me, and I knew I was going to be disappointed with the results.

When the last exam was finished, I emptied my locker and wandered the borrowed halls that I had known for only one year. A few other students were also leaving. Others still had exams to complete. We all seemed dazed by a mix of nostalgia and anticipation. It was a strange, anti-climactic ending to a long journey. With a conflicting sense of loss and anticipation, I walked down the hall, and out the doors for the last time.

THE SUMMER OF '65

As I returned to the tobacco fields at the end of high school, I possessed skills and confidence that that been honed by five summers of labour and dynamic social interactions with a diverse cast of characters. I still wasn't clear about where I was going, but I certainly knew where I had been.

I had experienced the death of close friends and grandparents. I had nearly lost my father. I had learned to work long hard days with no one to rescue me when I faltered. I had been pushed to my limits physically and emotionally and found the courage and strength to not only survive but to delight in the challenges and triumphs involved in overcoming.

Although we had not formally committed to marriage, Sharon and I were planning our lives as a couple. We spent most weekend evenings at a dance hall or beach together or with friends. The Belgian Hall in Delhi and the Highland Hall at Long Point were always lively venues. Sharon and I bought a small hibachi grill and would spend hours on the beach and dunes of Long Point Provincial Park. By mid-summer, we had started to smoke cigarettes. We chose Peter Jackson King Size Menthols because we thought they were cool. They had a white filter and were long and, in our minds, gave us a Clint Eastwood/Faye Dunaway look. After a long, hot week of working in the tobacco fields, my idea of bliss was spending a lazy Sunday evening swimming in Lake Erie and barbecuing on the sandy hill with my sweetheart, while overlooking the rippling lake well into the night.

As the summer began, I worked for the Flue-Cured Tobacco Growers' Marketing Board for nearly four weeks measuring crops and supervising cut-downs before returning to work at Steve VanQuaethem's farm. When I started with Steve, five years earlier, he and Nellie were newlyweds. Now, they had two beautiful children, Brenda and Brian, and they were experienced and respected tobacco farmers. At the start, I was inexperienced with work and diverse personalities. Now, I could do any job on the farm and I had learned to work effectively with people of all ages and all walks of life. What an incredible education.

My friends from North Carolina, Jerry, and Billy, did not return, and instead, the other primers consisted of three Spaniards and two guys I knew from high school. All of us were experienced primers and we worked well together from the first day. Harvest proceeded quickly. There were several days where, because Steve had less acreage that year, we went to Tillsonburg to prime for Steve's dad, Joe VanQuaethem.

I was a little wary when I realized how often we would be working for Joe. My first impressions the day he chased a primer down Broadway made me apprehensive. As I got to know Joe, I realized what wonderful people he and Adrienne were. They worked hard and treated others fairly, and they expected the same of everyone they worked with.

Our crew worked well all summer and soon another harvest was coming to an end.

My five years working with Steve VanQuaethem and his family had taught me much more than how to work in the fields. As I said goodbye at the end of the summer and headed off to university, the fierce hug I got from Steve felt more like a graduation than my last day at high school.

UNIVERSITY

I went right from the tobacco fields to my new home away from home at the University of Western Ontario (UWO). I had paid for a year of residence with meals included. I was notified I would be at Sydenham Hall. When I arrived, I was shown to my room on the third floor, and introduced to Bill, my roommate for the year. Our rooms were simple.

There was a closet, a single bed, and a small desk on each side. There were two male residences side by side on University Drive, each housing about three hundred male students at all levels of study. The other residence was Medway House.

The hazing began almost immediately with older students inviting, demanding, and, in a few cases, dragging the frosh guys into the open square in the middle of our dorm. These older UWO comrades used a mix of fun and intimidation to get us to march around the square chanting, "Sexy Sam from Sydenham," playing to our egos as our neighbours were dubbed, "Mickey Mouse from Medway House." After a couple of 3:00 a.m. "fire drills," and a midnight walk to a women's residence where we were required to serenade the women from the street before stumbling back to bed, our initiation was complete and we settled into the serious work of getting a degree.

I was totally unprepared for the university experience. When I went up the hill to register for my six classes I was already overwhelmed. There were so many choices. My uninformed strategy was based on avoidance rather than passion. Other than continuing to climb the academic ladder, I had no clear goals. By avoiding Mathematics and French, I quickly moved out of the Arts and into a narrow set of Sciences. I ended up registering for Botany, Zoology, Physics, Geology, Chemistry, and English. The huge classes of three hundred or more were impersonal. The lectures were monotonous. My choices were a disaster and I struggled for the first time in my school history. To cope, I went home almost every weekend, and, by the end of September, I was often smoking a pack of cigarettes a day. When we did our tests, the results would be posted in rank order in a hallway for all the world to see. As I blanched at marks in the fifties, I soon learned that the most important measure was not my mark but my standing on the Bell Curve. Other students assured me that, as long as I was in the top seventy percent, there would be an adjustment made to move us from dismal to dim. I had been at the top of my classes in high school with eighties, now my marks were often in the sixties, and I had neither the skill nor motivation to do much better.

It wasn't all misery. Sharon and I were very much in love. My friend Jerry DePlancke ended up on the second floor of my wing of the residence and he and I spent many hours together. I soon made friends with several of my Sydenham colleagues who were just as confused and homesick as

I was. We made the best of our situation. Mealtimes in the cafeteria and TV times in the Common Room were filled with lively conversation and laughter. We had to dress in a jacket and tie, with dress shoes, or we would not be allowed into the dining hall for the evening meal.

During the first month, this led to some hilarious confrontations as guys tested the limits and tried to get away with Converse runners and string ties. One of my third-floor neighbours was a huge Dutchman who arrived at Western with only sandals. When he was blocked from entering the dining hall I happened to be nearby as he plead his case. After reminding our proctors that sandals had been good enough for Jesus Christ, Carl was given three days to get real shoes.

The meals were awful. They were repetitive with breaded veal being presented so often that there were uprisings and protests with mushed food and flaming napkins returned to the kitchen. Even the chicken legs and pork chops were more breaded covering than meat. The mashed potatoes seemed artificial, and a rumour soon spread that they were seasoned with saltpeter to reduce our sex drive. My favourite meal soon became pasta of any sort. That was one meal they couldn't seem to ruin.

In the Common Room, the popular TV shows were light entertainment like *Hogan's Heroes* and *The Beverly Hillbillies*. When Adam West's version of *Batman* debuted in January, the room was always full as the exaggerated acting along with its "*Biffs*" and "*Pows*" seemed perfect for derisive laughter, groans, and guffaws from our ragged group. Being in residence was like being a passenger on a large ship at sea. For many of us, we had lost sight of shore and were not sure the ship had a destination.

As I wandered the halls and music rooms there were interesting people at all hours of the day or night. One night each week, a third-year philosophy student, who always had a huge pile of unwashed laundry on the floor of his room, would host a gathering where a dozen or more of us would fill his room with smoke and debates about the meaning of life. Another night, a pop/rock pianist would entertain us for an hour or two with the tunes he played in bars to pay his tuition. Almost any time night or day there was at least one open door and an invitation to visit. Often, my room was a centre for discussions on war and religion. My roommate would quickly escape and find a place to study as the philosophizing went late into the night.

By Christmas, my roommate and Jerry's roommate agreed to a switch, and Jerry moved to the third floor. This change did not improve my academic success, but it allowed me to survive the rest of the year. Jerry managed to get passing grades despite missing classes and often finishing essays an hour before they were due. His bright nonconformist mind was a source of constant delight for me and the debating society that often ended up in our room. During the winter a postgraduate student from India, who moved in next door to us, taught us how to drink tea and play Bridge. As March brought warmer weather, Jerry and I went for long walks along the Thames River on campus. Jerry had found his passion in Mathematics and the new field of Computer Science. He loved the university environment, and he and his girlfriend, Joan, were happy in London. Since university had not lit a fire in me, I focused instead on my girlfriend Sharon and the life we were dreaming of together.

By the end of March, everyone was feeling the pressure of final essays and projects, and the impending exams. My friend across the hall slipped into a deep depression, often sleeping sixteen or twenty hours a day. Another acquaintance jumped from a third-floor window hoping to end it all. As the jumper limped into the cafeteria a few days later, his nicotine-stained fingers and hollow eyes hardened my resolve that I did not want to return in September.

I was determined to complete my year as well as I could, so I finished all my assignments and studied hard for exams. In late March, Sharon and I discussed getting married, and me going to Teachers' College. Soon we had a plan that I would save enough for an apartment and Teachers' College and, with Sharon working, we could get married in the fall of 1966.

I survived the exams with my last, the Physics exam, being two hours of total panic. Since there was no math involved every question was theoretical. As I began the exam, I knew what it felt like to be that tall boy in grade two so many years ago who never learned to read. Like a shipwrecked sailor, I managed to stay afloat and get enough answers to have a chance of passing. I walked out of the exam room into a fresh spring day. I had survived the worst year of my life. It could only get better going forward.

SUMMER OF '66

As my parents drove me home from university, Sharon and I sat in the back seat. I told Mom and Dad that instead of university I was going to attend Teachers' College in the fall. That was a disappointment for Mom, but Dad seemed okay. A few minutes later, I shared our wedding plans. At the time, I was twenty and Sharon was nineteen. My parents listened in sad silence and suggested we talk more later. It was a long quiet hour as we made our way back to Tillsonburg.

My heart and mind were in chaos as I sat at our supper table that night. It felt so good to be home with Mom and Dad and my brother. The aroma of the food filled me with joy and warm memories. Yet, my plan to marry chilled the room. As we ate, trying to ignore the elephant in the room, I tried to reassure my family that I had thought it out carefully, and that everything would be all right. Partway through the meal, my mother declared that, if I went ahead with this ill-advised plan, she would not be at the wedding. My father sat in uncomfortable silence, and, for the moment, my brother chose to side with Mom.

For the next three months, it was as if none of this had happened. My plans for September were never mentioned. Our family meals were filled with good food and conversation, and brother Larry and I enjoyed being back together. My marks arrived in early May. I was relieved to find I had passed all my courses with Bs, Cs, and Ds in Chemistry and Physics. The results just emphasized my poor choice of courses. I looked forward to resuming university studies once I had become a teacher, but I knew my focus would take a dramatic shift.

I got a summer job at Livingston Industries in Tillsonburg along with my friend Jerry DePlancke. Livingston's packed car parts from Ford and General Motors to be sent to South American assembly plants. My orientation session lasted about fifteen minutes. I was taken to a small office beside a packing line where huge wooden packing boxes were being filled by husky men, then rolled out into the yard to be loaded onto waiting rail cars. My job was as a stock checker.

Each box had a list of the parts that were to be packed. My job was to check off the parts as they were packed and sign my name to say that everything was included. As soon as I gave the thumbs up the wooden lid was nailed on, and the box was shipped. I was responsible for two packing lines. One packed smaller parts, and the other dealt with heavy pieces like hubs and axles. Between them, the lines completed over fifty shipping containers a day, and I quickly learned that no matter how hard I worked I couldn't keep up with all the paperwork during a normal day. As I put in ten-hour days and worked weekends, I learned that the people Jerry and I had replaced were family men who had said, "Enough is enough," and had been immediately fired. The truth was, we were pawns in a labour dispute, but the work was steady, and the pay was good, so I did my best and put my money in the bank.

I worked every day until mid-July when the whole factory slowed down. One Monday, there was an eerie silence, and no boxes were packed. I was told that the model year had changed and until the 1967 parts started to ship many workers would be on lay-off or holidays. I was assigned sweeping and clean-up duties and, when that was completed, I was told to stay out of sight of the supervisors. I endured a week of skulking around in the quiet warehouse and decided the tobacco fields were calling. I quit Livingston's and joined Norm Williams' harvest crew.

Since Norm only had Marketing Board rights to grow eighteen acres, he used a half gang. The gang was made up of his daughter, Marguerite, tying, and two leaf handers, a kiln hanger, and two Georgia Boys and me in the field. My Georgia priming mates were experienced primers and good workers, but they were definitely good ol' boys, more interested in pay and play than in the work. Throughout harvest, they wore fleece-lined aviator hats that they had bought "cheap" at a surplus store with the chin straps hanging beneath their constant smiles. Early on I made the mistake of encouraging them to prime a few armfuls for the next day. They looked at me as if I was insane. They replied almost in unison, "Hell, boy, we might be dead by tomorrow. We need to git to town and have some fun." We worked well together, and harvest sped by.

By mid-July, I had enough money to ensure the rent for the next year in a furnished basement apartment in Tillsonburg, costing eighty-five dollars a month. In August 1966, my fiancé, Sharon, moved in. Although I spent much of my time at our new love nest, I still slept in my shared bedroom with my brother until the day of my wedding. By August, Larry had accepted the upcoming wedding and agreed to be my groomsman. Most of the time Mom and I avoided the wedding topic and our family meals were as enjoyable as in earlier years. A couple of times, when only Mom and I were in the house she reminded me that I was making a big mistake. As Sharon and I completed our wedding plans Mom was not involved.

By late August, Sharon's Ford Falcon was burning oil and sputtering at intersections. One Saturday we drove to London, adding oil halfway, and explored new car possibilities. We agreed on a white 1966 Chevrolet Chevelle SS. It had an automatic floor shifter and blue bucket seats. It cost $2800, and, with our Ford Falcon trade-in, we were able to get credit and monthly payments we were sure we could manage. Now we really were a couple—we were in debt together.

As soon as I began classes at London Teachers' College, I knew I was on the right path. I enjoyed the courses, especially Child Psychology, and my confidence soared. My newfound contentment must have shown at home as the icy chill with Mother melted, and by the end of September Mom was helping us list and invite her side of the family to our October 22 marriage.

Sharon and I enjoyed planning our fall wedding at First Baptist Church in Tillsonburg and our reception at Mil-Mar Manor on the edge of town. We had four sets of bridesmaids and groomsmen. We had a miniature bride and groom and a ringbearer. We found a wonderful seamstress for the women's dresses, and soon the big day arrived. We were married at First Baptist Church with Reverend Chubb presiding. After a meal, speeches, and dancing at the elegant Mil-Mar Manor, we headed to Buffalo for a weekend honeymoon.

On Sunday, as we drove home from Niagara Falls, we sang Patsy Cline's song, *Side by Side*. As the song said, we didn't have much money, and we certainly didn't know "what's a-comin' tomorrow," but we intended to meet whatever did come our way "side by side."

I had no idea of the challenges and opportunities that awaited me. *With a little bit of luck*, I had been hatched and fledged, and now I had left the nest ready to test my wings.

~ A Selection of Photographs ~

Top left: Howard and Lillian Lester on their wedding day, April 7, 1945. Top right: Lillian and Doug, 1946. Below: Baby Doug on the Lowrie farm, Spring 1946.

Top left: Howard and Doug, 1946. Top right: Dad and Mom with baby Doug at the Chipps farm in 1946. Lower left: Gramma Chipps with me before she was crippled with arthritis, 1946. Lower right: Doug at the Rutherford farm, 1947.

Top left: Mom on vacation while Larry and I were at Aunt Mabel's, 1949. Top right: Cousin Val and I at the Buchner farm, 1949. Below: Dad and I fishing on the Otter River, 1950.

Top: Dad, Larry, and I with our pre-owned 1948 Dodge sedan in 1950. Centre left: Mom, Larry, and I on the beach in Port Burwell, 1951. Lower left: Larry and I with a proud catch in Midland, 1953. Lower right: Dad with Larry and I on a fishing expedition at Little Lake in Midland, Ontario, 1953.

Top left: Doug as horse and Larry as driver while one of the Jordan girls rides in the back, 1953. Centre left: My last tricycle, 1953. Lower left: Larry and I, Christmas 1954. Top right: Doug and Rex, 1954. Lower right: Larry and I with two-wheelers, 1955.

Top: Grade three class photo, Tillson Avenue Public School, 1955. My friend Hugh Hawkins is in the front row, sixth from the left. I am in the second row, seventh from the right. Photograph by the John Seldon photography studio, Tillsonburg. Centre left: Larry and I at the Hawkins farm with Lassie, 1955. Lower left: Lassie with me, Larry, Heather, and Jennifer Jordan at the Hawkins farm, 1956. Lower right: The "building crew" as Mom and Dad started to build their house in 1956.

Above: Setting in at our new home. Gerald Beaman (standing, left), Bob Beaman and Larry (sitting), and I are in front of our backyard rabbit pen. The two-bedroom bungalow was situated on the front corner of the Grimmet farm. We spent many hours each week with our neighbours, the Beaman family.

Below: Grade seven at Tillson Avenue Public School in 1959. I am in the second row, second from the right. Ross Andrews was our teacher (standing, far right).

OPPOSITE PAGE. Top left: Looking to the future (Grade 9 at Glendale High School, 1960). Top right: Vacation at Beatties' cottage, 1960. Centre right: Larry, Mom, Dad, and I at Beatties' cottage in Summer 1960. Lower centre: Maple Lane Senior Public School staff in 1968; I'm in the back row on the far right. The school opened in 1965 and, after several reorganizations under county and regional school boards, finally closed its doors in 2015. Principal Irv Horton is seated in the centre of the front row.
THIS PAGE. Top centre: My first homeroom class at Maple Lane Senior Public School in 1968. Lower centre: Daughter Stephanie and baby brother Jason with me in Otterville, 1973.

Top left: My second Ottawa marathon, 1987. Top right: Cheryl on our wedding day, May 20, 1988. Below: Our blended family in 1988: Heather and James next to Cheryl, and Jason and Stephanie next to me.

Above: Dad shooting trap from the sixteen-yard-line in Vandalia, Ohio, in 1990.
Below: Cheryl and I in England in 2020.

Above: I celebrate the completion of my second lap of the equator—49,804 miles (80,150 kilometres)—on February 24, 2024.

~ Part Two ~

MARRIED LIFE

Our first year of marriage was a joyful time as we lived in our little furnished basement apartment with just enough money to survive. For our first Christmas, we each had a budget of ten dollars. Decorating our home and getting by with bare necessities was a wonderful adventure.

MORE THAN A BIT OF LUCK

During my first year of marriage two near-death experiences reminded me once again that a bit of luck is required in order to survive.

When Sharon moved in, I eagerly went into cleaning mode. As I scrubbed the little stove, I was washing deep in the oven when, with a purple flash, I suddenly found myself flung to the wall. I had failed to unplug the stove and a fuse kept me from being fried.

My second brush with death came on a beautiful spring morning in 1967. During my year of Teacher's College, I commuted to London with three other students. Rose was driving her big Oldsmobile and Tom and I were chatting in the back seat. As Rose sped along our familiar Highway 401 route at sixty miles an hour, she crested a knoll and suddenly realized something was very wrong. Three cars in front of us careened into the ditches and, as Rose tried to slow on the black ice, we headed toward the median ditch. I was on full alert as the car entered the median and started to head toward the east bound lane. I did not see my life flash before my eyes—instead I saw two large transport trucks side by side. If the car went another fifteen feet, we would be directly in their path. I crouched with my arms over my head and waited for the crash. At the last possible moment Rose's Olds' long tail had caught the bottom of the median and swung us to safety. When I lifted my head, we were sitting in the median facing toward home. After a tow truck pulled us out and pointed us in the right direction, Rose somehow calmly drove us to London.

BUILDING A LIFE

As Sharon and I started building a life together I realized that like most people I was ad-libbing my way through life. Each step along the path had involved more than a little bit of luck.

My year of Teachers' College went well, and in April of 1967, I was hired to teach at Maple Lane Senior Public School in Tillsonburg, starting in September. Now with a clear goal in mind, I returned to university studies that summer, taking French and Psychology. I knew immediately I had found my home in the Arts. Suddenly, university was easy, and studying was fun. I was excited to be learning and helping others learn too.

Maple Lane Senior Public School was sparkling new when I arrived. The concept of having all Tillsonburg's grade seven and eight students in one school was a solution to overcrowding in the three previously K-8 schools, and it was also a bold experiment in providing French, Physical Education, Home Economics, and Industrial Arts at a level that only city schools had previously provided. Principal Irv Horton, who had been the star quarterback of Tillsonburg District High School in the fifties, had assembled an all-star teaching team. As the newest and youngest addition, I realized I was privileged to be part of the staff.

I proved to be a natural teacher and I loved the challenges and learning opportunities at Maple Lane. My colleagues were an exceptional collection of unique people and skilled educators and to my surprise in the new industrial arts room was my grade seven teacher, Ross Andrews.

I taught Math and English to thirty-nine grade eight students in the mornings, and in the afternoons five classes of grade seven Science and all the grade seven Boys' Physical Education classes. Irv Horton was a great principal and coach. My colleagues worked hard. I learned new approaches to teaching and character development every day. My self-awareness soon increased. When I yelled at a student in the hall or chased a defiant tough across the playground, I realized I was on display, and I quickly decided that humour and finesse were just as necessary in a school as in a tobacco field.

As the lease for our Tillsonburg apartment came up for renewal, father-in-law Norm Williams offered to rent us the hired man's house on the corner of his farm for forty dollars a month. We moved into our country home with a card table for our kitchen and a potpourri of other furnishings. I loved our new home surrounded by fields and trees. It was a short walk to the woods and the Otter River just beyond. I took up photography and spent hours hunting, exploring, and photographing nature in the miles of riverside just out my back door.

With a home and a job, graduating from university became my next goal. I commuted to London for two courses every summer and two each winter. There were some white-knuckle drives in fog or blizzards during the forty-mile commutes, but I was young, and life was an adventure. One fall night as I was ready to head home from class, a dirty hound followed me to my car. She had no I.D. or collar and seemed hungry and lost. I looked at her long floppy ears and her bowed legs and smiled as she looked at me with big dark eyes. I invited her into my car and without hesitation I had an adopted dog. I graduated in 1970 with a B.A. in Psychology and English and a Bassett-like hound named Lolly.

LIFE MOVES ON

Our rural house was hot in the summer and cold in the winter. After three years on the edge of the farm we moved back to Tillsonburg. Our beautiful apartment was the upper floor of a grand old red brick house on a hill. We had two bedrooms, a balcony overlooking the town, and a huge yard. Our hound Lolly had a batch of six pups that we kept in the attic until they were weaned and found homes. With the help of a student who worked at the local golf course I became a member of Tillsonburg Golf Club and spent many evenings practicing or playing a leisurely round. I taught Sunday School and became an active member of Tillsonburg Little Theatre. I built flats and sets and acted in plays. When our daughter, Stephanie, was born in the spring of 1971 we suddenly became much more aware of the nearby truck traffic, the steep stairs, and the apartment neighbours below us. We knew we needed to move again.

Our house search led us to an old brick house in Otterville, a nearby village. We decided that we could afford the purchase if we stretched ourselves to the limit. The house had good bones, but it was very old. Making it a home would be an adventure in survival. The wallpaper was faded and peeling. There was no real kitchen, just a large pantry with a sink. Finances were painfully tight as we immediately had to update wiring and plumbing. In the fall of 1971, after some basic repairs and painting we moved into our "fixer-upper."

Even though our budget was tight we were constantly improving our furnishings and surroundings. During our second year of marriage, we had discovered Bill Hilliker Furniture and started to upgrade our furnishings one piece at a time. I refinished a dining table and chairs and we checked regularly at Bill's for a bargain.

Each morning, I headed to my teaching position in Tillsonburg while Sharon managed a baby and a tight budget in a house with no kitchen. For nearly two years, the main feature in the kitchen area was a large table saw. For us this wasn't a hardship since we now had a dining room and a dining room table. Sharon sewed frilly curtains and we dined like royalty on macaroni and beans.

By the time Stephanie could walk we had an old upright piano that Bill Hilliker had sold us and moved to our home. Stephanie wasn't two when she demonstrated her climbing skills. Sharon heard the piano protesting and rushed into the living room where she found Steph standing proudly on the top of the piano.

In the spring of 1972 our old wood furnace, which years ago had been converted to natural gas, failed its annual inspection and was condemned. Sharon stood in the basement with Stephanie in her arms as the gas man sealed off our furnace. She wondered how we would cope.

That summer, in order to pay for a furnace and learn the building trade, I took a job as a carpenter with Tillsonburg builder Richard Epple. During July and August, I progressed from shoveling dirt and wheeling cement to laying out studs and acting as sawyer for all the rafters in one of the final houses we framed that summer. Richard was not only a master carpenter, but he was also one of the most well-organized and effective leaders I had ever encountered. The carpentry skills and work ethic I gained that summer have allowed me to build and renovate with confidence ever since.

Despite the challenges, having our own home was a never-ending delight. In the evenings and weekends, I took on the renovation and yard maintenance challenges. I tore out the old furnace and we purchased a new one through Union Gas with monthly fees we could afford. Outside, I built fences and a covered deck. I found a sawmill where I could buy inexpensive boards and fenced part of the yard. During the winter I built and installed kitchen cupboards with a sink and counters.

Aside from managing our curious toddler along with sawdust, Sharon learned to paint, sew, and decorate. She loved creating a beautiful home and did it well. One evening as I was working on the stairs leading up to the bedrooms, I heard a thump-thump and looked up in time to see our little girl bouncing down the stairs. I rushed to pick her up off the living room floor fearing the worst. She smiled and goo-gooed and headed off on another adventure.

In June 1973, our son Jason was born. He arrived a bit early and had to spend two weeks in London hospital. Since he was born at the end of the school year, Sharon and I had the summer to get used to two little ones. By the time I returned to school, Stephanie and Jason were well known in our small village.

By 1974 we had renovated every room in the house and cleared and established a large garden.

In the spring of 1974 my brother, Larry, who had married in 1972, began developing plans and poured the foundation for a house on a large country lot he had bought on the south side of the sixth concession just north of Springford. Larry, who was now also a teacher, was living in Woodstock with wife Nancy, and they were looking forward to welcoming their first child in November. When he asked me to help him build their little house in the country I was eager to use my carpentry skills. The foundation was already in when we started construction on July 1. For the next two months "Lester Bothers Construction" framed, closed in, and roofed his house. We worked hard every day with my "Epple learning" and a big book on house building being in constant use.

It was joyful and empowering to be spending every day with the brother with whom I had built forts in the woods, now building a real house, and building it well. A little luck was involved the morning Larry skied off the wet porch onto the ground below. Our dad helped us when he could. By September, we had everything except siding and trim completed and I left Larry on his own as I took on another challenge.

CREATING COMMUNITY

That September, I became a school principal. After seven years at Maple Lane Senior Public school, I had been chosen to be the teacher/principal at Elliott Fairbairn, the smallest of the three Tillsonburg schools. It was on the east side of town in an area that had in the past been the least prosperous. In the days before Maple Lane, the school's eight grades numbered a crowded two hundred and four students. Now the kindergarten to grade six school had less than one hundred and forty students.

Just before I arrived, two developments changed the student mix in a way that made my eight years there much more challenging and rewarding. Two new subdivisions brought business owners and professionals into the school area. Then, the summer before I arrived, a new social housing initiative brought a street full of single parents on social assistance who lined up to register their children on my first days of my principalship. The mix of students and parents was eclectic, and both sides of the wealth divide benefitted from the mingling.

I loved the community and the challenges. The school had a large playground and a wooded area at the back of the property. As principal of one of the smallest schools in Oxford County, I taught grade five/six most of the time, with a part-time teacher giving me three half-days a week to attend meetings and perform my administrative responsibilities. The teachers were caring and effective, and classroom and school routines were well established. However, there was no sports equipment, and like my experience as a boy at Tillson Avenue, Physical Education had not been part of the curriculum. I wanted to change that.

In August I bought a small collection of sports supplies—a starting pistol, stopwatches, four marker cones, a soccer ball, and a few gym mats. I marked out a two hundred metre track on the schoolyard. In September I invited parents to help clean up the woods and asked the community to help add playground equipment. Parents and local businesses responded enthusiastically. We soon had a fort and slide on the edge of the woods and a swing set in the front yard with an adventure playground of posts and chinning bars. That fall I was able to add a mini-trampoline and real gym mats to our physical education equipment and through the winter we did gymnastics in the school hallway. The first two years went quickly.

In the fall of 1976, as I worried about a lack of budget for equipment, I was privileged to attend a gymnastics workshop where Romanian gymnastic coaches told us that Nadia Comăneci, who had just wowed the world at the Montreal Olympics at age fourteen, had trained in a barn with tarps filled with hay. Inspired, I designed a large canvas container that was sewn by a local business and then filled it with foam seat material donated by a nearby manufacturer. This landing pad became our mat for gymnastics and high jump. Then I used cement blocks, two-by-fours drilled every inch with nails, and bamboo poles, as our high jump standards. Soon, Elliott Fairbairn students were setting records in running and high jump at the Tillsonburg Track and Field Championships.

A HOME OF OUR OWN

By the time I started at Elliott Fairbairn, Sharon's parents had sold their tobacco farm and moved to a large lot where they built a new house, and, in the vacant lot next door, Norm's little greenhouse hobby—starting flowers and vegetables—had quickly grown into a thriving business. We asked Norm if he might one day sell us the lot next to his house and he agreed. We began making payments on the future site of our dream home. With my increased salary as a principal, we realized that we would soon be able to build our forever home. Sharon and I began looking at house plans and dreaming of building a house on this hill overlooking the Otter River.

Since Norm wasn't quite ready to give up his greenhouse business and we weren't ready to pay for construction, there would need to be a transition before we built. We decided to sell our Otterville house and move back to Tillsonburg while we waited to build. Our old house had been completely renewed inside and out. Our hard work had paid off. Our Otterville house sold quickly for a good price. We could now afford a new home in Tillsonburg. The sale, and subsequent need to purchase, happened fast. Sharon did the house shopping and we ended up in a brand-new home on Stoney Court in the new Lisgar Heights subdivision. Life was good. We bought a new white Chevy Malibu. We wallpapered and painted and settled into our new home.

I completed Principal's Courses and started work on a Master of Education degree. I was thriving as a school leader and principal. I took our students skiing at Ski-Hi, and winter camping at the Outdoor Education Centre. I took them golfing at the Tillsonburg Golf Course and to Toronto to see international gymnastics meets at Maple Leaf Gardens. I had just turned thirty, and Sharon and I were about to celebrate our tenth anniversary.

Then I made a fateful choice.

THINGS FALL APART

I had recently helped start Tillsonburg's first day care centre at First Baptist Church to help address childcare needs, and now, with growing awareness of the drug and alcohol issues of young teens, I became concerned about the young people in our community. Our local high schools had so many problems with unruly youth that they discontinued high school dances. Young people I had taught were using drugs, dropping out of school, and drifting to Hamilton and then Vancouver. My school students and church youth told me disturbing stories about older family members. Seeing myself as some sort of "Catcher in the Rye," I organized a teen dance at the local Legion. It went well, and then a local restauranteur contacted me and suggested we open a disco. George Szilagyi, who owned the Mocha Restaurant, and I formed a partnership. With Sharon's permission, I invested our nest egg savings of $10,000 and George and I turned an empty building on Brock Street that had once housed a charismatic church into the "Disco Palace." Infected with *Saturday Night Fever*, I thought I would help guide and protect local youth and become a successful businessman at the same time. That is not how it worked out.

I went to Toronto and purchased a mirror ball, projector, and worked with a sound specialist, Bill Irving, to create a control room for our DJs, with large speakers and huge woofers mounted on the dance floor wall. The sound was amazing. For three years, 1975–1978, at the height of the disco craze, I spent Thursday to Sunday evenings managing as many as four hundred youths from ages fifteen to thirty, as they filled the space with smoke and gyrated to the sounds of Captain and Tennille, the Bee Gees and other groups, often ending the evening swaying slowly to Led Zeppelin's *Stairway to Heaven*.

Dan Curren became our manager and lived in an apartment above the Disco. He, and one or two other big guys, helped maintain order. Downstairs, we created pinball heaven with a tuck shop that sold cigarettes, pop, and snack food. The machines brought in huge bags of coin as they happily dinged all night long. The place rocked and all seemed great—for a very short time.

Almost immediately after the Disco Palace opened, George Szilagyi offered my wife Sharon a job at his restaurant nearby. Sharon worked one hundred hours the first week. Her book-keeping role soon transformed into a management position, and she loved it. For most of the next three years Sharon was at the Mocha from dawn until the bar closed seven days a week. George seldom came to the Disco, and when he did it was on a Saturday night to show "his" disco off to one of his friends.

Somehow, amid the chaos, I was a fairly good principal and teacher at Elliott Fairbairn Public School. I helped get our children to and from daycare. During the Disco years, I completed a Master of Education Degree, organized town-wide school sporting events, and managed to be active at First Baptist Church.

At the Disco Palace, I managed the staff, bought supplies, cleaned, paid bills, and did the accounting. I liked the young people that came to the Disco. Although we had some sort of incident almost every night, these moments were handled quickly. I set an example of non-anxious consistency that created a safe and enjoyable environment. Young people who showed up drunk or high were asked to leave and, when they spewed their "@#%&!" vocabulary at me and my "henchmen," instead of openly escalating the situation, I learned to respond with something flippant like, "and a happy birthday to you too." Most came back another night and respected our rules.

On New Year's Eve 1976, Sharon joined me at the Disco, and we had a magical evening. The dance floor was filled with happy youth. Our cash box was filled, and our DJ made the countdown to 1977 dramatic and joyful. I thought that the good times could only get better. As the crowd started to leave, one young man helped us clean up and seemed to linger. A bit of probing led us to realize he had nowhere to go. We invited "Fletch" to spend the night at our home, and he accepted. Over the next few days, Sharon and I quickly came to appreciate Chris Fletcher's wit and intelligence, and Jason and Steph welcomed him into our home. Soon, with a bed, and a few other pieces of furniture from Hilliker's placed in our basement, the "Fletch" was serenading us to Alice Cooper as he settled in for the night.

Word of the Disco's success spread in the community. The bar owners and community leaders came to see what grooving could look like in 1977. I was about to discover what G. K. Chesterton meant when, in 1905, he wrote, "There is nothing that fails like success."

I was moving too fast in too many directions, and Sharon's constant involvement with my invisible partner and the Mocha restaurant became a major irritant. By the end of April, Sharon and I were no longer able to host Chris, and I asked him to leave. Although the Disco Palace still did well, in the summer of 1977, trouble was brewing.

As we showed the way, local bars updated their lighting and their music. In the summer of 1978, the Town of Tillsonburg sponsored a live dance at the Community Arena every Saturday night. Soon our numbers started to dwindle. As the Disco struggled, I seldom saw Sharon. I was tired and discouraged.

In September the Tillsonburg high schools reinstated their school dances. Attendance at the disco plummeted and, by early fall, it became clear that the business was doomed. We gave notice to our landlord and prepared to close the doors. The last weeks were painful as a few of our young friends would come waiting for the crowd that never came. I knew it was over. I was financially and emotionally exhausted.

Shortly after the Disco Palace closed, Sharon left the Mocha. I had lost our savings, and our marriage was in tatters.

During the next seven or eight years we did a lot of things well, but serious damage had been done—there was an unspoken emptiness somewhere deep in my marriage.

STUMBLING TO THE FINISH LINE

After the Disco disaster, Sharon and I reconnected, and we recommitted as friends and parents. We started attending a Pentecostal church and found joy in a renewed faith. We both tried hard. I bought a black Dodge Maxi van and created our version of a Winnebago. I bought the parts and transformed the empty cargo van, adding captain's chairs, a CB radio, roof vents, a microwave, cupboards, beds, and Porta Potti. We spent the next two March Breaks in Florida. We went to Nashville, and Disney, and swam in the ocean. We laughed and enjoyed being a family.

As we recovered from our Mocha/Disco era we sold our Tillsonburg house and rented a farmhouse near the New Road lot where we would build the next year. I think I hoped at some deep level that we were reinventing ourselves and that this new house would bring life back into our wounded marriage. I imagine Sharon hoped for a similar miracle. Sharon and I had dreamed up the plan and I drew it to scale. I developed a bill of materials and received a package deal with Allen's Lumber in Woodstock.

In the spring of 1979, we marked out our house on the lot, got a building permit, and on July 1, I started to build. I contracted things like the excavation, foundation, wiring, plumbing, bricking, and plastering. With my brother Larry's help, and Norm and Dad's when they could, I did all the rest myself. All summer I worked six days a week from 7:00 a.m. to 5:00 p.m. By the time school started and Larry had to go back to his teaching job, the windows were in, and the roof was shingled. Working nights and weekends, I finished the insulation and plaster board. Once the house was plastered, we were able to have cupboards and flooring installed. Then I trimmed and hung the interior doors. As I finished the exterior siding at 11:00 p.m. on a November evening, I was content. We were re-inventing ourselves. All would be well. By mid-December our new home was heated and ready. We celebrated Christmas 1979 basking in the warmth of a roaring fire, in our new home beside our new wood stove.

We started 1980 in a new house with new hopes and dreams. The next three years went well as I finished up the house and Sharon decorated. We enjoyed our backyard pool. I started running regularly.

BUTCH AND SUNDANCE

Shortly after we began our new life on New Road, I met a man who would have a profound influence on my running and my resiliency during the eventful next decade. I met Albert in a restaurant in Toronto as I decompressed after a day at an educational conference. As I waxed eloquent to Sharon about politics corrupting education and life being too end-loaded, the guy at the next table leaned in and joined the conversation.

Toronto city bus driver Albert Kerek became a precious friend. He and his wife Nellie had a son, David, who was an age mate for Jason. We were soon spending weekends in each other's homes. Albert and Nellie and their Italian neighbours were the most generous people I had ever met. As we got to know their neighbours, they too became friends. Our family was invited to attend an Italian twenty-fifth wedding anniversary that had more food, laughter, and dancing than any of our family had ever experienced.

By the time Albert first visited me at New Road, I was running two or three miles most days, but I had gym shoes and improvised running gear. On our first run, Albert asked me how fast we had run our two miles. I looked at my dress watch and guessed about twenty minutes. His response was, "Have you ever heard of Cassio?" Within a month, I was timing every run with my new Cassio watch. Albert was extremely fit, mostly due to his winter hockey and summer cycling. It was common for Albert to do a century ride several weekends between April and November. Albert followed the Tour de France and all the major marathons. With his influence my running became more disciplined, and my speed and efficiency improved. By 1981, I was running almost every day and contemplating making it a daily discipline.

Running with Albert was unique. There was no sense of competition or envy. We nicknamed ourselves Butch and Sundance and spent hours philosophizing. "On November 28, 1981, somewhere between 1:00 and 2:00 a.m.," I noted in my journal, we discussed the possibility of running a marathon in 1982. By the end of the hour, we were both talking seriously about the New York City Marathon. We decided the make 1982 the "year of the run."

As the new year began, I committed to run every day, with two guidelines. First, I would run each day no matter what, and second, the minimum distance would be one hundred miles every month. I logged every run with time and conditions in *The Complete Runner's Day-by-Day Log and Calendar* by James Fixx. Although we had our own running routines, Albert and I kept each other updated on our progress. He introduced me to *Runner's World* magazine, and I added *Canadian Running*. We both read every issue from cover to cover and shared our insights. For me, it was like the owner's manual for a machine in need of regular tune-ups. I kept every copy in a banker's box for years. Through the first six weeks of the year, I grew in confidence.

On February 14, I visited Albert in Toronto to assess our fitness levels. We ran over nine miles—the longest run of my life. Although we both realized we could not be marathon-ready in 1982, by the end of the weekend we had agreed to run the Metro Toronto Road Runners' Eglington Flats Ten-Miler on April 25. This was the first road race of my life. The day was hot, and the course was much hillier than advertised. Albert and I ran side by side for much of the race and then I encouraged him to leave me behind and finish strong. I finished in seventy-ninth place with a time of 78:49 minutes. Albert finished fifty-sixth in 70:14. That was our one and only race together, but my mentor had done his work. I now had the skill and confidence to continue on my own.

In 1982 I ran every day for a total of 1542 miles. Although I was still hoping all would be well in our marriage, 1982 ended on an ominous note as I helped Sharon move into an apartment in London so she could return to school to complete a business diploma at Fanshawe. I realized she was on her way out, but I tried to convince our children and myself that this absence was only temporary.

RUNNING FOR MY LIFE

As 1983 began, it became apparent that Albert and I were not going to run a marathon together any time soon. I couldn't wait. I needed a goal to get me up in the morning and keep me focused on something positive. I signed up for Canada's National Marathon in Ottawa to be run on May 15. Running became my safe place. I ran alone. I gradually increased my pace and my distance. I adopted Amby Burfoot's twelve-week marathon preparation plan and mapped out the three months leading up to the marathon. I planned my mileage for each day. My mantra became, "Plan the work and work the plan." Regardless of weather or my physical condition, I followed the plan.

On April 16, I ran the Tillsonburg 10K in 42:25. By the middle of April, I was running sixty miles a week, and before marathon day, I had run eighteen miles twice. I was ready. On May 15, 1983, I completed the Ottawa Marathon in three hours and twenty-nine minutes. Sharon, Steph, and Jason were there at the finish line cheering me on. That evening, as we celebrated with a restaurant meal and began our trip home, I basked in the joy of my family. All seemed well. I had no clue that two years later I would be in our dream home as a single parent.

WISHING DOESN'T MAKE IT SO

Like T.S. Eliot's *Hollow Men*, our marriage ended not with a bang but with a whimper. Mostly, our life went smoothly. I told myself Sharon just wanted a chance to prove herself in the business world, so I encouraged her in every way I could. Meanwhile, Sharon was trying to leave with as little damage as possible. Then in 1985 Sharon met a businessman in Woodstock and started working with his office supply business. Even as Sharon set up an office apartment in Woodstock I was still in denial. Soon, Sharon was spending most of her time at her new apartment.

As the inevitable end came, we were still doing many things as a family. We celebrated birthdays and special events without tension. It wasn't difficult because Sharon and I were still friends, but I reluctantly realized we no longer shared the same hopes and dreams.

We were already living apart when, in July 1986, I helped Sharon trade in her old Pontiac 6000 and purchase a brand new 1986 Pontiac Firebird. I even bought her a personalized licence plate that said SHAR. That Firebird turned out to be her getaway car, and by September 1986 Sharon had officially moved out of our home.

Now I knew the marriage was over and our children knew it too, but we played a charade with family and friends for almost another year before everyone knew we were divorcing. Probably during that time, the only one being fooled was me. After Sharon officially moved out, I lived in denial for months with Sharon's wedding dress and many of her clothes still hanging in our closet. I couldn't comprehend that it was over. There had been no big fight. I convinced myself that it was a temporary malaise, and that one sunny day Sharon would return. I prayed and hoped. I helped Sharon with expenses and car insurance. My confusion was maintained as Sharon would arrive on a Friday evening or Sunday afternoon and share a meal as if all was well, and then leave for her other home. At some point in the process my anger and confusion were too much for our daughter Steph, and she moved to Woodstock to be with her mother.

My happy ending illusions dimmed when I started getting material from Sharon's divorce lawyer. Finally, the ultimate wake-up call sent me scrambling to a lawyer of my own. A legal document arrived demanding Sharon's exclusive custody of our son. Up until then, I had relied on faith and *a little bit of luck*. Now I had to face the reality that there would no "happy ever after" ending to the Doug and Sharon story.

The lawyer I found was compassionate and unflinching as I sat in his office sobbing. I needed his calm presence as much as I needed his legal expertise. His involvement helped pause the slippery slope Sharon and I were on now that we were part of the divorce industry. With opposing lawyers, we were rapidly losing control of our destiny and moving toward an inevitable legal battle. I started paying monthly support for Steph and we agreed to a custody process so that Jason could regularly visit his mom.

Accepting the reality of divorce, I itemized all our possessions and debts. Sharon had no interest in the house. She wanted to move on. I calculated what I was confident was a fair settlement, with me taking full responsibility for the house and mortgage. While our lawyers squabbled, Sharon and I came to an agreement on our own on finances and custody. Neither lawyer was particularly happy, but they helped us finalize details. My lawyer did a double-take as he saw us sitting outside his office holding hands as we waited to sign the final papers.

The divorce was painful, but it wasn't ugly. Sharon and I had been friends, parents, and life companions for over twenty years. As we ended our marriage, we had two children we loved, and precious memories that we would carry with us. It was time for each of us to move on with as much dignity and respect as we could.

NOW WHAT?

As I accepted my freedom and let go of my teenage dreams, it was time to start dreaming a new life into existence. That was not easy. Since I was seventeen life with Sharon had been my primary focus. Now I was like an astronaut cut loose from the mothership, floating in space.

To keep from falling apart, I used routines to create stability. I focused on being a good parent and an effective teacher-principal. I got up at the same time every morning. I made my bed. I ran. I cooked. I shoveled snow in the winter and mowed lawn in the summer. I washed our clothes and cleaned the house. I took garbage to the dump, swept the garage, washed the car. Little routines filled empty hours. I often spent Saturday night ironing clothes—my dress shirts had never been so well cared for. In the summer of 1986, I started riding my bike to town every morning for a weight training session at the Community Complex.

In the spring of 1987, although money was scarce, as an act of hope I planted a few scraggly jack pines on the hillside by my house. I dreamed of a better future. I ran every day, and in May, Jason and I flew to Ottawa where I ran my second marathon.

I was still in right relationship with my ex-in-laws, Norm and Gladys so, as long as I could afford it, I hoped to continue to live next door. My mother and father invited Jason and me for meals, and when I isolated myself, they just happened to drop in. I wrote to my daughter, Steph, and slowly started to heal our relationship. Jason and I started going to the gym Complex in Tillsonburg at least two mornings a week for weight workouts. I bought a yellow fiberglass canoe and a 750 cc. Suzuki motorcycle. I continued my church routines at Springford Baptist and took Jason and his age-mates camping, skating, skiing, and on other adventures.

My involvement in Springford Baptist Church was a steadying influence. I attended choir practice every Thursday night and sang in the choir every Sunday morning. Pastor Paul Stade was a confidant and support as I sought to maintain balance. Our pianist/choir director was an amazing older woman named Lilian Broad. I visited her home to practice, and soon she became my mentor and friend. Often on the way home from work, I would stop in for tea with Lilian and her budgie, Peetie. As our friendship grew, I told her that if I ever entered into another romantic relationship she would have to approve before I proceeded. I had no idea how synchronistic her approval would be.

The dissolution of the relationship with my wife and the alienation of my daughter made it clear to me that I still had much to learn about relationships and communication. In the fall of 1987, I signed up for the Ontario Ministry of Education course, Guidance Part 1. Driving with another colleague each week to Brantford for our course was a welcome break in my rigid routines. The course teacher was excellent, and soon I was learning about interpersonal psychology and names I had never heard, like Alfred Adler, Eric Berne, Carl Rogers, and William Glasser. I was especially captivated by William Glasser's concepts of Quality Education and Reality Therapy. I was encouraged by Glasser's focus on improving present relationships and circumstances while avoiding dwelling on past events.

As I focused on the future, I began to dream of a woman to share my life with.

THE SUNSHINE THAT CHANGED MY LIFE TO SPRING

The way that my wife Cheryl came into my life was subtle. As I started to visualize a new life partner, I dreamed of a tall athletic blond and kept hoping somehow our paths would cross. Meanwhile, I enjoyed parenting, working, running, and singing in the church choir. One Sunday morning, in the fall of 1987, a new woman assisted our choir director, Lilian, by playing the organ. I couldn't see her face from my location, but the foot and ankle that I caught sight of during the sermon were intriguing. After the service, I discovered that this attractive divorcee had just returned to Tillsonburg with her two young children. I was impressed with her musical skills but immediately labelled her as too young and "not my type." Life continued.

As the 1987 Christmas Break came, we started the week with a Christmas concert. I did a production with our youth group, and this woman, who I now knew as Cheryl Mansfield Kempston, did some cute piano pieces with her daughter, Heather, and son, James. I was impressed by the way Cheryl treated her children. At the social hour after the concert, I learned that Cheryl needed to change employment and that she had administration and technology skills. I wished her well, and Jason and I headed off for the rest of our Christmas Break.

My life was full. On Tuesday morning I met with my pastor friend, Paul Stade, for a tune-up of his running as he prepared to carry the torch for a mile on January 4 in advance of the Calgary Winter Olympics in February. I was delighted when my daughter, Stephanie, came home for a visit on Wednesday. On Thursday, our disco friend, "Fletch", joined us. On Friday, the kids and I drove to Toronto and picked up Albert. My heart was singing as we drove home with lively banter filling the vehicle. On Christmas day, Albert joined Steph, Jason, and me as we enjoyed Christmas meals at my parents at noon, and Norm and Gladys' in the evening. By Sunday evening I had taken Albert back to Toronto and returned home to an empty house. Even though I was a single parent, it had been a very good Christmas.

The next week, as Jason and I returned to our routines, I realized how comfortable I was becoming as a single parent. Near the end of the week, I noticed an ad in the paper for an administrative assistant for the Town of Ingersoll. I thought of Cheryl Kempston and, after managing to find her number, gave her a call encouraging her to apply.

The next five weeks were cold and busy. At church, Cheryl thanked me for helping her find her new job. I quickly moved on. My life was full. Jason and I were going to Tillsonburg three mornings a week. Aside from my role as a principal-teacher in Ingersoll, I was leading our church youth group, singing in the choir, taking a weekly course in Brantford, and teaching the adult Sunday School class. As I celebrated my forty-second birthday, a romantic relationship was the last thing on my mind. Or at least that is what I thought.

On Saturday, February 13, I took Jason and twelve other young people skiing in Woodstock. After a long and enjoyable day, and a riotous Swiss Chalet dinner, many of the youth group members and I went to Springford Baptist Church, where Lilian Broad and Cheryl Kempston presented a Valentine's Music Night. I already knew Lilian was an amazing pianist. Now I had a chance to see her protégé's skills on display. Individually and together the women were amazing. Their fingers danced across the keyboards. They performed individually and in a piano duet. They led a sing-song of old love songs like *Don't Sit Under the Apple Tree with Anyone Else but Me* and finished with love-filled church hymns. As I drove home, and as I ran my four miles at 10:30 p.m., I thought of the quiet dark-haired young pianist and a phrase my father sometimes used to describe an intriguing person— "Still water runs deep."

CUPID SHOOTS HIS ARROW

On Sunday morning, which just happened to be Valentine's Day, I decided to invite Cheryl and her two youngsters for an evening meal. As far as I was aware, I had no romantic aspirations. It was just a chance for the only two single parents in our little church to share insights and perhaps develop a supportive friendship. I called, and Cheryl agreed to come.

I cooked a roast with browned potatoes, parsnips, and carrots. When she arrived, I asked Cheryl to make the gravy which, after some laughter, she proceeded to do. Apparently, that was her least favourite cooking task. Heather and James, ages seven and five, were well-mannered guests, and the meal was enjoyable for everyone. After supper, Jason entertained the younger guests with his vast supply of toys and construction materials while Cheryl and I talked. I quickly realized this woman was very bright and curious. By the end of the evening, we had agreed to go to the local theatre to see *Three Men and a Baby* on Tuesday night.

We were both very proper on our first public outing. It certainly wasn't a date! There was no handholding and nothing but a polite goodbye at the door. However, by Friday, I had asked if Cheryl might be interested in going dancing on Saturday night. Something was happening. By the time

I held her in my arms on the dance floor, the electricity was unmistakable. On Saturday, February 20, I wrote, "I went dancing with Cheryl. It feels like love."

Over the next five days, Cheryl and I spent hours walking and talking and dreaming about the challenges and possibilities of a blended family. We were open and honest about our past failures and future hopes. Cheryl was younger—there was an age gap of ten years. We discussed the challenges that age differential could bring in the short and long term. We discussed housing and work and the discipline of children. We discussed our preference for spirituality over religion. I felt I had met my soul mate, and Cheryl agreed. By Friday, February 25, we discussed marriage—no bended knee, just a realization it was the only sensible thing to do. On Saturday, February 26, we went to London to buy wedding rings—twelve days after our Valentine dinner.

The pace at which we moved must have been bewildering for our friends and family, but we never blinked. Like a well-planned process, instead of our ad-lib reality, we quickly began planning for the amalgamation of our families and furnishings. Getting married seemed like the only logical next step. We chose Friday, May 20, 1988, for our wedding day. We discussed the details of selling Cheryl's condo and renovating the New Road home. It almost felt like an arranged marriage where we had been informed of the wedding and now it was time to get acquainted.

SWEPT OFF MY FEET

Once the initial logistics had been taken care of, we began a swept-off-our-feet romance. For the month of March, we were together as often as possible. I visited Cheryl's Concession Street condo in Tillsonburg almost every night and, as we bid our farewells late in the evening, we stood on the doorstep like teenagers needing just one more kiss before I left. By the beginning of April, courting was curtailed as we had started to reorganize the house on New Road. With Doug Ludwig's help, I cut through the cement basement wall and installed a window in what would become Jason's new bedroom. I partitioned off a corner of the basement and quickly created his room. Cheryl sold her Tillsonburg condo to her brother, and by the end of April, we had moved her furniture to New Road. On April 16 Jason ran the Tillsonburg 3K and I ran the 10K in 40:19. On Sunday, April 17,

Heather and James moved in with Jason and me while Cheryl moved back home with her parents until after our wedding.

WEDDING BELLS

The wedding was at Springford Baptist Church on a Friday evening. Being allowed to remarry in a Baptist church was a privilege that would not have been offered in every church and we were very grateful to Pastor Paul Stade.

The service was attended by a small group of friends and family. As part of the ceremony, I sang a love song I had written to celebrate our love.

It was entitled *You Brought the Sunshine.*

Deep beneath the snow,
The flowers wait for spring.
Deep within my heart,
There were songs
I could not sing.
But when the summer sun
Begins to melt the snow,
The flowers start to bloom,
And the world begins to glow.

Chorus:
And you brought the sunshine
That changed my world to spring.
And you brought the music
That taught my heart to sing.
And even though the cold wind
Blows against my door,
There'll be sunshine
In my heart
Forever more.

I never dreamt that I could love
The way that I love you.
And I will thank the Lord above

Each day my whole life through.
I want you walking by my side,
No matter what life brings.
For you have filled my life with joy
And given my heart wings.
(Chorus)

The winds of change keep blowin'
But some things stay the same.
The daisies still need sunshine,
And the roses still need rain.
And I need you beside me
Every step along the way,
For you brighten every hour
And give meaning to each day.
(Chorus)

We enjoyed a limo ride, photos, and a delicious meal with a few guests at Elmhurst in Ingersoll and then headed off to Niagara Falls for a weekend honeymoon. On Tuesday morning, we had breakfast together back home as a blended family and headed off to work and school as if it had always been that way. Jason and I resumed our morning gym workouts, and on those days, I would take him to Annandale High School before heading to Princess Anne Public School in Ingersoll where I was the principal. Cheryl took Heather and James to Harris Heights Public School in Ingersoll, and each evening either Cheryl or I picked them up from after-school care with the Reed family. Heather, James, and I laughed and sang on the way home. They were especially impressed when I drove my old Chev truck that honked every time I made a left turn.

BECOMING A FAMILY

Being with Cheryl was magical. We connected on so many levels. She was physically gorgeous, and I was totally smitten. Yet it was a calm sincere *twinkerpation* that we both knew was the basis for a long and meaningful relationship. We were farm kids, yet we both wanted to continue to learn and explore the bigger world. She was bright and curious. She loved the fields and woods and country roads, yet her past included the ability to attend Officers Mess Dinners, perform before large audiences, and interact with high-ranking military leaders and guest dignitaries. She played the piano and organ effortlessly and, with her mentor Lilian Broad, Cheryl had heard the best of the gospel musicians at Massey Hall in Toronto. Even though she had a repaired knee from a serious injury at age thirteen, in our first years together she never let that stop her from running a mile with me or biking while I ran. As we sang, swam, cooked, cleaned, and parented together, everything seemed so natural. I had married my new best friend. I had found a kindred spirit.

THE LESTER-KEMPSTON BUNCH

The way our blended family bonded together was amazing. Right from the start, Jason was great with Heather and James. Although Stephanie was living in Woodstock, we made sure to involve her in family events as often as possible. My mom and dad and Norm and Gladys welcomed Heather and James into the family without the slightest hesitation. Cheryl's family was every bit as gracious, and we quickly settled into our new normal. Cheryl and her ex-husband Brad had ended their marriage amicably, and Brad had remained active in Heather and James' lives, taking them every other weekend for visits and outings. The interactions with Heather and James' father were supportive and the weekends and holidays away with him were always fun for them.

Like a Rube Goldberg machine our marriage set off a sequence of cascading events in 1988. As the school year ended many of our family experienced changes. I said goodbye to my colleagues at Princess Anne Public School in Ingersoll since I had been transferred to Hillcrest Public School in Woodstock. Heather and James said goodbye to their Ingersoll friends since they would be attending Southridge Public School in Tillsonburg. On July 9, Heather and James' dad, Brad Kempston, married a nurse named Judy on the hottest day of the summer. Stephanie's mother made plans to move to Indiana, and Steph had to bid farewell to her as Sharon left Woodstock for Indianapolis. On July 23, Sharon married business executive Joe Eller, whom she had met while in Woodstock. Steph decided that rather than moving in with us she would attend Hairdressing School in London. We helped her find accommodation and move to London, and every time we saw her for the next six months, she had new hairstyles with a variety of colours.

The summer of 1988 continued to be a summer of firsts. Cheryl had her first holiday from her job with the Town of Ingersoll where she had worked since January, and the two of us went for a short vacation to the hills of Ohio and West Virginia. Jason had his first trip to his mother's new home in Indianapolis. We had our first weekend away with Heather and James, with a day at Santa's Village in Bracebridge, and our first motel night as a family in Barrie. Jason had his first year working in tobacco harvest. Heather and James were natural swimmers, and they celebrated firsts regularly in our backyard pool as they went from paddlers to swimmers during that first summer.

As fall arrived, Cheryl's friend and mentor, Lilian Broad, was hospitalized, and when Lilian returned home it soon became apparent that she was no longer able to lead the church choir. It was another transition as Cheryl took on the added responsibility of church choir director. Then, at Thanksgiving, we loaded up the Malibu with all six members of our blended family and headed to Buffalo for our first weekend of shopping and family bonding with all four children. I didn't make reservations, and I confidently drove to the area where Sharon and I had stayed many times in the past. I was surprised to find the first motel was full, so I checked another. By the third "no vacancy," I realized that I had never visited the area on the Columbus Day weekend, and certainly not while the Buffalo Bills were playing a home game. After lunch we focused on shopping and had a fun afternoon. As evening came, I checked back with the Buffalo Motor Inn, hoping perhaps someone had cancelled a reservation. No luck. I explained again that there were six of us so we would need a very large room. I started to leave, ready for a long drive home, when the woman behind the counter said, "Well, we do have one unusual space available. I didn't mention it because it costs a bit more." Without hesitation, I took the room. It turned out to be a room within a room, with two double beds plus a single bed and a cot. It was perfect! We celebrated with good food and lots of laughter as our four children enjoyed each other's company. We didn't know it then, but our full house was soon to become the new normal.

Our first Christmas as the Lester-Kempston Bunch was amazing. I hadn't had a joyful family Christmas for several years.

Steph had come home, so we had all four children as we made our final preparations. It felt so good to have the added excitement of a six-year-old and an eight-year-old in the house. We had learned a bit about flexibility over the last year, but with three parent homes and four grandparent homes in the mix, "stay loose" became our new mantra. After a Christmas Eve breakfast and present opening, Heather and James headed off to Niagara Falls to celebrate Christmas and gather with their new stepmother's large Italian family. Heather loved Judy and her family and arrived back home remembering every name and most of the birthdays. Meanwhile, after spending a few days back at New Road, Stephanie asked me if she could move back in and complete her high school education. After consulting with Cheryl and setting out some very clear expectations, we agreed.

We would start 1989 as the Lester-Kempston bunch, with four children, two dogs, two cats, a rabbit, a budgie, and an amazing goldfish, "Survivor," which somehow survived Jason's infrequent care.

YEAR TWO

As our amalgamated family began our second year together, life was good. Brad Kempston's new wife, Judy, worked in London as a nurse. She had no children and immediately made co-parenting Heather and James a priority. From the start, Brad and I had gotten along well. He and Judy were thoughtful and consistent with their parenting time. Brad introduced Heather and James to skiing, and this activity became a precious time with local and resort experiences allowing their skill and confidence to grow.

There was no Reveille bugle, but as Stephanie defragged from a year and a half of unstructured expectations, January 1989 started out as a version of boot camp at our house. Monday to Friday, breakfast began at 7:00 a.m. with everyone expected to be at the table dressed and ready to start the day. Steph was accepted into the semestered program at Woodstock Collegiate Institute in Woodstock. This meant, if she stuck at it, she would complete high school by the end of 1990. Our concerns about Stephanie fitting in were short-lived. She took school seriously and we soon relaxed. With Cheryl's influence and feminine touches, the house once again became a home. As I finished up Stephanie's new room upstairs, it felt like the time we had lost during the family chaos was being beautifully reclaimed. Just before her eighteenth birthday, Stephanie got her driver's licence.

Once Stephanie had begun classes and our family routines were established, we divided the four children into two teams, with supper preparation being assigned to one team a couple of times each week, and, to the other, clean-up. Despite a little protestation drama to make it clear to Cheryl and me that they weren't servant labour, the arrangement worked well.

We soon learned some interesting things. Steph turned out to be an amazing cook. She also proved to use more dishes and utensils in preparation than anyone—much to the dismay of the clean-up crew. This was particularly unfortunate when Heather was not Stephanie's cooking partner. It turned out that Heather's disdain for clean-up matched Stephanie's gourmet delight. Once, when we pushed a little too hard on the clean-up inadequacies, Heather angrily declared, "I'm not Molly Maid!" The boys did their parts and the arrangement worked well.

In the spring, we traded our Monte Carlo on a low-mileage grey 1987 Plymouth Voyager minivan. This non-descript symbol of middle-class families became our adventure-mobile for the next decade. We used it often and we used it well. As summer began, James played soccer in Tillsonburg, and Jason played rural fastball on a Springford travel team. Stephanie began waitressing at Norfolk Landing restaurant. Getting people to work and attending games kept us busy. At the end of June, we celebrated Jason's sixteenth birthday with a surprise plane ride at Tillsonburg airport. Now, with four drivers in the family, vehicle insurance coverage and logistics became a regular part of our family dynamic.

Jason and Stephanie's maternal grandparents, Norm and Gladys Williams lived next door. They had a boat on Lake Erie at Booth's Harbour, and in the past, several times each summer, Jason and Steph had joined them for an afternoon of fishing. No fishing trip had been complete without hotdogs and fries at the Marina. By 1989 these trips were much less frequent and gramma Gladys needed a hip replacement. Another long-standing tradition was coming to an end.

In the busy-ness, my morning runs were a time of silence and reflection. New Road had been central to my life since my first days working in tobacco, and now, as I ran along the road past the familiar farms, I realized everything was changing. Jason and Stephanie were becoming adults and, although living close to grandparents had been a blessing, we knew Jason and Steph would soon need to move on. The realization of how quickly life moves along was emphasized as my father and mother both celebrated their seventy-fifth birthdays that year.

In July of 1989, Cheryl and I took Heather and James on a major family adventure. We drove to Cochrane, and then took the Polar Bear Express to Moosonee. As we enjoyed breakfast on the train while watching the wilderness outside, I was so thankful that this beautiful woman and these delightful children had become part of my life. At Moosonee, we took a small boat to Moose Factory and, after a short walking tour, made our way back to Moosonee and the train to return to Cochrane. In the following days we toured the Abitibi Paper Plant, Science North in Sudbury, and then drove from Espanola to South Baymouth, where we took the Chi-Cheemaun ferry to Tobermory and drove home. Our first family vacation with Cheryl's little ones had been a wonderful success.

GRAMPA NORM

Now retired from tobacco farming and his greenhouse business, Grampa Norm devoted himself to his acre of lawn. In the heat of the summer, it wasn't unusual for Norm to be moving his lawn sprinklers at 3:00 a.m. Even though we were on a hill with light sandy soil, we were blessed with good wells. At our house, the well was only twenty-six feet deep. In July of 1989, Norm set out to "wash" a new well near his implement shed so that he could devote one well exclusively to lawn maintenance. To do this, Norm had bought a "sand point" from a local well supplier and attached it to a twenty-foot-long 1.25-inch pipe that was intended to supply water from his new well. To wash his well, Norm used a larger pipe to help protect and guide the smaller pipe as it made its way down into the ground. It may sound complicated but, when it works, it is amazingly efficient. Norm had watched it done in my backyard in July 1979 as a local "well washer" started at 8:00 a.m. and was pumping water from my new well by noon. Unfortunately, Norm's well-digging program didn't prove to be quite so efficient.

On July 19, I helped Norm set up his well-washing process and then returned to my house to work on some of my own tasks. On July 21, Norm and I worked all day on his well. By the end of the day, we were down twenty-two feet, but we were both exhausted, and we had no water. Over the next two weeks, I vacuumed the pool, stained the fence, and worked on other projects. On August 1, as Jason began tobacco harvest, I was surprised to see Norm still working on his well project. I tried to assist, with no luck. By August 9, Norm was reminding me of Captain Ahab as he was now down nearly twenty-five feet in his third location, determined that, in the next hour, success would be his. Water eluded him.

Undeterred, Norm continued tinkering. On August 12, after four weeks on a project that should have taken four hours, Norm realized the original well pipe, which was to carry water from his newly discovered source, was defective. It had several very tiny holes that had caused it to constantly lose its prime. Once we changed to a new pipe, we had a successful well within a couple of hours. Norm then realized he had probably reached the water table on his very first attempt. Norm's "Summer of the Well" had finally come to a successful conclusion.

Looking back now, I realize that Norm needed the project as much as he needed an additional well. Norm's relentless work ethic and determination as an employer, mentor, father-in-law, and neighbour, had shaped and influenced me since I was sixteen years old. Now, as his next-door neighbour, I was constantly challenged to keep my yard in good condition. Because of Norm I watered our lawn, mowed the ditch across the road from our house, and fought the dandelions that threatened to besmirch Norm's pristine lawn.

The same year as the well, Norm took on another project that amused and astonished us all. One of the maple trees Norm had planted on his front lawn a dozen years earlier now impeded the view from his picture window, and he decided it should be moved. Two different professionals declined the project saying the tree was too mature to be moved. Undeterred, Norm recruited grandson Jason, and for a couple weeks they filled their spare time digging a huge hole for the tree's new home, and then, as we surreptitiously spied, Jason and Norm dug carefully to free up the transplant target. I managed to avoid being recruited and remained too busy to help as they brought in Norm's tractor for the final process. With tarps and ropes, laughter and grunts, Jason and his grandfather triumphed. Soon Norm had green grass growing where the tree had once stood and, with his care, the transplant not only lived but flourished. I am sure that every one of our family benefitted and learned things from Norm's tireless example.

SETTLING IN

That summer, both Jason and Stephanie worked in tobacco harvest and as harvest work, baseball, soccer, and summer holidays came to an end, we were all ready for some same-old-same-old. That fall, all of us were in school, including Cheryl, who had restarted part-time university studies and begun a Computer Science distance course with the University of Waterloo. On Thanksgiving weekend, all six of us loaded up our Voyager and headed to Buffalo for another weekend of shopping and good food. This time we had booked room number thirty-two at the Buffalo Motor Inn well in advance. What a joy to have our blended family laughing and enjoying each other's company. The only tension all weekend occurred late on Saturday afternoon as five of us excitedly watched the Blue Jays in a nail-biter playoff game against the Oakland A's, while seven-year-old James made it clear he was starving and couldn't care less about the outcome. Once the game ended and we found a restaurant with lots of good food, all was forgiven. On Monday afternoon, we returned home to a Thanksgiving meal with my parents. I was very thankful for all my blessings.

One Saturday in early December 1989, Jason, Dad, and I went hunting in the woods behind neighbour George Varga's farm. It was a beautiful afternoon filled with excitement as Jason shot his first ruffed grouse. It was also filled with the realization of how time moves on. As we walked home, Dad indicated that this would be his last hunting trip. His legs and heart could no longer climb the hills. As the year ended, we celebrated Christmas in multiple places with a mix of family members. Flexibility had become part of our lives. We had more Christmases that year than ever, starting with my parents on December 17 and the Mansfield's on December 19, before having Christmas at our own house on December 23. Heather and James then celebrated again in Niagara Falls with Brad and Judy.

TRANSITION TIME

The next two years were a time of major transitions.

The first few months of 1990 sped by. During the March Break, Jason and Stephanie took the train to Battle Creek, Michigan, to spend time with their mother. By then, Cheryl and I had decided that we could not afford to stay in the big house on New Road. At that time, we planned to stay in the area, but we hoped to cut our mortgage and expenses. We quietly listed our house for sale. We set the price high and, perhaps at that time, it was more about dreaming than really wanting things to change; however, the process served to desensitize us and the children to the thoughts of a move. It also allowed me time to begin to grieve the loss and start to accept the inevitable. I don't think either Cheryl or I were disappointed when the house didn't sell. We took the house off the market and continued on. By June, James and Jason were both playing baseball, and Cheryl and I were playing on a slow pitch team.

One evening early in the summer, we heard a loud rumble outside as Stephanie arrived on the back of a Kawasaki motorcycle. The young man driving was Joe Scaife. He lived with his mother in Komoka. It soon became apparent that this wasn't just a casual ride. Stephanie introduced her new beau and, within a short time, announced that they planned to wed early the next year. Stephanie had just turned nineteen. Soon after our initial introduction, Stephanie, driving Cheryl's little blue Charger, had a nasty incident in a Komoka parking lot and returned home after a weekend visit with Joe's family with a huge dent just behind the driver's door. After ascertaining that a proper repair would cost over $1500, I decided to take on the job myself. I bought gallons of Bondo fibreglass resin plus primer and touch-up paint. After a couple of weeks of hammering and filling, sanding, and painting, the dent was patched, the door would close, and, if we stayed out of the sunlight the paint almost matched. The Charger was functional. Jason drove it to Woodstock for school the next year and it served us well until 1992. We joked that if it was ever in another accident, the weight of the Bondo would cause a rollover.

Near the end of August, Joe and Steph arrived one evening excited that Joe had just been hired at a factory in Tillsonburg. They asked if Joe could stay with us. When we asked when he would start, we discovered he was to be at the factory at 7:00 a.m. the next morning. We agreed, as long as Joe's improvised bedroom in the basement and Steph's on the second floor were considered off-limits for any sort of rendezvous. With this understanding in place, we spent the next five months with seven of us in the house, heading off in multiple directions every day. Steph and Joe kept their end of the bargain. On weekends, when Steph and Joe went out on a date, Cheryl and I were amazed when they often returned home by 11:00 p.m., even though we had not tried to impose any kind of curfew. Joe fit in well, and along with visits from other family and friends, our kitchen table was always full of food and conversation. Meanwhile, Steph was coming to the end of her high school program and would complete her courses by year's end.

In November, Heather celebrated her tenth birthday at our house with a group of Southridge Public School friends. We were so impressed with how grown up these young women had become.

As Stephanie neared the end of her secondary school studies, she and Cheryl began to plan her January wedding. Cheryl sewed the wedding dress and bridesmaid dresses, and she and Steph created the flower arrangements. By December, Stephanie and Joe had rented an apartment in London near Fanshawe College.

As the new year began, the wedding activities increased, with a shower, and final planning for the ceremony and reception. On January 26, 1991, Stephanie and Joe were married at Springford Baptist Church. Steph was beautiful in her wedding dress. Later, as I danced with the bride at the wedding reception at Springford Hall, I was so thankful that Stephanie had returned to New Road and that she had graduated from secondary school.

On the Monday morning after the wedding, just five of us gathered around the breakfast table. It felt strange. Another transition.

As April arrived and the Blue Jays began their season, another family tradition began. Several times during the next two summers we would load up the van with the three still at home and often one or two friends and head to Toronto to sit high in the stadium and cheer on our team.

In May, Heather took up horseback riding. With her riding helmet and riding boots she looked elegant. She was a natural and enjoyed her weekly lessons. However, her opportunity was short-lived. Before the end of the summer, her teacher took a leave of absence, and we couldn't find a suitable alternative. We were learning that change is a constant.

At the end of June, Jason finished his high school studies at Annandale. He had decided his future was in design and illustration. As I helped him research future possibilities two things became clear—he didn't have enough quality work in his art portfolio, and his knowledge of Apple computers and design software was deficient. Jason decided to attend a fifth year of high school at Arthur Voaden Secondary School in Woodstock because of its reputation for vocational excellence. Here he would focus on preparing his skills and portfolio for post-secondary school.

MARY LAKE

At the beginning of July 1991, Jason headed south to Indiana to spend time with his mother. Cheryl and I and the younger two headed north. We had discovered a cottage rental on Mary Lake near Huntsville which would end up being our summer destination for several years. Owned by the Willows family, the "middle cottage" was the perfect summer vacation getaway for us. Dan Willows, Sr., was a London Industrial Arts teacher, and his son, Dan Willows, Jr., was a skilled carpenter. Together, they had renovated and repaired three old cottages on one beachfront property and named the middle one "The Belvedere." The Willows family spent much of the year in the largest of the cottages and rented out the other two. Perched on a hillside with a sandy beach and private dock, our rental was idyllic.

As we settled in at the cottage that first year we spent long lazy days swimming, canoeing, sunning, and having a bonfire on the beach in the evening. On July 1, we canoed across the lake and climbed the large, forested rock formations on the opposite shore. It was an experience to remember, climbing the tall cliffs and exploring the quartz-filled rock along the path. From our perch high on the lakeshore we could see all of Mary Lake. While descending to return to the canoe, Heather lost her balance. We watched in horror as she went rolling down the steep embankment towards the rocks on the lakeshore. Fortunately, she slid to a stop on a large rock formation just before it dipped into the water. Miraculously, she was not hurt at all. That same evening, we went to Bracebridge to see the Canada Day fireworks. The following day, Heather and James met our neighbours in the Willows' other rented cottage. A friendship blossomed and soon they were spending time with Jean Bickle, her son Josh, Amy Williams and her son Matthew. Together the children explored the lake, river, and surrounding areas. One day, Jean took the children by boat down the Muskoka River for lunch in Huntsville. Each night after a day of adventures, Heather and James were exhausted, but every morning they were up at dawn, eager for a new day of discovery.

Our hosts, Marg and Dan Willows' three children were all amazing athletes and loved the water. We only interacted a few times during each stay, but the family left a lasting impression on each of us. Their daughter, Deb Willows, had been born with cerebral palsy and needed a wheelchair, but that didn't slow her down. When we first met, Deb had just competed at the 1988 Paralympic Games and set a Canadian and world record in the fifty-metre backstroke. Seeing her manipulate her wheelchair, and swim, was an inspiration. Although Heather was only ten and James only eight, Marg and Dan's son Danny invited them to try waterskiing. With the assistance of Dan Senior and Dan Junior, by the end of the second day both Heather and James were confidently skiing behind the Willows' boat. Cheryl and I watched Heather and James' determination and pluck with joyful admiration.

CHERYL AND DOUG'S EXCELLENT ADVENTURE

At the end of July, Jason started tobacco harvest while Heather and James began a two-week vacation with Brad and Judy. Freedom called, and like giddy teenagers we started preparing for our first road trip. We refitted the Plymouth Voyager to be our travel home for an ad lib western journey. We had fourteen days. The only definite destination was to visit our friends Larry and Carolyn Larson in Wawota, Saskatchewan. We then hoped to make it into the mountains of British Columbia and head home through the northern United States. I took out the back seats of the van and put in a mattress and sleeping bags. Cheryl made privacy curtains for the windows. We borrowed a roof storage container from my brother, Larry. We packed a cookstove, utensils, and camping gear, with plans to keep our expenses low.

On the evening of July 28, we headed west. Without children or work responsibilities I discovered I really had married a kindred spirit. After sleeping for a few hours at a rest stop in Michigan, we crossed the Mackinac Bridge and headed north of Sault Ste. Marie, back into Ontario. The rocks and hills were beautiful as we enjoyed the freedom of the open road.

For nearly ten years I had run every day through sickness and bad weather but continuing my streak on our westward trip proved to be a challenge. Late in the afternoon, at the Montreal River Hill, along the same route on the Trans-Canada Highway where Terry Fox had run his last days of the Marathon of Hope in 1980, Cheryl drove four miles ahead and waited as I ran along the edge of the highway. I quickly discovered two things that added to my admiration of my Canadian hero. There was no shoulder on much of the pavement. A wrong step and the drop off to gravel would be a disaster. The second thing I learned is that what appeared to be a slight incline never ended. As I finished my sample of Terry's experience, I was relieved to see our van waiting beside the road.

We continued on to Marathon, Ontario—over 1100 kilometres from home. We found a campground where we were instructed to put our fee in an envelope and deposit it in the payment box. We cooked a meal and spent the night without ever seeing another person.

Although Cheryl and I had been married for three years, this adventure was unlike anything we had ever experienced. As we spent long days together, I realized several times each day that this woman was more amazing than I had ever imagined. Early on the third day, I set up our camp stove at the side of the road overlooking Lake Superior, and we had breakfast on a hill while enjoying the amazing view of forest and lake as birds sang in the sky. Mid-morning, near Thunder Bay, we saw a sign inviting us to an Amethyst Mine. I looked at Cheryl and she smiled in assent—this girl was a gamer. We spent the next two hours visiting a surface mine where they invited us to search for our own purple amethyst. Cheryl and I were discovering the joy of living in the moment.

As we entered Manitoba toward evening, we were nearing another 1000-kilometre day. When we saw a campsite beside the road, we were excited. We were a little surprised, however, when the manager just stuck his head out of his door and said, "Park anywhere," then disappeared. We found a level spot and Cheryl waited as I got out and opened the white topper to get our cooking supplies for the evening meal. When I looked up, my bare arm was black. There were hundreds of hungry mosquitoes beginning their evening meal! I quickly closed the topper, chased as many mosquitoes as possible off my exposed skin, and scrambled back into the van. Our questions about the quick disappearance of our campground manager had been answered. We made a hasty exit and drove toward Winnipeg, not quite sure what we would do next. Fortunately, we found a truck stop in the middle of the city.

Now late, at the end of the third day of our trip, I still had not had my daily run, and we were now parked at a Husky Truck Stop without having eaten supper, in the heart of Winnipeg, during a mosquito invasion. We discussed our options and decided this is where we'd spend our night. After finding a parking place that wasn't directly under the bright lights, I crawled into the back of our van and prepared for a run. I am sure Cheryl had questioned my maniacal devotion to running in the past, but even I had to admit this was pushing the limits. At 11:30 p.m. I ran two miles further west along the highway and back. My forgiving wife welcomed my return, and we had a midnight meal at the all-night truck stop.

After a surprisingly good night's sleep in our van, we awoke refreshed ready for more adventures. When we looked at the van exterior, we were amazed. The front of the previously white topper was black with mosquito carcasses, and our windshield and hood were so covered that we knew we would be investing in trucker-quality cleaner before continuing west. As we enjoyed a truck stop breakfast we were impressed by the service and quality. Perhaps we had discovered something. Then it got better. After visiting the washrooms and walking past several doors marked "shower," I enquired if the showers were for truckers only. The woman said they were available to travellers for three dollars but were free if you filled up with gas. Sensing Cheryl's reluctance, our host offered to show her a shower space. Suitably impressed, Cheryl went to shower while I filled up the van and started the process of removing mosquito detritus from our vehicle.

As we explored Winnipeg, Cheryl decided she would cut her hair. I followed suit and soon we both had shorter hair than we had had in years. To add to our new look, we both bought prescription designer sunglasses in a boutique next to the hair salon. Leaving Winnipeg, we headed southwest to Wawota, a village in southeast rural Saskatchewan. After two nights with our friends, the Larson family, we left on a quiet Saturday afternoon with Regina as our next destination. We were about to get a lesson in rural Saskatchewan life.

We were in no rush so we chose the scenic route along Highway 48 for the two-hour drive to Regina. With our gas gauge moving toward empty we came to the village of Vibank. We were surprised to find the gas station closed before 5:00 p.m. and continued on. When we passed through the next village of Montmartre our gas gauge was alarmingly low and, once again, the sole gas station was closed. By the time we coasted up to the Texaco station in the next village of Kipling our van sputtered and stopped almost in front of the station. Once again, the gas station was closed.

Realizing we might be camping in our van until Monday, I decided to check the station's hours. As I approached the building, I could see a light and someone inside. After knocking on a side door, a man answered. I told him our story and he good-naturedly assured me that he would provide gas and help us get on our way. The station owner explained that since most of the Saskatchewan farmers had their own storage tanks, the village gas stations often closed early on weekends. He told us that all the locals knew that the houses near his station had a key to the gas pumps—it would have been the same, he said, in the last two villages we passed through.

Thankful to be on the road again, as soon as we arrived in Regina we searched for a Husky Truckstop for our evening meal and a parking place for the night. In the morning, we headed west toward Calgary with no particular agenda. Our visit to Wawota had been our only destination, so from here on we were vagabonds enjoying the open roads. We drove through Medicine Hat and spent the afternoon at a rodeo in the town of Strathmore. After another night at a truck stop near Calgary, we began our morning in a beautiful park on the Bow River where Cheryl amusedly watched a "duck ballet" while I enjoyed a morning run.

As we continued west, we were awed by the mountains. In Banff our compatibility was confirmed once again when we turned a corner and simultaneously delighted in the discovery of a Harvey's restaurant for lunch. As we continued on, we spent a couple of leisurely hours bathing in a hot spring pool in Radium and then spent the night in Cranbrook, British Columbia. It was time to pivot and head toward home. We had travelled over 4,000 kilometres.

As we travelled south through the hills, from Cranbrook toward Montana, the number and frequency of small, white roadside crosses was unsettling. At first, we thought that the locals were showing their respect for animals killed on the road. However, as we entered Idaho and began travelling the most extreme hills we had ever seen, we realized these were memorials of human fatalities.

This was the most mountainous terrain we had ever experienced. At the tops of the hills, we were awestruck by the beauty while sobered by the signs reminding truck drivers to check brakes and ensure chains were secure before descending. Partway down the mountainsides, there were numerous escape routes for drivers whose brakes had failed. The bridge over the Kootenay River was breathtaking. After a day of hills, we arrived at Flathead Lake and spent the night at a Conoco Truck Stop in Laurel, Montana, relieved to once again be on relatively flat ground.

The next day we visited Cody, Wyoming, and its amazing Museum of the West. That night, we arrived at a truck stop in Bar Nunn, Montana, about 9:00 p.m. This had become an anticipated routine as we travelled. We would enjoy a late supper and then linger over decaf coffee as the locals arrived. It was the same in almost every truck stop restaurant. In the late evening, friends and family of the wait staff would fill the bar and booths discussing their day and sharing local gossip. There was always lots of good-natured teasing and laughter. These evening gatherings had been especially entertaining since we entered "cowboy" country. The guys and gals, with plaid shirts and boots, really did look like characters out of a Marlboro cigarette ad. That night by the time we returned to our van, parked close to the all-night restaurant entrance, we had learned that there was a campground, a saloon, and a strip club, all at the end of the parking lot. We set up our privacy curtains and snuggled into our sleeping bags.

We were both sleeping soundly when, sometime after midnight, we awoke with a start. There was a very loud yelling match happening right at the front of our van. We quickly deduced that the angry woman had come to check on her trucker partner and had been waiting in the parking lot when he emerged from the saloon when it closed. Now she had him caught in a lie, and they were having a donnybrook, ten feet from our bed. We stayed low in case bullets flew and were absolutely quiet. Fortunately, after about twenty minutes the angry woman made her final statements and left with tires squealing. As we settled back in, we were more intrigued than frightened. We had come to see the wild west and it had certainly delivered. We had just managed to drift back to sleep when we were awakened yet again, this time by a group of inebriated young men who hooted and hollered their way across the parking lot. We sincerely hoped they did not notice our out-of-country license plates. After fearfully envisioning our van being rocked to-and-fro, and windows broken, we experienced a deep sense of relief once we were sure they had moved on.

As morning dawned, it was time to get serious about getting back home. But first, we took a final southern tour. We drove through classic western towns like Casper, Douglas, and Cheyenne, and drove far enough into the outskirts of Denver to be able to say we had been there. Then we headed east, spending a night in Brush, Colorado before driving across Nebraska and Iowa to spend a night in Des Moines. On the last night of our "truck stop road trip," we splurged and stayed at a motel in Kalamazoo, Michigan. By the time we arrived back home the next night, we had travelled 8500 kilometres, and spent all of fifty-four dollars on accommodation. It had been the greatest adventure of my life and I was even more in love with this adventurous woman.

MORE TRANSITIONS

As August was coming to an end in 1991, Heather and James made the most of their days in the pool while I prepared to go back to work and Jason finished up another harvest. On a sunny Sunday afternoon on August 18, Jason and I went golfing at Mount Elgin. On the sixth hole, a golfer on the next fairway hit a ground-skimming drive that hit me in the left ankle. I fell to the ground. As I got up and limped in circles, I realized I could still walk. I decided to call it a day and went to the clubhouse to ice my wound. For the next nine days, I ran a slow mile or two, hoping the pain and swelling would soon subside. Finally, on September 3, after a sleepless night because of the pain, I realized my running streak needed to come to an end. I had run every day since January 1, 1982, a streak of nine years, two hundred and forty-two days. During that time, I had gone from an occasional runner to a marathoner, and I had logged 14,441 miles. Those miles on the road had transformed my body and my mind. I had become stronger and more disciplined while becoming more thoughtful and aware. Although my running streak was over, I knew that, as soon as possible, I would continue regular running.

In September, school routines began again. Heather was in grade six and James in grade four. Both were doing very well. Heather, who was able to read before she began school, was identified as gifted in Language Arts and participated in an enrichment program. James showed special skills in Mathematics and Sciences. Meanwhile, Jason was thriving as he focused entirely on Art at Arthur Voaden Secondary School in Woodstock.

I was beginning my fourth year as principal at Hillcrest Public School in Woodstock. Since I no longer had classroom duties, cross-country coaching provided a welcome opportunity to work directly with children. The teams I had coached over the last three years had been good, but this year our team was exceptional.

As our family celebrated Thanksgiving, there were only five of us on our annual trip to Buffalo. We knew this Thanksgiving tradition was also coming to an end so to celebrate we decided to go to the Buffalo Bills game on Sunday. None of us had ever been to an NFL game and we thought we were early when we arrived over an hour before the game. To our surprise we were late to the party. The parking lots was already filled with travel trailers, truck campers, and more barbecues and beer than any of us had ever seen in one place. It was a cold windy day, never getting above 5° C. We thought we had prepared by bringing winter coats, but we were wrong. Buffalo's Rich Stadium was all steel and cement—even in the washrooms. The Bills played the Indianapolis Colts. The Colts' rookie quarterback, Jeff George, was horrible. The Bills' Jim Kelly and Thurmon Thomas were the best in the league. As the Colts floundered and the Bills fans cheered, we shivered. We managed to last until the third quarter. By then the score was thirty-five to six, and we were becoming increasingly nervous about the drunken, rowdy, half-naked men in the row in front of us with "B-I-L-L-S" painted in large blue letters on their bare bellies. We made a hasty exit and went in search of a warm restaurant and a hot meal.

When we arrived back home, the leaves were turning colour and endings continued. As fall ended, both my boys' and girls' Hillcrest cross-country teams won county championships.

Although Stephanie had completed her secondary credits the winter before, and Jason had finished at Annandale the past June, both their high school graduations were on the same evening. On Friday, November 1, Cheryl went to W.C.I. with Steph for her graduation, while I went to Annandale High School to attend Jason's graduation ceremonies. Secondary school graduation wasn't our only reason to celebrate. Stephanie was pregnant. We would become grandparents the coming June.

At forty-five, the country boy was a long way from the early days at the chicken farm. Cheryl had brought stability and joy to our family and as

I watched our oldest children become adults, I realized how quickly life moves along.

THE YEAR OF MOVES

The year 1992 started quietly, but we all knew that this would be another year of major changes.

As Jason returned from a Christmas visit to Indiana, I resumed daily four-mile runs and James and Heather enjoyed skiing most weekends at Cobble Hills. I was making regular trips to Toronto to work with Jim Montagnes as I completed my third year of training in Dr. Glasser's Reality Therapy. Cheryl was now officially registered for September courses at the University of Waterloo.

Our house was back on the market again, and this time we ready to move. Cheryl and I had decided our future was in Waterloo where she would study music.

By spring we hadn't sold yet, but we were optimistic as mortgage rates fell as low as 8.5 percent. That may seem high now, but the year that I built the house in 1979 they had climbed into the double digits, and by the early eighties mortgage rates had peaked at over twenty percent.

In April everything started to move quickly. As we celebrated Steph's birthday on April 7, Steph and Joe announced that they would move from London to Tillsonburg at the end of May. On April 22, we got an offer on our house, and by the next week, the deal was finalized. On May 1, Jason received confirmation that he had been accepted into the Undergraduate Degree Program at Herron School of Art at Indiana University in Indianapolis so he would be heading to Indiana in August. Our time at our house on New Road was coming to an end.

I sold the 1968 Chevy truck that had served us so well, and we found new homes for our cats and dogs. We searched for a new home for us in Waterloo, but all the houses were more than we could afford. On May 9, we bought a townhouse condo on Keats Way in Waterloo. Fortunately for us, the former tenant's choice to flush their pet rabbit's droppings down the toilet had resulted in an expensive blockage in the city's sewer pipe that led the exasperated landlord to welcome our offer to buy.

In the midst of our busy-ness, we still needed to help Stephanie and Joe get settled in their new location. After work on Friday, May 29, I drove to

London and rented a twenty-two-foot Ryder truck. We helped Steph and Joe empty their London apartment and move to Tillsonburg. Cheryl and I crawled into bed at 3:20 a.m.

Thank goodness for the excitement of new beginnings because we had no time to rest. Every spare moment was spent packing and sorting. The next Friday, June 5, I rented a truck again, and Cheryl and I moved a load of boxes and belongings to Waterloo. Our move had begun but we were far from finished. We still had a lot of packing and sorting to do. The pace continued with a phone call late on Sunday, June 7. At 11:40 p.m., Stephanie's daughter, Katelynn Michelle was born. We were grandparents!

After celebrating with Steph and Joe, it was back to work for us. We filled the garage with furnishings and appliances that we were sending to Shackleton's auction, including Cheryl's beloved little blue Charger. When the movers arrived at 6:30 a.m. on June 18, they loaded a forty-foot truck that would head to Waterloo, and then as soon as they left, Shackleton's loaded a twenty-eight-foot truck from our leftovers to go to their auction near Springfield.

As our New Road home emptied, the moves continued. Cheryl left her job at the Town of Ingersoll to attend university starting in September, and I was informed that I would be leaving Hillcrest to become principal at Plattsville Public School. As June came to an end, Heather and James visited their new schools in Waterloo and I visited my new school in Plattsville. The next day, we drove to the cottage at Mary Lake. It was time to relax.

SUMMERTIME AND THE LIVIN' IS BUSY

As we settled into the scenic magnificence of Mary Lake, I was able to exhale. We relaxed and enjoyed time canoeing and picking wild blueberries. This year, Danny Willows had a new kind of watercraft — a Kawasaki stand-up jet ski. We watched in amazement as Danny did incredible maneuvers. He could even dive the craft underwater and pop back up. Watching, we realized it took a great deal of strength and skill to get started with this new machine. I was more than a bit intimidated when Danny invited me, Cheryl, Heather, and James to try it out. To make it possible, Danny brought us to the jet ski in his Zodiac boat. He helped me get into position and, since I had ridden a motorcycle, I was soon zooming around the lake with a goofy smile and a joyful heart. Heather and James also succeeded in operating this amazing watercraft. Once again, I was so thankful for the cottage and the Willows family. As the week progressed, we all went horseback riding, and my mom and dad came for a night. By the time we headed to our new home in Waterloo, we were rested and excited about the future.

As I had a week to reflect while at the cottage, I was so thankful for the last four years. Stephanie and Jason had been given a loving supportive home to finish their high school studies. Now, Stephanie was a mother, and Jason was headed to a prestigious art school to prepare for his dream career. Heather and James had learned how to water ski and swim, and both were doing well in school. Cheryl was now enrolled in the University of Waterloo's music program at Conrad Grebel and would be able to study full-time to complete her university degree. I had completed my studies in Reality Therapy and had started a part-time Master of Theological Studies program at Conrad Grebel.

Upon returning from our holiday, our family would be city dwellers for the first time. Our new condo had been neglected by the last tenant, which meant we got a bargain price and had an opportunity for renovations and painting. That was a bonus for us since this was the first home that Cheryl and I could make our own. I welcomed the fresh start. We updated the bathroom, replaced rugs and wallcoverings, painted, paneled, and purchased some new furniture. By the end of July, we had made the condo our own and were happily settled. The Keats Way condo complex had lots of low-traffic roads and green spaces, so James and Heather soon were zooming around the neighbourhood on new bikes and making new friends.

Our summer adventures were not over. I had completed my training in Reality Therapy and, to finalize my certification, I needed to attend a week of testing and proficiency demonstration. I chose August 1–5 in Kansas City, Missouri. Cheryl, Heather, and James would accompany me. We left early so we could tour Ohio, Kentucky, and St. Louis on our way. The Certification Week was held at the Hyatt Regency in downtown Kansas City. I didn't know anything about Kansas City or the Hyatt or I might have had second thoughts.

The Kansa City Hyatt was a beautiful forty-story hotel that had opened in 1978. It was also the site of one of the United States' worst disasters. We learned that on July 17, 1981, two walkways had collapsed, one directly above the other. They crashed onto a teen dance being held in the hotel's lobby, killing 114 and injuring another 216. It remains the deadliest non-deliberate structural failure in American history. When we arrived eleven years later, the hotel was filled to capacity and was the centre of culture in Kansas City. While we were there, the visiting baseball teams stayed at the Hyatt. We had just missed the Blue Jays, but on our last night there James met some of the California Angels and got an autograph from one-handed pitching sensation Jim Abbott.

The second thing I hadn't known about Kansas City was that in 1990 the United States had experienced eight months of devastating recession, and that Missouri was hit hard. When I went for a morning run on July 31, the city streets had numerous burned-out and boarded-up buildings and part way through the run I wandered into a neighbourhood that no Canadian country boy should have been in. When I saw iron gates on ruined houses and a man passed out on the hood of an old Cadillac, I made a hasty retreat. Our Hyatt hotel proved to be a safe island in a sea of decay. Other than a trip to Kauffman Stadium to see the Kansas City Royals play the Oakland A's, we stayed close to the hotel. My certification went well. I was now a Certified Reality Therapist.

One of the highlights of the trip home was a meal at an Ohio truck stop. When I declared that we were going to change up our evening meal with something other than fast food, our son James was not happy. James slouched into our booth at the diner. His attitude quickly changed when his trucker-sized chocolate milk arrived; he was suitably impressed. By the time James and Heather had also enjoyed trucker-sized main courses and desserts, our young travellers had learned another valuable lesson about delaying judgement until you had all the facts. Heather and James enjoyed the road trip experiences, and we returned home to Waterloo in early August, just in time for one more significant event—Jason's move to the U.S.

We helped Jason pack for his move to Indiana. His college program would take four years. He planned to live with his mother, Sharon, and buy a car to commute to Herron Art College. On August 10, Jason said his goodbyes in Waterloo, and he and I headed to my mom and dad's. After a good meal and a tearful farewell with his Gramma Lester, Jason, Dad, and I headed to Dad's summer highlight—the Grand American World Trapshooting Championship in Vandalia, Ohio.

Dad had been loading his own shells and shooting clay targets at the Straffordville Gun Club ever since he retired. In the 1980s, I had suggested he visit the big competition at Vandalia. We only stayed one day the first year, but we were suitably impressed. The event lasted a week and had over 3,000 competitors. The trap houses extended over a mile, and the main concourse was filled with vendors. There were gun traders, repair shops, clothing, food, art, and jewelry. It was a gun lover's paradise. Dad was hooked, and every year we would spend three days during the sixteen-yard championships, and Dad would compete with the best in the world. Jason had often joined us when sports or work didn't interfere. As part of his transition, Jason joined his Grampa at Vandalia before making his move to the U.S. to attend college.

We all shot some practice rounds on Tuesday, and on Wednesday Dad shot two hundred registered targets in the 16-yard competition. At age seventy-seven, Dad shot ninety-five out of a hundred on the first round and ninety-two out of a hundred on the second. Jason and I watched proudly. Although that was a good score, there were men with $10,000 guns who could shoot two hundred in a row and, at night, the shoot-offs for the trophy would go for a couple of hours before someone missed. On Thursday, August 13, we drove Jason to Carmel, Indiana, and helped him unload his belongings. More tearful goodbyes, and Dad and I returned home. I was excited about the future.

THE WATERLOO YEARS

In September of 1993, I started my twenty-sixth year as an educator with high hopes. Plattsville was my fourth principalship. The school, built in 1961, had been the centre of a quiet rural village until the 1980s when new subdivisions doubled the village population in just a few years. As I began my assignment, new house building was continuing at a rapid rate. Most of the new residents commuted to work each day.

Plattsville Public School was a challenge right from the start. The school was overcrowded with four portables and new students kept coming. There was a mix of very religious rural students who were bussed in and street-smart ex-city kids who now lived in the village. The staff had expanded quickly with many of the teachers in their first teaching assignment. With kindergarten to grade eight, well over three hundred students, and a staff of over twenty, this was the largest and most complex school I had supervised. It was hard work.

As a full-time administrator, many days were no fun at all. Dealing with suspensions, frustrated teachers, and angry parents wasn't the dream I had of changing the world through teaching. Although the teachers were polite, and most did good work, they made it clear from the start that I was going to have to work hard to gain trust and cooperation. In a September interview I asked one of the brightest young teachers to tell me about his philosophy of education. Without hesitation, he looked me in the eyes and said, "I don't have a philosophy of education. You tell me what to do and I do it."

After my first year at Plattsville, the summer of 1993 started with another great holiday at Mary Lake, this time with Jason joining us. Both James and Heather spent a week at the Mennonite Brethren's Camp Crossroads that same summer—their first time away from parents. In August, Dad joined me as I drove Jason back to Indianapolis for his second year at Herron. Again, we spent a day at the Grand American World Trapshooting Championship in Vandalia, Ohio, before dropping Jason off. With Jason and I as his assistants Dad shot two hundred rounds of trap, but it was hard work, and as we drove home, Dad said this would be his last trip to Vandalia.

This time as I took Dad home and returned to Waterloo, I realized that even with luck on our side change is relentless. My oldest son was building a life far from his birthplace. My father's health was failing. My wife was finishing university with no particular career path. I was struggling to be an effective principal. I was starting to learn that life is always a mix of joy and sorrow, of grief and anticipation, of fear and triumph.

During my second year at Plattsville, a tough assignment was made even more challenging as the newly elected NDP government, facing huge deficits, froze teachers' wage increments and instituted twelve days of unpaid leave each year. These "Rae Days" hurt us all. This austerity program hit my young teachers particularly hard since most of them were still paying off student debt and at the lower end of the teacher's wage grid. Although the established teachers weren't happy to be reminded that they were civil servants, their paychecks didn't suffer much because they were already at the top of the wage grid—a fact that created even more tension and dissatisfaction with the younger teachers. My relationship skills were tested every day.

Our involvement in Waterloo Mennonite Brethren church became a welcome refuge. In the fall of 1993, I had the privilege of singing in a presentation of Handel's *Messiah*. I sang tenor in a large group directed by Rob Shuh. It was the most technical and challenging choir experience of my life. Backed by an orchestra, over a thousand people attended our performance in December. This experience and a family celebration for Heather's thirteenth birthday at the end of November were bright spots in a challenging time in my life.

Cheryl's parents brought my mom and dad to Heather's party. During the evening I was saddened to realize how quickly my father's health was deteriorating. In December Dad spent time in Tillsonburg Hospital dealing with heart and blood pressure issues. He was able to be home for Christmas and my mother insisted on hosting the whole family and, at age seventy-eight, still preparing the usual Christmas dinner. With my brother's family and all of our children, we had a wonderful time together.

Shortly after Christmas, Dad was readmitted to hospital. It seemed he was rallying and would soon be home again as Cheryl and I drove from Waterloo on the Sunday afternoon of January 29, 1994. In the hospital we discovered Dad had been moved to Intensive Care. Here I found my mother and brother and soon we were making end-of-life decisions. Within a couple hours, Dad's sons and their wives comforted my mom as my father peacefully died. He was seventy-eight.

After a week in Tillsonburg, helping my mother and brother with the funeral and legal details, I returned home and plunged back into work and church activities. The loss of my dad was profound. Stephanie and Jason had moved on. I had just moved away from the fields and woods I loved and now I had lost my loving and supportive father. I didn't grieve much because I didn't know how, and because life was too full for "sentimental" sidetracking. I had lessons to learn about loss.

Just four months later, Stephanie completed her second pregnancy, and our grandson, Matthew Dayton Scaife, was born on June 7, 1994, the same day as his sister Katelynn's second birthday. Heather finished grade eight, Cheryl had completed her final university courses, James had a tonsillectomy, and Jason arrived in Waterloo for a six-month sabbatical.

Looking back and retelling this part of my story is informative. I realize that for each of us life, as Dickens described it, is both tragic and magical. Tears and laughter, heartache and joy are so intermingled that, during the rush of events, we often don't experience life fully. For me, much of the time in Waterloo was like rafting down a fast-moving river.

There were many times during those years when I lay awake at night, rehashing a conversation at work or home wishing I was a better husband, father, son, principal, man. There were many more nights when I drifted off to sleep filled with joy and gratitude for my many blessings.

The move to Waterloo placed me in a multicultural city where my simple faith and patriarchal views were being challenged every day. As I continued to learn and grow, I watched our four children become citizens of a larger world. Our children were amazing. Heather and James were hardworking and fun to be around. Jason was doing well in college and was becoming a very capable man. Stephanie was doing great as a mom with two little ones.

By July 1994, Cheryl had completed her courses. She finished her B.A. with a Dean's Honour List standing. She had studied piano under the direction of famed Liszt specialist, Philip Thomson, and sang in two prestigious University of Waterloo choirs. Upon graduation Cheryl worked for a few months as the office manager/bookkeeper with a graphic design business, before taking a position with World Vision Canada. On January 5, 1995, Cheryl began her role as executive secretary for the president of World Vision Canada. Cheryl's opportunity would require more changes in family routines.

Cheryl's new job was filled with prestige and expectations. Each day, she commuted from Waterloo to Mississauga, leaving very early and often returning very late. Within the first month Cheryl had to stay over a few nights in Mississauga, either because of weather or demanding workloads associated with the organization's Annual General Meetings.

Often Heather, James, and I were on our own to prepare our evening meal. Most of the time we did very well, but there were nights when I wasn't able to give the love and support the children needed. Despite some of the challenges, our lives were overflowing with activity and wonderful friendships. Waterloo Mennonite Brethren Church was good for all of us. The Sunday services were filled with music and helpful messages. Both Heather and James enjoyed the friendships and activities of the church youth group. They made enduring friendships. Each summer, James and Heather spent a week at Camp Crossroads near Torrance, on Black Lake.

I helped start a Christian Men in Action group that held monthly breakfast meetings with inspirational speakers. A kitchen crew would cook a hearty breakfast for over a hundred men. Cracking dozens of eggs, toasting loaves of bread, and creating a huge pot of porridge led to riotous kitchen adventures. With these men I was able to share my fears and failures and grow in resiliency and wisdom. Our men's group helped people move and renovate and we attended men's conferences.

In June of 1995, a provincial election changed education again. Mike Harris' Conservatives won a huge majority, pushing the NDP into obscurity. Rae Days were gone, but teachers were still under attack. Now, the message to the public was that teachers were not only overpaid but that we were too lax. Wages remained frozen and payments to local school boards were reduced. As the school year ended, I no longer felt like I was an idealistic educator inspiring young minds. I felt like an overworked manager caught in a system that was under siege.

My concerns about work were quickly, although temporarily, left behind as Cheryl, Heather, James, and I packed up and headed to the East Coast. Other than getting to the ocean, we had no particular destination. It ended up being the most joyous and adventurous holiday the four of us ever had together. In Prince Edward Island we tented on the edge of the Atlantic. We swam in the ocean and basked on sandy shores. James and I joined a charter for a day of Cod fishing in the Atlantic and barbecued our catch at our campsite. After upgrading to a two-level motel room in Charlottetown, we attended the Anne of Green Gables attractions and the Charlottetown theatre. James and Heather spent an evening racing on a go-cart track as Cheryl and I watched from the bleachers.

Starting in Charlottetown, and for the rest of the trip as we travelled through Maine, New Hampshire, Vermont, and New York State, we sought out motels with three beds. We had no reservations, so the discoveries were a delight. The serendipities and unique rooms became an exciting end to each day. Our last motel room was the most amazing of all. There were three double beds in what easily could have been a bowling alley. The rest of the summer went quickly as Cheryl returned to work, and Heather and James enjoyed time with their father, and at camp.

In January of 1996 we purchased a beautiful large house on Old Post Road. We moved in March. In April the Oxford County Board of Education, facing uncertain funding, issued layoff notices for the coming school year. Once again, this impacted the younger teachers. On the Thursday before the Easter weekend in 1996, I had the unpleasant task of handing out twelve September layoff notices to teachers at Plattsville. I tried to assure the teachers that this was just a formality, but it was a horrible experience. Then it got worse. On May 13, I was told that I had been transferred to Chapel Public School in Woodstock for September. Then on May 25, I fell off a ladder at our home on Old Post Road and broke my left heel. I did my best to finish well at Plattsville, and by the time the new principal arrived for an orientation, the teachers' jobs were secure and much of the fear had been abated.

As I said goodbye and left Plattsville on crutches, I left a school that was much better equipped and organized than when I arrived, yet it had been very hard work. As the school year ended, I visited my new school and met the staff. Chapel Public School, built in 1893, was a much smaller two-story kindergarten to grade five school in the centre of Woodstock. Administration and discipline would be much easier, but I would now have an hour commute on the good days.

I was beginning to think it might soon be time to leave the teaching profession. I had a lot to think about as I convalesced during July. The broken heel was serendipitous, even though I wondered if I would ever run again. The pause was needed. I rested and realized how demanding the last four years had been.

As I read and reflected, I had few regrets. Leaving our small town and moving into the bigger world had changed us all. Each of our family had learned and grown. I thought back to little Dougie, and all the other boys and girls born at the end of World War II. I realized that my journey was not unique. For many of us there is a curiosity that leads us along unknown paths—and with *a little bit of luck* we discover new and exciting things.

By fall I was able to walk with high top black runners and during Christmas break I jogged a slow mile. By early 1997 I was running again and enjoying my role at Chapel Public School.

In May 1997, Heather, James, and Stephanie travelled to Indianapolis with Cheryl and me to attend Jason's graduation from Indiana University.

It was a great weekend. The night before the ceremonies our blended family sat around a table in a Ruby Tuesday restaurant in Indianapolis, laughing and enjoying each other's company. I looked at Cheryl with a contented smile.

After a year at our big house on Old Post we moved to a tenth-floor condo on King Street. In the fall of 1997, I did something I had hoped never to do. For two weeks I went on strike. I joined the teachers and principals of schools all across Ontario as we protested sweeping changes to Ontario education. That was it for me. I decided to leave public education. I resigned from the Oxford County Board of Education at the end of 1997.

We stayed in Waterloo for another four years. As Heather and James completed high school, I trained in Personality and Grief Recovery Skills. I ran workshops and did individual counselling. I did supply teaching and taught summer school for the Waterloo Region District School Board. I ended my time in Waterloo working as a labourer for Mardel Commercial Refrigeration.

LIFE GOES ON

By the time Cheryl and I moved to Brampton, in early 2001, Heather and James had completed high school and were off to post-secondary education. We were empty nesters and the move ended Cheryl's long daily commutes. We had just settled into out seventeenth floor condo when Cheryl's father died suddenly just after his seventieth birthday.

In Brampton I found work as Manager of a youth counselling and support service. As part of Rapport Youth and Family Services my team of counsellors were located in Bramalea City Centre. Each day was an adventure as we dealt with homelessness, abuse, addiction and family dysfunction. We provided educational and vocational support to over 1200 young people each year for the four years I was there.

By 2005 both our mothers were widows with health issues, so Cheryl and I resigned from our jobs and moved back to the Tillsonburg area. During the next ten years there were many moving days, graduations, weddings, births, hospital visits, deaths, funerals, anniversaries, reunions, and special occasions. My mother died in 2007 at the age of ninety-two. Cheryl's mom died in 2010.

As I finish writing this in 2023, Stephanie has a daughter and son, Jason has two boys, Heather has a daughter, and James has a son and a daughter. Our seven grandchildren range in age from newborn to thirty.

That little farm boy who tried to follow his dad to town has exceeded his wildest dreams.

Work and recreation have taken me to Trinidad, London, Dublin, Paris, Amsterdam, Lesotho, South Africa, and most of the large U.S. cities. In recent years Cheryl and I rode VIA Rail from Toronto through the Rockies and did extended road trips from coast to coast.

I have enjoyed every adventure, but nothing gives me greater joy than a walk along a beach, a river, or a country road with Cheryl by my side.

I still run four miles most mornings although my pace slows a bit each year. Over the last forty years I have logged over 48,000 miles and in February 2024 I completed my second lap of the equator.

At age seventy-seven, living in an apartment in central London, Ontario, I can look back over the years with compassion and grace toward a younger Doug, and toward all the people who have challenged and enriched my life along the way.

Through sharing my life journey, I hope you've smiled and remembered your younger days and the many ways your own story has been enriched and rewarded with *a little bit of luck.*

www.ingramcontent.com/pod-product-compliance
Lightning Source LLC
Chambersburg PA
CBHW072000070526
44583CB00015B/1269